Progressive Politics and the Training of America's Persuaders

ᏸ✦ᏻ

Progressive Politics and the Training of America's Persuaders

ဆာ ◆ ෆ

Katherine H. Adams
Loyola University New Orleans

LAWRENCE ERLBAUM ASSOCIATES, PUBLISHERS
1999   Mahwah, New Jersey   London

Lawrence Erlbaum Associates, Inc., Publishers
10 Industrial Avenue
Mahwah, NJ 07430

Cover design by Kathryn Houghtaling Lacey

Library of Congress Cataloging-in-Publication Data

Adams, Katherine H.,
Progressive politics and the training of America's persuaders / Katherine Adams.
    p.   cm.
Includes bibliographical references and indexes.
ISBN 0-8058-3236-X (cloth : alk. paper). — ISBN 0-8058-3237-8 (pbk. : alk. paper)
1. English language—Rhetoric—Study and teaching—United States—History. 2. Persuasion (Rhetoric)—Study and teaching—United States—History. 3. Rhetoric—Political aspects—United States—History. 4. Progressivism (United States politics)—History.
    I. Title.
PE1405.U6A35   1999
808'.042'07073—dc21   98-41195
                                                        CIP

Books published by Lawrence Erlbaum Associates are printed on acid-free paper, and their bindings are chosen for strength and durability.

Printed in the United States of America
10 9 8 7 6 5 4 3 2 1

For Vick

Contents

Acknowledgments ix

Introduction xi

1 The Current/Traditional Paradigm and the Powerless Citizen 1

2 To Create a New Social Order: Progressivism's Three Tiers of Education 21

3 At Wisconsin: A Progressive Writing Curriculum for Advanced Students 39

4 Professional Writing Instruction Crosses the Country 70

5 University-Trained Persuaders Sell Reform, Consumerism, and War 95

6 After World War I: A Cacophony of Persuasion 132

7 "The Unknown Citizen": A Conclusion 145

Works Cited 151

Author Index 161

Subject Index 165

Acknowledgments

I would like to thank Loyola University's Grants and Leaves Committee for a grant that allowed me to travel to Madison, Wisconsin, to use the university archives and the state archives located there. The university also granted me a sabbatical that provided me with the extra time needed to pursue this project.

My colleagues David Moore of the history department, Peggy McCormack of the English department, and Larry Lorenz and Cathy Rogers of the communications department helped me to understand the Progressive era although any mistakes herein are of course my own. Alice Templeton gave me invaluable assistance with structuring and editing this manuscript. I also thank the fine library staff at Loyola University and especially Pat Doran, our exceptional interlibrary loan officer.

Introduction

University instruction in rhetoric changed drastically during the nineteenth century. At the beginning of the century, college students generally studied rhetoric for four years, learning precepts from Aristotle, Cicero, and Quintilian that they applied through regular oral performances. This curriculum had meaning in a smaller United States, in which well-educated male citizens might lead their town governments, serve as lawyers, or enter the clergy, working within small communities where they would need oral persuasion skills to succeed. In the first half of the nineteenth century, the work of British rhetoricians Hugh Blair, George Campbell, and Richard Whately caused alterations in this curriculum by increasing interest in literary genres, stylistics, and organizational patterns for written essays, but students generally still received four years of rhetoric instruction, and the focus remained on memorizing precepts and performing orally in class.

After the Civil War, however, the four-year curriculum in rhetoric was disrupted by the trend toward separate majors and general education requirements and by changing economic conditions that fostered this new form of higher education: College graduates would be entering a new array of careers like engineering and accounting, products of the Industrial Revolution for which classical rhetoric and oral practice seemed irrelevant.

To fill their own slot in the new general education, college English teachers developed a single year's composition course in which students learned to write short essays with well-organized paragraphs and correct grammar, obtaining transferable skills deemed applicable to a variety of majors. Discussion of human faculties and of appeals to the will, reason, and imagination in George Campbell's *The Philosophy of Rhetoric* (1776) provided impetus for four separate forms of discourse—argumentation, exposition, narration, and description—although most classes emphasized exposition. Teachers like A. S. Hill and Barrett Wendell of Harvard planned for this one remaining rhetoric requirement, labeled there as English A, to prepare students to write competent informative papers in whatever field they chose.

But at the beginning of the twentieth century, when this freshman composition course was becoming a national requirement, American social and political life necessitated another change in the rhetoric curriculum. In the period between 1890 and World War I, as big business and government garnered more shared power in an industrializing United States, many educators, social critics, and politicians began to question this power and its effect on the citizenry. Reformers who envisioned a new style of modern democracy, such as Robert La Follette of Wisconsin, worked to institute a new advanced writing curriculum by which a few persuaders could be trained to bring information and "right" thinking to a more active electorate. This book concerns the resulting changes in college instruction, the profession—that of persuader—these changes created, and the impact of these programs and these trained specialists on American society. For whereas the freshman class taught four separate forms of discourse and especially emphasized exposition, the new courses, which were given labels of professional work such as journalism, advertising, public relations, creative writing, and technical writing, looked at all formats and techniques as subsumed by the only real goal of any rhetoric: persuasion. Whereas freshman composition valued correctness, advanced composition stressed effectiveness. By developing these specializations, Progressive politicians and educators hoped to train the rhetors who could persuade people to reform both government and business and create a better United States. By the end of World War I, however, teaching methods and professional practices created to fulfill social reform goals had also proven infinitely useful to big business and big government. Reformers might have intended to create only muckrakers and consumer activists, but they could not control the uses to which their new persuasive techniques might be put.

Although the early curriculum in rhetoric and the reduction from four years of rhetoric study to one have been well studied, the development of advanced writing majors during the period from 1890 to World War I has not been thoroughly examined. Certainly no history is researched or told in a vacuum. The colonial tradition and the nineteenth-century movement toward a sole freshman requirement have been described frequently because they provided composition and speech teachers with an academic history and a means of explaining the worst of current practice; the history of advanced classes, which entered many different departments, has served no comparable function.

In the 1940s and 1950s, speech teachers began writing about the history of rhetorical instruction to verify the place of their specialty in the college curriculum. Although their predecessors had founded speech departments, these academic units were being taken over by drama, speech therapy, communications, and other additions to the curriculum. Historical studies could reinstate speech's centrality in undergraduate education and provide research topics for an increasing number of graduate students. In a five-article series in *Speech Monographs* appearing from 1946 to 1951, for example, Warren Guthrie surveyed "The Development of Rhetorical Theory in America," broadening the number of key texts to be taught and researched. He argued that in colonial America the theories of Peter Ramus (1515–1572), as presented in Omer Talon's *Audomari Talaei Rhetorica* (1549) and William Dugard's *Rhetorices Elementa* (1648), were more popular than Ciceronian rhetoric. Then, after 1730, precepts from Cicero, Quintilian, and Aristotle did shape the American curriculum, but the most influential versions of these theorists' principles appeared in textbooks, such as Antoine Aroauld's *Art of Speaking*, translated from the French in 1708. After 1785, Guthrie claimed, study of Blair, Campbell, and Whately, of treatises by American teachers such as John Witherspoon of Princeton and John Quincy Adams of Harvard, and of textbooks such as Henry Day's *Elements of the Art of Rhetoric* (1850) and M. B. Hope's *The Princeton Text Book in Rhetoric* (1859) replaced the attention given earlier to classical treatises and to textbook versions of them.

In Karl R. Wallace's influential anthology *A History of Speech Education in America*, from 1954, various scholars surveyed the rhetorical theory and pedagogical practice of the eighteenth and nineteenth centuries to further reveal the worthy past of college speech instruction and the many texts available for study. In "English Sources of Rhetorical Theory in Nineteenth-Century America," Clarence W. Edney informed readers of the classical treatises on proper pronunciation used in American classes. In "Rhetorical and Elocutionary Training in Nineteenth-Century Colleges," Marie Hochmuth and Richard Murphy divided the century into quarters leading to the triumphant creation of separate speech departments: first, classical rhetoric became "systematized and ensconced" in American colleges; next, interest in elocution developed; eventually, rhetorical training was linked with literary training; and finally, a complete curriculum arose, first within English departments and then in the more friendly environment of separate departments of speech (173).

As study of the rhetoric curriculum gave speech teachers a new legitimacy and research site, it also provided composition teachers within English departments with a new sense of disciplinarity. In the 1950s, literature teachers had complete control of English departments; to gain tenure-track jobs, composition teachers worked to professionalize their field, by connecting it with the history of rhetorical theory and pedagogy. These teachers also had a second purpose in examining their past, for while they wanted a new status, they also wanted to repudiate many of the current teaching methods, especially the obsession with five-paragraph themes, modes of exposition, and grammar rules. Thus, historical interpretations could both assert past greatness and cure recent ills.

The first study fulfilling those goals was the 1953 dissertation *Rhetoric in American Colleges, 1850–1900*, by Albert Kitzhaber, a student of Porter Perrin at the University of Washington, a place where even respected writing teachers fought for a secure status in the English department. Using careful analysis of textbooks, Kitzhaber first explained rhetoric study at the beginning of the nineteenth century as an attempt at fostering general mental discipline as well as rhetorical skill. He then traced the ascendancy of the forms of discourse, the paragraph, and grammar in the work of his "Big Four" textbook authors at the end of the century—A. S. Hill and Barrett Wendell of Harvard, John Franklin Genung of Amherst, and Fred Newton Scott of Michigan—and concluded that in the resulting freshman course, "good writing" came to mean "not effective writing, but writing that violated none of the rules" (319).

In *Writing Instruction in Nineteenth-Century American Colleges* (1984), James Berlin continued this criticism of a reductive course that diluted earlier rhetorical instruction. Berlin argued that with the ascendancy of George Campbell's version of rhetoric during the nineteenth century, emphasis switched from developing ideas fully through the topoi or other heuristics to adapting a previously learned piece of information for the reader. He also traced another less influential approach to rhetoric, labeled in his book as Romantic rhetoric, which found its theoretical grounding in Emerson and its strongest classroom advocate in Fred Newton Scott of the University of Michigan, whom Kitzhaber had also praised for his teaching and professional service if not for his textbooks. This Romantic approach, in opposition to the accepted paradigm, stressed the writer's own thinking processes and discoveries, not organization of established data. In Berlin's analysis, labeled by Robert Connors as a "kings and battles" interpretation of good and evil in pedagogical history, Scott as the lone knight could not win the day but his example did lead by the 1960s to an empowering form of writing instruction that Berlin scripted as the final victor ("Historical Inquiry").

Subsequent studies have further analyzed the texts that created the scientific, objective approach to composition that Berlin criticized. In *Nineteenth-Century Rhetoric in North America* (1991), Nan Johnson reviewed the rhetorical treatises of Blair, Campbell, and Whately and the American texts based on their principles to look at the odd ways in which "firm classical foundations" and "belletristic interests in 'criticism and literary taste'" combined with "epistemological approaches to rhetoric as a 'science' closely related to the study of the'mental faculties'" (14). Sharon Crowley in *The Methodical Memory* (1990) discussed the scientific approach to invention as "a review of the mind's contents and operations" with the intention of presenting results clearly to readers (68). Invention became simply a matter of "select, narrow, and amplify," she asserted, and emphasis in instruction shifted from discovering the content and appeals needed for particular situations to learning set organizations that could present information held in memory to any reader. In *Composition-Rhetoric*, Robert J. Connors reviewed this devotion to "narrowing and channeling experience" while also discussing the assignments, texts, student population, and institutional realities of this required course (313).

Recently historical studies have also focused on the cultural significance of college composition instruction. In "From Rhetoric to Composition: The Teaching of Writing in America to 1900" (1990), S. Michael Halloran noted that as a sole requirement in writing, the freshman course seemed adequate in the 1880s and 1890s because power was shifting away from local courts, churches, and town meetings where the oral rhetoric of the few college-educated leaders had dominated, and toward national industries and political parties where internal directives were replacing public speaking as the primary means of influence. In hiring college graduates, entrepreneurs could get technical expertise along with correct formulaic writing, without the dissension and activism that might be caused by well-trained rhetors. In the introduction to *Oratorical Culture in Nineteenth-Century America* (1993), Gregory Clark and Halloran pointed out that the earlier nineteenth-century focus in the United States on communal and then on individual growth was transformed by the culture of professionalism of the late nineteenth century, and the schools reflected that trend.

Although these writers have been fully investigating freshman composition, they have failed to truly consider what the subtitle to Berlin's book on the twentieth century, "writing instruction in American colleges," promised because they do not cover the advanced courses developed in the Progressive era. Concerning Progressive education, Berlin noted in *Rhetoric and Reality: Writing Instruction in American Colleges, 1900–1985* (1987), that Fred Newton Scott, in his articles more than in his freshman texts, expressed a concern for the social situation of the writer, creating at least theoretically a democratic rhetoric that was "never dominant." In a chapter on "The Influence of Progressive Education: 1920–1940," Berlin concentrated on how an increased faith in science and in the development of citizens led in the freshman course to placement tests, ability groupings, and readings on social issues. He mentioned that some creative writing courses appeared, but did not further consider the advanced curriculum. For Berlin and these other historians of rhetoric, "writing in American colleges" meant freshman composition and not advanced instruction.

Although history of the freshman paradigm has helped teachers evaluate their methods and understand their academic role, it alone will not tell the story of university writing instruction and its impact on public rhetoric. The more influential story, in fact, is the one that involves not the change from four years to one year of training for all students, but the creation of writing as another of the twentieth-century specialties. An accurate analysis of writing instruction must include a study of advanced as well as introductory courses and a consideration of the politics, social climate, and educational priorities that led to the development of advanced courses in the decades after the freshman course became established in almost every school.

The period between 1890 and World War I was a time of changing values. Americans began to respond to the consolidation of power that had oc-curred after the Civil War, when, as historian Eldon Eisenach has noted, political parties had ruled "almost without challenge, dominating political communication and policy agendas, organizing the electorate, and dictating to office holders, both elective and appointive, the public policies to initiate, legislate, administer, and adjudicate" (8). By the 1890s, reformers hoped to create a new style of national democracy, involving strong but more trust-worthy leaders responsible to an educated electorate. To end the era of the city and state boss and the favoritism shown to business, political reformers concentrated on voter registration and citizenship requirements, primary elections, and nonpartisan municipal governments as well as railroad and antitrust legislation. Social reformers supported the rights of labor, women's suffrage, and universal education. Politicians like Theodore Roosevelt and Robert La Follette, economists like John Commons and Richard Ely, edu-cators like John Dewey, and social activists like Jane Addams led in these efforts. They viewed themselves as *Progressives*, defined by historian Thomas R. Pegram as "those reformers who attempted to transform the partisan, selfish institutions of politics and government into compassionate, efficient agents of the public interest" (xiii). In their vision of progress, new leaders would work with a well-educated populace, giving them the right informa-tion to choose the right nominees, laws, and national reforms. The newly reconceived "people" would thus gain a new type of national power. Although recent historians such as Eldon J. Eisenach, David Sarasohn, and Morton Keller have argued about the role of each party in this movement, its cohesiveness, and its ultimate impact, this period was clearly a time in which an older view of governmental and business power was being questioned and that questioning led to the desire for a more active and complete form of education for citizenship.

To secure a proper education for the masses, reformers such as John Dewey sought universal enrollment in elementary schools in which students would function as groups of citizens, combining new information with their own experience and working together to solve problems. In this environment, as was true at Dewey's elementary school at the University of Chicago, which opened in 1896, children would practice speaking skills in their small groups much more than they would write because as citizens and voters they would need to read, listen, and respond orally, not to write treatises or fiction. Dewey did not give as much attention to a curriculum for older students, perhaps because in 1900 only 6.3% of Americans graduated from high school (*Historical Statistics* 379). But, like elementary students, high school students would be involved in experiments and projects that more frequently involved spoken interaction than written work.

Although the high school and entry-level college classes on writing never became their focus, Progressive reformers did work on writing curricula for the final college years, shaping majors to train the experts needed for social and scientific progress. In a larger democracy with a more active citizenry, politicians, governments, newspapers, corporations, and scientists would rely on professional communicators who could gather facts and create emotional appeals and thus inform citizens of events and of the of proper means of judging them. These experts were thus necessary colleagues of college-trained engineers, political scientists, and sociologists, providing citizens with information from all fields upon which they could act locally. Starting in midwestern strongholds of Progressivism such as Wisconsin, Illinois, Kansas, and Michigan, advanced classes on professional genres created new specialists in persuasion, who could enable citizens to improve their lives and American democracy.

However, as these new courses spread out from the Midwest and as their graduates sought employment, businesses realized that the persuasive techniques being taught at colleges could also be used to enhance other messages and to quell the power sought by the people: These tools of democratic enlightenment could also further the consumer manipulation of national firms and any sort of goals that a government might devise. Thus, when mine owners such as John D. Rockefeller, Jr., wanted to deny having initiated a bloody vendetta against striking workers, when Westinghouse or Ford Auto wanted to create a market for a new luxury item, and when the government wanted to sell an unpopular war, these methods also served them well. Ironically, methodologies developed to educate and thus empower citizens would soon be used to control them. The Progressive belief that the average American did not need rhetorical skills and could trust in trained persuaders was ultimately not good for democracy.

Just as this powerful public rhetoric developing at the beginning of the twentieth century was indeed persuasion, so is any attempt I can make at describing it. Like the speech and English teachers discussed here, I also have a purpose for investigating college instruction, a belief that historians of rhetoric need to look not just at the history of a single course but at the larger history that has rendered the freshman course inconsequential and ineffective. Although scholars have considered the history of separate parts of the rhetoric curriculum, as De Forest O'Dell, James Melvin Lee, Albert Sutton, and others have done for journalism, they have not looked at the larger subject of how these specialties arose from political and educational goals of the Progressive era and how they interact to tell Americans what to think and do. Rhetoric historians need to move beyond the freshman course to the scene of greater influence, the site where professional writers who create the rhetoric of our country learn their trades. Journalism, advertising, creative writing, and public relations are not discrete professions, even though they may appear to be so today and their practitioners may deny their connections with each other. These real forms of discourse derived from the same sources and share the same goal, of persuading citizens whose own rhetorical education gives them little understanding of the techniques being employed on them.

Of course, creating causal arguments to explain the creation of a curriculum and a mode of public discourse is an enterprise fraught with difficulties. Certainly, as Dominick LaCapra has written, such historical writing should not be viewed as a monological "authorial voice providing an ideally exhaustive and definitive (total) account of a fully mastered object of knowledge" (36). Instead, like all public rhetoric, it is "a 'dialogical' exchange both with the past and with others inquiring into it" (9). I hope here to offer research and interpretation on the history of advanced writing instruction and thus to invite new conversations on the Progressive era and its impact on the forms of public rhetoric that still affect our schools, businesses, government, and homes.

1

The Current/Traditional Paradigm and the Powerless Citizen

Rhetoric is an art tied to its times, to the political and legal forums available to its educated citizens. In the American colonial period, college students studied rhetoric for four years to improve their knowledge of Latin and to prepare for the oral persuasion practiced in their professions and communities. At the beginning of the eighteenth century, this curriculum was modified by the addition of materials from British rhetoricians such as George Campbell and Hugh Blair, but rhetoric remained a central part of the liberal arts college curriculum.

After the Civil War, however, this requirement quickly lapsed from four years to one. The new freshman composition courses de-emphasized persuasive rhetoric and thus reflected a different perspective on how skilled at writing and speaking students should become. The change from classical rhetoric to a system often labeled the *current/traditional paradigm* (although Robert J. Connors rightly noted in *Composition Rhetoric* that it is no longer current and was not based on traditional rhetorical texts) signaled a reduced public role for citizens, even the elite few with college degrees. Within a larger, industrialized nation, fewer Americans would participate in the arena of power, and, not coincidentally, the rhetoric curriculum no longer offered them the means for such participation. Although many critics have decried the lack of social relevance in the new composition courses, the course work may have been very relevant to the role business and government envisioned for college graduates: In new middle management jobs, they would contribute to the smooth workings of large organizations without causing any trouble. The necessary precursor, then, to the Progressive era and to writing's role in it was the constriction of rhetorical power to a few as colleges trained workers to not talk back.

THE CLASSICAL CURRICULUM IN RHETORIC

In the first decades of the nineteenth century at eastern colleges and at a growing number—around 500 by 1850—of schools in other areas, the curriculum in writing and speaking reflected the colonial model: Study of

1

classical rhetoric was combined with oral performance as part of a curriculum that also included mathematics, history, logic, theology, natural science, and moral philosophy. In the colonial period, this four-year rhetorical study gave the very few who entered college (less than 1% of the population) a grounding in rhetoric as a liberal art and as a means to succeed in the pulpit and in the law court. Although more specialized career preparation occurred through apprenticeships, college study did prepare students to succeed within their communities in this smaller world of business and politics.

As an industrializing society began changing the liberal arts college into the professional university, this older rhetorical curriculum lingered. When John H. Lathrop was inaugurated in 1850 as the first chancellor of the University of Wisconsin, he spoke of the importance of the library, scientific apparatus, and a practical education for the average citizen of the state, causes shared by state universities across the country. Even though Wisconsin's curriculum included modern languages, surveying, geography, hydrostatics and pneumatics, electricity, magnetism, chemistry, mineralogy, constitutional law, and political economy, the university adopted a traditional program of classical rhetoric and oral disputation. As the college catalog for 1858 indicates, for example, students studied Cicero's *de Oratore* as second-term sophomores; juniors studied Quintilian's *Institutio oratoria*, Plato's *Gorgias*, and logic; and all classes performed orations in Latin and English and participated in debates.

At Wisconsin and elsewhere, professors and tutors involved with this traditional curriculum offered students theoretical knowledge of persuasion as well as practical training. Their lectures focused on invention as the discovery of valid or seemingly valid arguments to support a point of view. They taught this first step as the key to successful rhetoric, which also consisted of arrangement, expression, memory, and delivery, undertaken for three separate rhetorical purposes: the forensic (legal accusation and defense), deliberative (public policy), and epideictic (praise and blame). This instruction presented the writing process as similar to oral performance, with handwriting (*orthographia*) replacing oral delivery as the final step.

In this system, invention proceeded by status or issue questions (fact, definition, nature of an act, or procedure) or by topics or commonplaces, such as division, consequence, cause and effect, and definition. Arrangement specified the six parts of a persuasive oration: exordium or introduction, narration or statement of facts, division or the outline to be followed, confirmation or proof, refutation, and peroration or conclusion. Expression, or style, included wording and specific "figures" like synecdoche, metaphor, antithesis, and isocolon. Memory and delivery, often taught together as elocution, further prepared the student for oral performance (Welch).

For the recitations, debates, and orations in their classes, for college assemblies, and for literary society meetings, students had to invent ideas, arrange them, choose an appropriate style, memorize their speeches, and repeat them well in sound, expression, and gesture. Practice assignments also included translations, imitations of models, and written compositions, with many more done in English than in Latin by the late nineteenth century. Since students were learning the rhetoric of law and politics, they were often assigned practical topics on current moral and social issues. In 1767 at King's College (which later became Columbia University), for example, students debated whether a man ought to fight for his country if he were not persuaded of the justice of the cause. In 1779, Yale seniors centered their commencement presentations on the justice of imposed taxations (Rudolph 45–47). In the 1850s at Harvard, forensic exercises stemmed from ongoing political and social debates: Does the isolated United States need army and navy fortifications? Should a Congressman submit his own opinions to those of his constituents? Can a lawyer be justified in defending the guilty? Was the state legislatures' confiscation of Tory property justifiable? (Potter).

This curriculum in classical argumentation would become less common after 1850 as time given to Latin studies contracted and as separate majors developed. Although the University of Wisconsin adopted the traditional rhetoric curriculum at its opening, its teachers, like those at other universities, would soon experiment with newer approaches that seemed more relevant to a developing nation with a wide array of new careers.

BELLES LETTRES AND EPISTEMOLOGICAL RHETORIC

Before the Civil War, other types of rhetorical study were gaining favor, shifting the focus away from the court and pulpit, from argumentation, and from oral work. One popular alternative was known as "belles-lettres," inspired by Hugh Blair's *Lectures on Rhetoric and Belles Lettres* (1783) and by Matthew Arnold's argument that literature was essential for a national identity, for an understanding of shared history, priorities, and goals. Blair's widely studied lectures—which appeared during the nineteenth century in

62 complete editions and 51 abridgments with exercises—introduced students to genius, beauty, the sublime, and figurative language as well as to a broad array of genres, including poetry, drama, historical and philosophical writing, and literary criticism. These lectures fostered the first American courses in literary history as well as writing classes focusing on literary analysis and style. At Wisconsin, as the university catalogs indicate, the *Lectures* served as the rhetoric text for juniors from 1862 to 1866. The tradition remained in President John Bascom's lectures to seniors on aesthetics from 1874 to 1887, and in new courses on literary history, analysis, and taste.

Also influential was George Campbell's *The Philosophy of Rhetoric* (1776), which incorporated new findings from the social and behavioral sciences, labeled as faculty psychology. In analyzing the brain's processes, Campbell added imagination and passion to John Locke's categories of understanding and will and concluded that each of these means of processing information occupied a separate site in the brain. Thus a speaker might employ a unique rhetorical practice to engage each capability of an audience. Persuasion aimed at the will was thus just one of four choices and not the sole aim of discourse, as it had been viewed by classical rhetoricians. Expository prose might affect the understanding; fables, parables, allegories and poetry could stir the imagination and passions. Campbell believed that, instead of relying on classical heuristics or topoi to gather information, writers naturally drew on knowledge gained by previous intellection and experience: Thus invention had more of a managerial than an investigative function. Because all brains functioned similarly, the rhetor's major task was to order previously learned facts and opinions for the audience.

A NEW PARADIGM

Although Blair and Campbell brought new psychological theories and genres to the university, thus reinvigorating college study of rhetoric, no approach to extended training could survive the educational changes of the late nineteenth century. By 1900, at the 1,000 universities, colleges, and technical institutes across the country, students pursued majors in agriculture, business, and engineering as well as the liberal arts. For this larger and more varied group of students, neither oral disputation nor literary appreciation nor theoretical consideration of human faculties seemed relevant. And rhetoric study no longer occupied English professors, who like their colleagues in other fields were becoming specialists, in literature and philology. These changes led to another model for rhetorical instruction after the Civil War, primarily involving rhetoric and grammar texts written in the United States.

Constructing a new type of writing course provided a challenge for teachers. The goal was by then a general one: to prepare students to write well in college and in any career. The approach would concentrate on writing and not on oration since the new careers in a larger United States would not involve much disputation; it would de-emphasize persuasion since the new writing would be more scientific and factual. The stress would not be on specific types of investigation or on actual genres because the class would prepare students to write about such diverse subjects as agricultural developments and military campaigns. The resulting plan for instruction at first involved courses during all four years, as earlier rhetoric study had. But in a curriculum increasingly filled by electives and majors, composition study soon devolved into a year's work for freshmen that included rhetorical study, readings, and grammar. This requirement had little connection to the real discourse of any career, but it seemed to English professors to be manageable and broadly relevant. Although recent studies of writing teachers, such as JoAnn Campbell's work on Gertrude Buck of Vassar and Robin Varnum's on Theodore Baird of Amherst, reveal that such an approach was not universal, it certainly controlled the multi-section freshman composition programs at state schools such as the University of Wisconsin and at most private colleges.

Rhetorical Study

As academic generalists, English teachers and textbook writers who were creating the new requirement emphasized psychological theories and teachable categories over the traits of real genres. Their prefaces and book structures show that they were fashioning methods of controlling discourse so that it could be captured in a term or year, through rules that could be imposed on students and their writing. Because the rules and formats called "the basics" were not integral to any advanced curriculum, they were not being taught as a final step or goal. Thus students were not being prepared to write professionally but to learn real writing at some later date—although they would take no more writing courses and there might be little writing instruction within their majors. The most successful composition textbooks created a new system, which was separate from any discipline or degree.

At the University of Wisconsin in 1866, for example, second-year classes used Henry Day's *Elements of the Art of Rhetoric* (1850). Day's stated purpose was to elevate the teaching of invention, "the art of supplying the requisite thought in kind and form for discourse," and treat it as "a distinct and primary department of the art of Rhetoric" (iii, 35). He began by quickly discussing the general nature and parts of invention, but then divided discourse by following George Campbell's *The Philosophy of Rhetoric* and precepts of faculty psychology. Day thus devoted the bulk of his text to discussing discourse as explanation (narration, description, analysis, exemplification, and comparison and contrast meant to appeal to the reason); confirmation (argumentation directed at the will); excitation (meant to appeal to the feelings); and persuasion (aimed at the passions). Throughout the book, he taught by principles and exercises, not by studying audiences, purposes, or appropriate techniques for real occasions.

From 1870 to 1878, sophomores and juniors at Wisconsin learned writing from Alexander Bain's *English Composition and Rhetoric* (1866). In this text, the stated goal for students was "the discrimination between good and bad in expression," not forceful writing on any real subject (3). An associationist psychologist, Bain also used Campbell's *The Philosophy of Rhetoric* to form his categories: Description, narration and historical composition, and exposition were addressed to the intellect; persuasion or oratory to the will; and poetry to the feelings. For each category, Bain insisted on set principles whose careful study could create a syllabus. To explain description, for example, the text introduced enumeration of parts, statement of the form of the whole, statement of magnitude, and statement of branching parts. For exposition, it taught general laws, specific facts, definition, contrast, analysis, and examples. In the preface, Bain made clear the distance that the class should maintain from real writing: Writing of papers should not be emphasized since they require "the burden of finding matter as well as language" (6). He instead suggested that students revise subject matter presented in a poorly worded format, abridge or summarize texts, and parse the writing of various authors.

From 1886 to 1893, sophomores at Wisconsin studied A. S. Hill's *The Principles of Rhetoric*, which was printed in its original and a revised edition 21 times between 1878 and 1898. Following its reductive definition of rhetoric as "the art of efficient communication by language" (iii), this popular text offered basic explanations and rules for each feature of prose except invention, which Hill considered too complicated to be taught in one course to a heterogeneous college population: "[Rhetoric] does not undertake to furnish a person with something to say; but it does undertake to tell him how best to say that with which he has provided himself" (iv). This book divided discourse into narration, description, and argumentative composition. The 1895 edition also included a lengthy chapter on exposition.

The first edition of *The Forms of Discourse*, written by Wisconsin's William B. Cairns and used at the university for over fifteen years after its publication in 1896, focused on narration, description, exposition, argumentation, and persuasion. Cairns based his forms of discourse on primary laws of association: contiguity (the basis of description), continuity (narration), likeness and contrast, and cause and effect (both of which are used in exposition, argumentation, and persuasion). Whereas the preface paid attention to invention, most of the text concerned these forms.

All of these texts neglected invention, audience, and situation and instead stressed an array of formats derived from psychological analyses. By the late 1890s, writers settled on the now familiar four forms (narration, description, exposition, and argumentation or persuasion) and modes of exposition (such as comparison, cause and effect, and exemplification) to organize their books and suggested syllabi. Under each form, the required elements were fully stipulated, so that students could use a fill-in-the-blank approach to a paper's overall format and its paragraph-level structure. In all these texts, emphasis was not on persuading a certain audience but on conveying material to any general audience clearly. Even in the sections on argumentation, students found information on supporting a thesis logically, not on persuading readers through combinations of facts, examples, and appeals geared to specific characters and needs. In delineating fallacies such as hasty generalization, either-or choice, and appeal to pity as mistakes to be avoided, these texts failed to recognize the effects of strong emotional appeals on real audiences.

Readings

The first current/traditional texts had short excerpts from professional writers, usually no more than a paragraph, that provided examples of techniques being discussed. A. S. Hill's *Principles of Rhetoric* included excerpts from Homer, Arnold, Macaulay, Huxley, Webster, Newman, and Lamb. Its quotations on logic and argumentation came from Whately, J. S.

Mill, and others. Alexander Bain's *English Composition and Rhetoric* contained paragraph-length examples from Milton, Macaulay, Shelley, and Paley.

By 1910, a few separate readers and rhetorics with full articles began appearing. Wisconsin's Karl Young, Norman Foerster, and Frederick A. Manchester published *Essays for College Men,* which contained articles by Wilson, Newman, Huxley, William James, and Arnold. Young's *Freshman English: A Manual,* a 1914 revision of Frances Berkeley Young's *A College Course in Writing from Models* (1910), had rhetorical information with readings from Huxley, Wilson, William James, Lamb, Carlyle, Dequincey, Dickens, and Stevenson as well as newspaper articles and student themes.

The nonfiction reader became common within the freshman course for several reasons. In a course focusing on writing as products to be graded, and not on drafts and revisions, readings allowed the class to discuss something beyond the topic sentence and paragraph unity, and thus provided a more intellectual content for the course. Such readings could also suggest themes for writing although their subjects might seem distant to the student. In his book about college education, *The Goose-Step,* Upton Sinclair recorded his own frustration, at Columbia studying under George Rice Carpenter, with what he judged to be meaningless writing assignments derived from class readings:

> Our professor would set us a topic on which to write a "theme" : "Should College Students Take Part in Athletics"; or perhaps, "A Description of the Country in Winter." My own efforts at this task were pitiful, and I was angrily aware that they were pitiful; I did not care anything about the matters on which I was asked to write, and I could never in my life write about anything I did not care about. I stood some six weeks of it, and then went to the professor and told him I wanted to drop the course. (9–10)

Teachers also attempted to give students formal models of organization and prose style by using selections from literary nonfiction although published works could be hard to emulate and they often violated rules mandated in the texts. In *Freshman English: A Manual,* the Youngs admitted that their samples did not conform to the rules of discourse that the book taught: "To assume, however, that any form of writing may be found in isolation is merely a fiction of teachers, for the purposes of the class-room" (145). In trying to classify readings by technique without discussing their larger persuasive purpose, textbook authors often found their precepts divorced from actual practice.

Grammar

As teachers began using texts that included both instruction and readings on college forms of discourse, another new emphasis entered the freshman course: grammar. Earlier texts, such as those by Alexander Bain and A. S. Hill, covered classical precepts on style because these authors assumed that college students did not need basic work on punctuation and spelling. Language study at first evolved separately from composition, as part of the growing interest in philology and literature. In the 1870s at Wisconsin, students studied George L. Craik's *The English of Shakespeare*, John Mulligan's *Structure of the English Language*, and Wisconsin professor Stephen Carpenter's *An Introduction to the Study of the Anglo-Saxon Language*. By the late 1880s, they took Anglo-Saxon and Chaucer as requirements and Advanced Anglo-Saxon as an elective.

But entrance examinations, introduced first at Harvard in 1874, as well as classroom experience, began to show that earlier stylistic materials were aimed above the level of the more varied group of students entering college. Harvard's influential "Report of the Committee on Composition and Rhetoric" of 1892, based on an examination of writing in the freshman class, decried high school preparation in the basics; other investigations and reports quickly followed. At Wisconsin in 1910, nearly 20% of students, numbering 150 to 200 annually, could not pass freshman composition. A new departmental bulletin aimed at high school teachers, *Requirements for Admission to the Freshman English Course*, stated the necessary features of "mental grasp"—in vocabulary, grammar, reference, sentence and composition structure, and mechanical correctness—expected from entering students. In an article concerning the department's standards, Professor Edwin Woolley labeled this "serious weakness in spelling, punctuation, grammar" as "simply illiteracy" ("Admission to Freshman English in the University" 239). These criticisms indicated that students needed more practical grammar work than could be included in a course on the history of the language, a judgment that teachers at Wisconsin and elsewhere readily embraced.

As early as 1877 at Wisconsin, in composition classes listed separately from study of the language, students reviewed grammar rules by using Edwin Abbott's *How to Write Clearly* and *English Lessons*. Abbott's texts were written as short manuals for students at the City of London School who were having trouble translating Greek and Latin. His 56 stylistic rules stayed in print for 30 years because they met a new American instructional need. Until the end of the century, the other choices for stressing grammatical correctness included rhetoric textbooks with short sections on grammar and style or theme cards, which listed shortened forms of rules and the abbreviations for them and could be handed out to students with their graded papers.

These makeshift materials, however, were swept away by the publication of Edwin Woolley's *Handbook of Composition* in 1907, subtitled "A Compendium of Rules Regarding Good English, Grammar, Sentence Structure, Paragraphing, Manuscript Arrangement, Punctuation, Spelling, Essay Writing, and Letter Writing." Woolley's handbook, with its 350 numbered rules, was the first to thoroughly cover mechanical correctness, providing rules, examples, and exercises that could become a substantial part of a freshman course if not the entire course. It also contained diction rules and short sections on manuscript arrangement, outlines, letter writing, and essay forms. In the preface, Woolley stated that he was not creating rhetorical principles or suggesting the means for addressing various audiences in various situations, but instead he was listing enforceable rules for freshmen classes.

Throughout the text, Woolley made his statements unequivocally if not always clearly or simply: "Do not use a simile or metaphor which is incongruous with the expression preceding" (11); "The subject of an infinitive and the predicate substantive completing an infinitive should be in the objective case" (17). The rules were followed by examples, with mistakes labeled *wrong, bad,* or *crude.* A short second section, "Exercises for Breaking Certain Bad Habits in Writing and Speaking," began with the conjugations of difficult verb forms (such as *sit* and *raise*) and then provided further work on grammar rules, mainly "fill-in-the-blank" sentences, correct spellings to copy, and error-laden passages to correct. No exercises corresponded with the sections on diction, outlines, letter writing, and essay forms. The appendixes defined grammar terminology, conjugated additional verbs, and gave the correct pronunciations of frequently mispronounced words.

Woolley next published *The Mechanics of Writing* (1909) to cover spelling, compound and derivative words, abbreviations, numbers, syllabication, capitals, italics, punctuation, and paragraphing, bringing in information contained in the *Handbook* but offering fuller explanations and more detailed exercises. The 590 rules, with numerical references to grammatical definitions at the end of the book, were terminology dense: "a non-restrictive[2] adjective[1] element following its principal should be preceded by a comma; and it should also be followed by a comma unless some other point is required by another rule" (150); "An interjection[1] or a parenthetic expletive[1] introducing a simple predication[2] (separate or component)[2] should usually be followed by comma or an exclamation mark, according to whether the writer wishes it to appear slightly, or decidedly, exclamatory" (181).

In the preface to this text, Woolley made clear the pedagogical theory behind this book and the *Handbook*. His intent was to help students master that "certain body of rules" needed to write English as "befits an educated person" (v). He clearly noted that college students and graduates as well as members of the learned professions did not know these "necessary rules"; in fact, he was presenting "rules that, so far as I had observed, were unknown to any considerable number of the class of people mentioned above" (v–vi). Thus he was teaching rules that were not required for professional writing. He also admitted that because students could not handle several choices, he had created rules to resolve stylistic options, like the placement of adverbs and participial phrases: He did not want to trouble these readers who needed "a short, quick answer" with "a discussion of permissible alternatives" (xii). And so "*in framing the rule cited*" (xii; emphasis added), he was creating one answer that the teacher would enforce: "These things so threateningly forbidden are, it will be said, done by every good writer of flexibility and spirit" (xii-xiii), but for Woolley, in highly moralistic and disciplinary language, "violation or lax observation of them by inexperienced writers means incessant blundering, and a slovenliness of style which is abominable in the present, and which can lead to no good in the future" (xiv).

And this preface also made clear the proper use of writing in freshman composition courses:

> The chief benefit derived from theme-writing lies probably in the instructor's indication of errors in the themes and his showing how these errors are to be corrected; for by these means the student may learn the rules that he is inclined to violate, and thus may be helped to eliminate the defects from his writing. (vii)

The problem for the teacher became, in Woolley's appraisal, the best means of indicating all the errors in the exercise/paper: perhaps 800 errors in 50 short themes. Thus this book, like the *Handbook*, advocated use of the number system in marking so that students could be led to an explanation of each fault and to exercises.

In *Exercises in English* (1911), Woolley provided additional drill materials. The 120 exercise sections contained frequent references to the *Handbook* and to *The Mechanics of Writing*. In *Written English* in 1915, he attempted to use simpler grammatical terminology and more exercises to cover manuscript arrangement, grammatical correctness, punctuation, letter writing, and spelling, for an audience of younger students. In the preface, he blamed writing problems on one key deficiency: "Instruction in the principles of elementary correction is largely desultory, irregular, and insufficient" (iii).

Woolley's books and their immediate imitators, and the courses across the nation that employed them, created expectations for freshmen far beyond those of learned writers; they made grammar into an academic obsession. Although professional writers might violate these rules and consider various stylistic choices, students did not have the knowledge or right to do so. The elite college group, still only 3% of the population by 1915, had clearly become beginners to be dogmatically instructed and corrected until some unspecified point in their future. For Upton Sinclair, studying at the City College of New York, the grammatical emphasis led to another dreary and pointless ritual of the course:

> The tired little gentleman who taught me what was called "English"; I remember a book of lessons, each lesson consisting of thirty to forty sentences containing grammatical errors. I would open the book and run down the list; I would see all the grammatical errors in the first three minutes, and for the remaining fifty-seven minutes was required to sit and listen while one member of the class after another was called on to explain and correct one of the errors. The cruelty in this procedure lay in that fact that you never knew at what moment your name would be called, and you would have to know what was the next sentence. If you didn't know, you were not "paying attention," and you got a zero. I tried all kinds of psychological tricks to compel myself to follow that dreary routine, but was powerless to chain my mind to it. (*The Goose-Step* 4-5)

By emphasizing grammatical correctness in the freshman course, however dull the resulting class periods might be, teachers could rely on their own academic strengths; they could teach the rules students would need to reach remembered linguistic standards. And, in the more practical and professional university in which the liberal arts were quickly losing ground, this instruction made English powerful: It could be the gateway to success or failure—if not because of the importance of the skills to future work, then because of the students' need for a passing grade to continue college.

A GENERAL FORM OF ADVANCED COMPOSITION

Although extended study of rhetoric began to disappear from the college curriculum after 1850, additional opportunities for advanced writing training did occur at the advanced level. The first model of advanced writing—as distinct from the classical rhetorical study of earlier generations—originated at Harvard and soon spread to other schools, especially along the eastern seaboard. These advanced courses developed as Harvard's Barrett Wendell and A. S. Hill came to grips with the limitations of the model that they had suggested for freshman composition at Harvard and had made popular throughout the nation with their textbooks. Although both men encouraged the few advanced students with literary aspirations, they primarily aimed at undoing some of the poor habits engendered by the freshman course and improving the students' general skills, not at providing specialized career training for writers (Adams 36–60).

A. S. Hill taught the first year-long advanced elective course, English 5, in 1877 to 20 seniors and 11 juniors. Hill designed this class, as he wrote in 1887, to teach his students to "put forth naturally and with the force of their individuality." He especially wanted them to get away from an abstract school voice or "theme language" that dominated the high school and even his own freshman course. Hill structured his class sessions to evoke a more natural prose: He allowed students to develop their own topics in daily 10-minute in-class sessions, an experiment that he found "unexpectedly successful":

> Having no time to be affected, they are simple and natural. Theme language, which still haunts too many of their longer essays, rarely creeps into the ten-minute papers. Free from faults of one kind or another these papers are not; but the faults are such as would be committed in conversation or in familiar correspondence. The great point has been gained that the writers, as a rule, forget themselves in what they are saying; and the time will come, it is to be hoped, when they will be correct as well as fluent, and will unite clearness in thought with compactness in expression, and vigor with well-bred ease. ("English in Our Colleges" 512)

Besides these short papers, students wrote longer essays once a fortnight, either on assigned topics or topics of their own choosing.

In 1884–85, Barrett Wendell introduced a second advanced composition course, English 12, another general-skills course that was one of Harvard's most popular electives (Morison 75). Wendell required that a page of work be written each day and be turned in before 10 a.m. Students chose their own topics for their "daily themes," but he recommended that they write on current occurrences. Each year, as his teaching notebook indicates, he began the class by discussing the value of these daily themes for achieving regularity of habit, gaining the power to hold attention, learning an efficient style, cultivating the power of observation, and correcting habitual errors (Notes of Lectures). He especially wanted students to see the possible writing material all around them and to improve their descriptive powers:

> What I bid them chiefly try for is that each record shall tell something that makes the day on which it is made different from the day before with the result that each new bundle of these daily notes that I take up proves a fresh whiff of real human life. (Notes of Lecturers)

In addition to these page-long themes, students submitted longer fortnightly themes, poems, or stories, which Wendell's class presentations helped them to plan and revise. In 1885–1886, as his teaching notebook indicates, students did a short article or story on a current topic for the first "fortnightly" and a piece of fiction or nonfiction based on ideas from the works of Macaulay for the second. The third fortnightly, in November, could be anything "of a literary character—a criticism, or an original work of belles lettres." The fourth theme, in early December, was a story concerning something the students had recently witnessed (Notes of Lectures).

Other private east-coast colleges, such as Amherst, Colgate, Columbia, Hamilton, and the University of Pennsylvania, soon began to offer advanced classes that involved daily themes and longer assignments, individual attention, and a chance to experiment with a variety of genres. At Hamilton College, the Seminar for Writing English, in which students criticized freshman themes as one of their ongoing assignments, served a select few. At Princeton, an elective entitled Advanced Composition was open only to superior seniors who could profit from individualized work. In this course, students could choose to write personal essays, arguments, drama, or verse. At Dartmouth in 1920, Practical Composition covered book reviews, editorials, articles, essays, and business correspondence. Dartmouth also offered Advanced Practical Composition, an intensive course in writing articles, essays, and literary criticism. From 1880 to 1890, only seven eastern colleges had advanced electives. By 1920, however, 29 of 37 eastern colleges offered one or more of these courses (Wozniak 129–32).

As advanced offerings spread out from these private schools, they also assumed another form: more freshman or remedial composition—the four forms of discourse, grammatical correctness, and lectures—for sophomores, juniors, and seniors who had not fully mastered the basics, students who might be advanced in class standing but not in skill level or interest. At the University of Wisconsin in 1899, such offerings included Advanced Composition and Advanced Rhetoric. By 1908, Fred Newton Scott and his colleagues at Michigan had instituted several general advanced composition courses following the forms-of-discourse approach to instruction: one covering description and narration, one on exposition and argument, and a more advanced class on the theory and practice of argumentation. In 1909 at Penn State, Advanced Rhetoric, a sophomore course, covered grammatical purity, diction, structure of sentences and paragraphs, and essay forms. By 1911, the department also offered an advanced course on argumentation and two advanced courses on exposition.

In subsequent decades, most colleges continued to offer two or three advanced courses, to provide remediation for students who needed more freshman composition or to challenge highly skilled writers—or to offer an unwieldy combination of the two. At some schools, these courses were requirements for education, English, or business students, but they generally remained as electives taught by literature professors or instructors, rarely by teachers who considered writing or rhetoric to be their academic specialty.

SOCIAL PURPOSE AND THE CURRENT/ TRADITIONAL PARADIGM

This combination of rhetoric instruction, readings, and grammar review at the freshman and advanced levels certainly fulfilled educational needs. It offered English teachers an organized way of teaching the basics of writing to a larger college population. With a growing store of rule-governed textbooks, composition courses could be turned over to instructors and graduate students who provided general guidelines for writing, some readings to engage the student, and grammatical instruction to insure a basic level of competency or exclude those who could not reach it.

But not just rebellious students such as Upton Sinclair or a few lines in textbook prefaces pointed to weaknesses of the new methodology: Teachers also immediately began enumerating its liabilities. As early as 1887, A. S. Hill felt that English A at Harvard had made the students into slavish devotees of forms and rules. He especially criticized their "theme-language":

> I know no language—ancient or modern, civilized or savage—so insufficient for the purposes of language, so dreary and inexpressive, as theme-language in the mass. How two or three hundred young men, who seem to be really alive as they appear in the flesh, can have kept themselves entirely out of their

writing, it is impossible to understand—impossible for the instructor who
has read these productions by the thousand, or for the graduate who looks
at his own compositions ten years after leaving college. ("English in Our
Colleges" 511)

Barrett Wendell also criticized the course in 1908 for "wasting the very
blood of their hearts" through its emphasis on formats over audience and
purpose ("Of Education" 243). In 1915, Edward A. Thurber of the
University of Oregon satirized the quickly chosen topics used to fill in
the blanks of the forms of discourse:

> Sometimes topics are assigned, or rather hurled out of mid-air. These
> topics have no relation to the students' other studies, but are something
> extra, which he must cram up upon as quickly as possible and then
> transport to paper. And the more frequently he writes the better. Let not
> the sun set upon an unexpressed idea. (10)

He also criticized the course's haphazard combination of readings: "Yesterday the class studied about a steam engine; today it takes up the history
of a piece of chalk; tomorrow it is to examine how well a man gives the
impression of height of a cathedral" (11). In "As to the Forms of
Discourse" from 1914, Wisconsin's Sterling Leonard stated that writing
students would find no guidance in forms of discourse: "For, useful as this
doubtless is for sorting completed pieces of writing, it does not view the
process of composition from the side of the thoughts or ideas the writer
has to express, and particularly of his purpose in expressing these" (202).

Many critics of the period also denounced freshman composition's
reliance on grammar study and drill. Gertrude Buck of Vassar College
thought that the study of sentence constructions apart from meaning
should be eliminated from the curriculum:

> Thought which is living, growing, organic in structure, cannot be con-
> veyed or represented by a lifeless, static, artificial construction. Nor are
> we studying language by studying such a construction. The sentences
> which grammar presents to us have in very truth ceased to be language,
> once they have been cut off from all reference to the various acts of
> thought-communication which gave rise to them, so that they seem to
> exist in and for themselves, mere mechanical congeries of words, brought
> together only to fulfil [sic] certain arbitrary requirements of the sentence
> form as such. (25)

An empirical study in 1923, by William Asker of the University of Washington, found no meaningful correlation between performance on grammar tests and the students' ability to correct their own sentences or write persuasively.

Later critics have viewed the current/traditional paradigm as lacking in social purpose, as endorsing a narrow view of structure and grammar that appealed to teachers but did not prepare students for active citizenship or for careers. In 1953, Albert Kitzhaber clearly enunciated this judgment: The course, he wrote, "meant the end of any tendency there might have been to recognize the communicative function of language, and the office of rhetoric in ministering to social needs." Writing thus became "an academic exercise to illustrate certain abstract principles or fulfill certain specifications imposed neither by the needs of the student nor by the requirements of the subject or situation" (347). Echoing Kitzhaber, James Berlin wrote in 1987 that this rhetoric "denied the role of the writer, reader, and language in arriving at meaning" (*Rhetoric and Reality* 36).

But this paradigm thrived even as influential teachers denounced it because it did have a very clear social purpose in the late nineteenth century, although not a purpose that Kitzhaber and Berlin would favor. After the Civil War businesses began growing from local shops into national concerns, an effect of the Industrial Revolution spurred by laissez-faire economics and a popularized view of Darwin's theories of survival of the fittest. The nation was increasingly run by industrialists such as Rockefeller, Morgan, Gould, Vanderbilt, and Carnegie who controlled the series of weak presidents that followed Lincoln. Federal and state governments awarded contractors, like Leland Stanford, enormous subsidies of money and land to build railroads across the nation, without monitoring what they charged farmers for crop transport or how they used the land. John P. Morgan's railroad fortune grew so large that he could refuse to loan money to the federal government because it lacked sufficient collateral. By 1879, Rockefeller's Standard Oil controlled from 90% to 98% of the nation's oil refining. Twenty years later Standard Oil had been transformed into a holding company, with diversified interests including the Chase Manhattan Bank, through the invention of the trust. This form of conglomeration allowed 5,000 separate companies to organize into 300 powerful ones by 1890. Morgan's railroad trust, for example, by then owned all but 40,000 miles of track in America (K. Davis 203).

Instead of being an era of active citizenry, this was an era of active businesses and acquiescent governments. During Grant's two terms (1868–76), corruption reigned supreme in government construction contracts, tax collection, funding for the Bureau of Indian Affairs, and railroad legislation. Grover Cleveland (1884–88; 1892–96) chose as Secretary of the Navy a man who had married into Standard Oil and who enlarged the Navy primarily by buying from Carnegie Steel at inflated prices. Although during Benjamin Harrison's tenure (1888–92) the Congress passed the Sherman Anti-Trust Act (1890), this law was virtually abandoned after the Supreme Court ruled in 1895, during Cleveland's second term, that a company owning 98% of the nation's sugar-refining capacity was a manufacturing concern and therefore exempt from this law of commerce. This court also ruled that no anti-trust laws could be used against railroads because to do so would restrain trade. It even declared that the Fourteenth Amendment, passed to guarantee the rights of freed slaves, provided protection for corporations against anti-trust legislation because businesses could be viewed as "persons deserving the law's due process" (K. Davis 204). With this kind of governmental backing, trusts and monopolies could keep prices artificially high, prevent competition, and set wages scandalously low. The victims of this governmental and business power were many: urban poor working in factories and living in slums, farmers whose profits were being eaten up by rate increases and whose homesteaded lands could be granted to railroads, and small business owners floundering in their attempts to compete with national firms.

Power in America was held by families, like the Vanderbilts and Du-Ponts, and by their entrepreneurial businesses. A few college graduates worked with reformers such as Eugene V. Debs and Samuel Gompers or returned to family farms, but the vast majority sought roles within these powerful family-controlled businesses, in that period's equivalent of middle management: in banking, stock brokerage, manufacturing, trade, railroads, lumber, oil, and law. They generally joined the establishment instead of either heading it or opposing it. In America in the Age of Titans, Sean Dennis Cashman refers to these graduates as "the teams of salaried managers who reorganized industrial enterprises of the most efficient and economic scales" (4). Even if they decided to enter politics, their positions would generally be assured by their allegiances rather than by their rhetoric or independent thinking.

Many business and government leaders, in fact, were rather skeptical of the college degree, and viewed it as effete and irrelevant to their world of gain and loss. Brown University's Francis Wayland recorded their prejudice in his 1850 report to the college corporation:

Lands were to be surveyed, roads to be constructed, ships to be built and navigated, soils of every kind, and under every variety of climate, to be cultivated, manufactures were to be established…What could Virgil and Horace and Homer and Demosthenes, with a little mathematics and natural philosophy, do towards developing the untold resources of this continent? (12–13)

Also in 1850, the Massachusetts General Court urged Harvard to establish a new image by abandoning its classical curriculum, giving citizens the more practical, open curriculum they wanted, and paying professors by class size: "Those only would succeed who taught … in a manner acceptable to the public. That which was desired would be purchased, and that which was not, would be neglected" (qtd. in Rudolph 102). At that time Ralph Waldo Emerson often spoke at college literary clubs, usually at off-campus meetings, complaining of the liberal arts college's neglect of individual talents and ambitions, of its dullness that left graduates disillusioned and unfit for careers (Bledstein 259–68). He recognized that college graduates, immersed in Latin and Greek and fraternity exploits, were not being prepared to lead their country or control its industry.

As small parts of a growing machine, then, these young employees would not need the oral training that could prepare them to address audiences of different ages and interests, sway opinion, or fight for a cause. In fact, such knowledge might be viewed as dangerous by the power establishment that made its decisions "through a network of bureaucracies and other complex organizations, by processes almost imperceptible to the 'citizen' and certainly inaccessible to him through official politics" (Ohmann 158). Young middle managers would, however, need mastery of report and memo forms, of correct sentences supporting the company's creeds and assertions—of the expository skills favored by the current/traditional paradigm.

In colleges separated from the real corporate action, where technology specialists and managers received their training, this paradigm thus did have a social purpose. The forms of discourse and modes of exposition guaranteed a basic knowledge of structure but not an expansive understanding of the rhetoric of any one discipline or of powerful techniques of persuasion: These courses taught students to follow a format without questioning its effectiveness. The varied readings did not foster too great an ability at critical analysis; in fact, their focus on personal narratives further removed writing from the arena of decision making. The freshman course's grammatical emphasis might insure that native speakers wrote correctly and that immigrants and others with irregular speech patterns learned the national language (or they would be ejected from the university), but it did not prepare students to use language effectively with various audiences. As Richard Ohmann declared, these courses were "affirming the prestigious language habits of society and discouraging or shaming other habits by ruthlessly applying a few rules of usage and shibboleths of grammar" (167). Beyond the freshman year, engineering, business, and the other majors that students could pursue generally offered too little writing instruction and practice to significantly alter the skill levels with which they left the freshman class. S. Michael Halloran argues that with current-traditional freshman instruction "the greatest loss was of the sense of a large social purpose for writing, a social role for which rhetorical art was necessary equipment" (177). Such a loss was perhaps an intentional one. At a time when the college curriculum was being carefully examined and new majors created, this freshman course came to every university and college, even though it was almost universally criticized, because it was purposeful in American society. It fostered neither the argumentation and leadership skills of classical argumentation nor the literary taste and cultural awareness of belles lettres. Instead it led to a kind of plodding affability—knowledge of how to take any subject and discuss it in five correct paragraphs without regard to its practical purpose, the needs of the audience, or social responsibility. It could thus create pliant business employees, not those who would lead or initiate reform.

2

To Create a New Social Order: Progressivism's Three Tiers of Education

As one of the sole requirements for students across the country, the new freshman composition course obviously served political and social as well as educational goals. The forms of discourse and grammar provided a rule-governed methodology that de-emphasized individual thinking and expression, thus helping to produce the competent but complacent employees needed for an industrial society.

As industrialists assumed power in the late nineteenth century, however, they were met by a strong reaction, now labeled as the Populist and Progressive movements to denote the earlier rural and the later urban reform efforts. This denunciation of powerful corporations and the weak governments that backed them implied a new role and curricular philosophy for writing—not as a matter of formal standards but as a tool of reform and empowerment. For the Progressives, writing courses at the high school and college freshman level held little interest: They did not use their energies to fight against the current/traditional paradigm thriving there but instead targeted the lower schools and advanced college curricula in writing. At the elementary level, reformers wanted to give students more experience with active language use, with the oral communication skills citizens would need to work together and effect change. Because only 1 in 25 Americans progressed beyond elementary school in 1900, citizens would need to learn in the lower grades how to judge new concepts and act responsibly, using their reading and speaking skills much more frequently than writing (*Historical Statistics* 369). Along with forming programs for doctors, engineers, and other specialists who could create progress, colleges began training communication experts to further educate citizens and persuade them to accept new political principles that could improve their lives.

THE POPULIST AND PROGRESSIVE
MOVEMENTS

The Populist and Progressive movements have proven difficult to define, and their meanings and effects have been much debated. The general consensus, however, is that their dominant legacy was an emphasis on social reform, on regulations and party allegiances that would privilege the rights of citizens. As reformers attempted to make government more socially responsive, they broadened education's mandate by extending opportunities to a larger group and by insisting on active learning and problem-solving. At the elementary level, the children's day would be shaped by the language arts of reading, speaking, and listening, key skills for active citizens. And they would learn from college-trained persuaders the "right" information and political values, a form of indoctrination that would create a populace dependent on the Progressive perspective, of course, but independent of the old bosses.

The rationale for the new advanced writing courses, therefore, can only be understood in the context of the political and social climate of this era. As industrialists tightened their hold on the American economy after the Civil War, they began to meet opposition across the country and especially in the Midwest, an area that felt victimized by eastern banks, railroads, and governmental policies. Midwestern farmers and small business owners wanted control over their own economic life, not subservience to eastern monopolies and the federal trade regulations that supported them. Jay Gould, J. P. Morgan, and others used a creed of self-reliance to justify themselves and their enlarging trusts; Darwin's *On the Origin of Species* (1859) seemed to support their survival-of-the-fittest mentality. But this laissez-faire order clashed with the belief in democracy and the American dream held by farmers paying exorbitant fees to transport their crops and by the small factory owners trying to compete with new conglomerates.

In the 1870s, small Populist groups in the Midwest, called Grangers and Liberal Republicans, began to form in response to eastern dominance, and especially to unfair railroad policies. Grange organizations created a third party, the Greenbacks, that endorsed a platform involving better currency regulations, railroad and monopoly legislation, farm and small business credit, and land conservation. By 1878 this group had elected 15 men to Congress, but it was unable to maintain its momentum beyond 1880 when farmers again began to work through local associations.

Rural alliances from several midwestern states, including South Dakota, Kansas, Minnesota, and Nebraska, regathered enough power by 1890 to again send representatives to Congress. But these men felt keenly frustrated by their lack of impact on the tyranny of big business. The alliances met together in 1892 and nominated James Weaver of Iowa as a third-party Populist candidate for president, yet they posed no serious threat to the successful candidacy of Grover Cleveland. William Jennings Bryan, a Congressman from Nebraska, drew their support in 1896 when he ran as the Democratic party candidate on a platform of equal rights for all Americans, anti-trust legislation, and de-centralized government: Bryan lost by only a half million votes.

By 1900, when McKinley again won over Bryan, midwestern alliances were beginning to change their goals: Instead of just seeking the cessation of preferential treatment for industry and business, they wanted the government to place firm controls on America's powerful capitalists. In 1860 there had been only three millionaires in the United States, but 40 years later there were 3,800: One-tenth of the population owned nine-tenths of the wealth of the nation (Weinberg and Weinberg, xiii). Businesses had begun what Sean Dennis Cashman referred to as their "great merger movement," leading in 1901, for example, to the creation of the U. S. Steel Corporation and the Northern Securities Company, a railroad conglomerate (3). Power was centered ever more securely and openly in the few. New sociological research, however, provided reform leaders with theoretical grounding for stringent legal controls on this growing capitalistic power. Ins *Dynamic Sociology* (1883), Lester Ward spoke of human beings as existing above Darwin's laws, able to work together to eliminate unnecessary competition and advance the state for the good of all. Thorstein Veblen and Edward Alsworth Ross also protested laissez-faire policies, arguing that businesses should be regulated and that social welfare should be protected.

The first signs of change came from city governments that endorsed a new, more powerful democracy. Local leaders who resented the corruption and inefficiency of party machines set off a wave of municipal reform campaigns, triggered by disclosures of fraud and by the breakdown of city services during the depression of the 1890s. Mayors William L. Strong of New York, Hazen S. Pingree of Detroit, Mark M. Fagan of Jersey City, and Tom L. Johnson of Cleveland strived for more honest, efficient government and better city services: Johnson forced Cleveland's utilities, railroads, and trolley companies to pay more taxes and won a fight for lower trolley fares; Fagan secured better schools, sewers, hospitals, and playgrounds. These officials believed in extending the power of the mayor, before usually a figurehead or party lackey, to tackle urban waste and create a better standard of living. Some cities instead chose government by civil-service appointees, breaking a pattern of highly partisan elections and paybacks. After a hurricane devastated Galveston, Texas, in 1901, the mayor and council were replaced by an administrative commission, a decision made by hundreds of medium-sized cities in the next decade.

State governments also began to adopt reform platforms, especially after 1905. The New York legislature investigated life insurance companies that year, revealing years of protection and payoffs by the Republican party. Democratic reform candidates won the governorships in South Dakota, Georgia, Alabama, and Mississippi by exploiting the issues of business and railroad control. Many states greatly expanded their regulation of railroads, utilities, and other corporations, creating new administrative structures to make the laws work. From 1905 to 1907 alone, 15 states established commissions to govern railroads and utilities.

This more aggressive view of government's proper role was endorsed and furthered by Robert La Follette, an 1879 graduate of the University of Wisconsin who attended law school briefly and apprenticed in a Madison firm before being admitted to the state bar in 1880. That year, when he ran as a Republican for district attorney in Madison, the Republican boss Colonel E. W. Keyes, postmaster of Madison, informed La Follette that he needed to withdraw because he was not the party's hand-picked candidate (La Follette and La Follette 47). After La Follette was twice elected as district attorney by taking his reform message directly to the citizens, he entered the Congress in 1884, again against the will of Keyes, his lieutenants Philip and John Spooner, and Senator Philetus Sawyer whom John Dos Passos described as "the Wisconsin lumber king who was used to stacking and selling politicians the way he stacked and sold cordwood" (424). In 1891, La Follette made his final break with this power group when Sawyer offered him money to influence his brother-in-law, a judge, to dismiss a case against state treasurers and bondsmen who had invested state monies and pocketed the profits. Sawyer, the principal bondsman, may have absconded with up to $300,000. For the rest of his career, La Follette viewed his refusal as carrying great symbolic import: In this act, voters could witness his commitment to stand by the people, serve their needs, and fight the political machine. He publicized this incident in frequent speeches and retold it to journalist Lincoln Steffens, who included it in his 1904 *McClure's Magazine* article on reform in Wisconsin entitled "Wisconsin: Representative Government Restored." In taking this moral stance and asserting his independence, the ambitious La Follette hoped to secure his own position as the people's advocate and hero.

In his three terms in Congress (1885–91), La Follette worked to release the country from the grip of corrupt industrialists and politicians: by opposing the frequent grants of Native American lands to railroad magnates, by passing a bill establishing an Interstate Commerce Commission for the regulation of railroads, and by instituting agricultural experiment stations that would provide legal and technical assistance to farmers. Having lost his reelection bid in 1890, a year when Democratic candidates swept the state, La Follette returned to Madison to practice law. He supported a friend for governor in 1894, and then he ran in 1896 and 1898, all three times without success, but he was building public support for his platform of honest government. After he was finally elected as governor in 1901, he worked for railroad taxation and regulation, fair income taxes, inheritance tax laws, anti-lobby laws, workman's compensation, regulation of work hours for women and children, and banking reform.

As the earlier theme of less favoritism toward business was replaced by regulation and social legislation, this new Progressive movement began reaching Americans across the country. It especially appealed to millions of lower-class urban voters who had come from rural areas and from other countries for factory jobs and a better life: In New York City, for example, the tenement population had increased from 21,000 in 1879 to 1,500,000 in 1900 (W. N. Davis 745a). After 1900, these workers began to join with small business owners and farmers to support candidates in both parties who would overthrow the political bosses and regulate industry. As President and national leader of the Progressive cause from 1901 to 1908, Theodore Roosevelt filed an antitrust suit against the Northern Securities Company, helped strikers in coal mines, regulated railroads, prosecuted offenses of the meat packaging industry, and promoted conservation. In these efforts he was seconded by such Progressive "Gladiators of the Senate" as Edmond Madison and Victor Murdock of Kansas, Charles A. Lindberg and Moses Clapp of Minnesota, Albert Beveridge of Indiana, and Bob La Follette, who became a Wisconsin senator in 1906.

Ever since this Progressive era, of approximately 1890 to World War I, historians have debated its meaning and impact. The spread of a Progressive vision led to a flood of new regulatory laws on trusts, conditions of labor, voting rights, and railroads. But, as historian Morton Keller has noted, Progressive initiatives had a decidedly negative impact on some disenfranchised groups: Southern African Americans were victimized by the Jim

Crow laws that stemmed from white Southerners' desire to extend their own power, and immigrants faced new restrictions on citizenship because they were judged as most susceptible to the movement's radicalism. Long-term gains against wealth and power, Keller argued, were actually few. But even though, as David Sarasohn wrote, the movement has "taken a considerable battering" with harsh judgments made of its cohesiveness and ultimate results, he noted that for contemporaries it was a significant "effort to limit the power of wealth in America and to provide some protection to those who lacked it" (viii). For Morton Keller, the period's social thinkers engendered "a shift of emphasis from community to society, from ethnic and other tribalisms to larger social units, from a natural, unconscious order to a conscious social one—one subject to social control." Although Keller recognized that older traditions and an increasingly pluralistic society created a tension with "the Progressive thrust to restore social cohesion," he concluded that the movement did shape early twentieth-century social policy (3). Eldon Eisenach also acknowledged the "increasingly convoluted and often frustrating conversation regarding the meaning of Progressivism," but described the legacy of the Progressive era as "the establishment of a new regime" (19).

PROGRESSIVISM AND WRITING INSTRUCTION

Part of this growing Progressive movement was a new vision for education. Progressive leaders agreed that corporations should be allowed to continue their quest for profit, but they should be overseen by a powerful, honest government, strong enough to regulate business and initiate social programs for the good of all. This view necessitated a well-educated, clear thinking populace, who could elect independent leaders instead of being controlled by local party machines that offered protection. Citizens would need the ability to work in groups within their communities, interacting with others to make improvements. They would also need career-oriented education that would allow their farms and small businesses to prosper, ending their dependence on the powerful and creating real progress for all. For the vast majority, formal education ended after the lower grades—in 1900 only 6.3% of Americans finished high school and 2.3% enrolled in college. With such a small amount of people going to high school and with 36% of high school graduates attending college, high school was not viewed as basic education for the majority but as a pre-college curriculum for a select group (*Historical Statistics* 385). For reformers, then, the lower grades, along with continuing education opportunities, held the key to a new active citizenry.

Progressive theorists intended to change the passive curriculum of drill and memorization—on Latin and English grammar, spelling, and mathematics—that had been common in lower schools. In this new vision, students would become active learners, able to associate their school work with their own experiences and with the values of their families and communities. In English, their curriculum would primarily involve the three language arts of reading, speaking, and listening needed for creating informed citizens who could read the latest research, study candidates, and interact locally to insure progress. Less emphasis would be given to writing although children would use it infrequently to report their research results and reach outside audiences.

In this effort to change the lower schools, many Progressive teachers were influenced by European reformers who advocated an active education in problem solving to prepare citizens to be lifelong learners. Through his writings and the widespread reputation of his school for young children in Switzerland, Johann Pestalozzi (1746–1827) argued for universal education, which would develop the best inner powers of the individual and thus would aid the child and the community. His method involved a progression from everyday experience to more complex acts, from the child's dots and lines, for example, to concepts of geometry, reinforced by direct experiences in a classroom community. His ideas soon spread to other schools in Europe and eventually to the United States. The first Pestalozzian school opened in Philadelphia in 1809, and then some of its staff members created a second school as part of a cooperative socialist experiment in New Harmony, Indiana. Many other American schools adopted Pestalozzi's theories during the Progressive period.

Another influential reformer, who visited Pestalozzi's school, was Friedrich Froebel (1792—1852), a German who saw all education as a process of self-activity in which the native endowments of the individual unfold naturally in accordance with laws of human development. His theories led to the kindergarten, which would help young children to use their inborn potentialities to think and act independently. In his kindergarten, self-active behavior included clay modeling, paper cutting, weaving, and manipulations involving the ball, cube, and cylinder, with kits and instructions available for teachers who were forming new schools and classes. His book *The Education of Man* (1826, translated to English in 1887), like his schools and materials, dealt with children only up to 10 years old. The first kindergarten in the United States was established in 1855 in Watertown, Wisconsin, by a brother and sister who had been trained by Froebel. Its instruction, in German, was quickly emulated in other German-speaking communities in the state. In 1873, the first public school kindergarten opened in St. Louis. Many kindergartens were later established in city slums by Progressive philanthropic organizations.

German philosopher Johann Herbart (1776–1841), who also studied with Pestalozzi, further stressed the child's role in society, viewing "dynamic morality" or the dominance of socially desirable ideas as the ultimate goal. Real character could only be achieved through action, through the testing of experience, which the school could provide through well-chosen situations and analysis of them. Herbart began teaching history, literature, language, math, and natural science instruction in the lowest grades through presentations and immediate practical applications so that children could assimilate operating principles to relate to their experiences. His American disciples in the 1890s, such as Charles and Frank McMurry, stressed the use of experiential subject matter appropriate for various levels of child development, compared to stages of development of the human race.

The most influential American reformer, however, was John Dewey. He did his college work at the University of Vermont and graduate study at the new Johns Hopkins University and then began a teaching career at the University of Michigan in 1884. From 1894 to 1904, he taught at the University of Chicago and directed a laboratory school where he could test and demonstrate his educational theories. He then went to Columbia University where he taught for 25 years.

Through his laboratory school and his writings, Dewey experimented with education that emphasized content related to children's own experiences and future role in society. Dewey believed that education should convey knowledge of the past to children so that as adults they could use it to cope with their environment. Instead of concentrating on rote memorization—or just the personal development of the child—he stressed the primacy of learner and content, of involving student groups in the discovery processes of each discipline, through active learning as well as through reading. He thought such an approach would bridge three contrasts or barriers that had stymied education:

First, the narrow but personal world of the child against the impersonal but infinitely extended world of space and time; second, the unity, the single wholeheartedness of the child's life, and the specializations and divisions of the curriculum; third, an abstract principle of logical classification and arrangement, and the practical and emotional bonds of child life. (*The Child and the Curriculum* 7)

Many schools, he asserted, had concentrated on content at the expense of the child, subdividing the subject matter into set categories and marching through them, creating a conflict between discipline and interest. He hoped that learning would no longer be a "routine or mechanical procedure" for which teachers had to create involvement through gimmicks or punishment (28). He advocated the use of occupations, like gardening, cooking, textile work, and carpentry, so that students could deal with problems, acting in ways that creatively connected school life with home life. For the child from ages four to eight, the curriculum would stem from actual experiences, like cooking and gardening. With the teacher's guidance, popping corn could reach to principles of physics, weaving could introduce Indian culture and traditions, and mail delivery could lead to a focus on interdependency in a society. From ages 8 to 10, children would use experience to study the processes by which each discipline worked. Measuring materials for a club house, for example, could lead to principles of mathematics or social intercourse. After age 10, by which time students would have investigated many of the processes involved with reading, mathematics, social studies, and science, they would be ready for further inquiry into each specific field.

Dewey's emphasis on experiential education and active communication was shared by other Progressive educators; many of them, however, focused not on the child as a member of society but as a developing individual, a viewpoint that became especially influential after World War I and until the Depression brought about a new emphasis on social responsibility. At Margaret Naumburg's Children's School (later the Walden School) established in 1914 and at other New York City Progressive schools, such as Elisabeth A. Irwin's Little Red School House and Caroline Pratt's Play School, music, art, and free discussion served as vital means of expression. In the child-study movement, centered in Illinois and led by G. Stanley Hall and Edward Lee Thorndike, students of William James, reformers fostered growth at each natural stage of verbal communication and action. These educators, like Dewey and like earlier European reformers, valued the language arts of reading, speaking, and listening. Instead of relying on drills or exercises, teachers stressed communication as the child needed it, to discuss a field trip, consider the results of an experiment, solve a problem, or probe their own experiences. Within their community, children would naturally express themselves in talk much more frequently than in writing.

Dewey and other American Progressive reformers, following predecessors such as Pestalozzi, Froebel, and Herbart, did not concentrate on high school or college instruction: In their quest for a better educated populace, they worked with lower schools, the beginning and end of education for most Americans and certainly for immigrants and the poor. When Dewey's school at the University of Chicago closed in 1903, only a few students in the third and last stage, ages 12 to 15, had been enrolled. For this age group, he advocated study of the various disciplines, with students learning to draw from each to analyze their culture ("The University Elementary School" 332). But he wrote only generally about those years and never fully tested his ideas within a school. The high school years, it seems, were beyond the priorities of Progressive education and more difficult to structure by its principles: The divisions of subject matter at this level and the amount of material to be learned about each one made a fully integrated curriculum unlikely; these subjects were not as clearly connected to the students' lives; and school administrators had to be concerned with the students' preparation for America's traditional colleges.

Had Dewey given more attention to the high school level and to writing specifically, he could have initiated important change in secondary education. In his view of active learning was couched a strong criticism of the faculty-psychology approach that had led to organizing writing instruction in the high school according to forms of discourse and modes of exposition as at the college level. In "Psychology and Social Practice," Dewey argued for the collaboration of psychological and educational theorists with classroom teachers to insure that schools were guided by the best approaches to education instead of by diluted versions of out-of-date theories. He especially eschewed any educational endeavors based on categorizations of separate brain sites, which had shaped composition's foursome of description, narration, exposition, and persuasion. Instead of endorsing any abstract approach, teachers needed to conduct experiments—going "back to the mother soil of experience"—that would probe the complex relationships between individuals and their changing culture ("The New Psychology" 278–81). Although he did not elaborate, Dewey viewed high school writing assignments as part of an organic active curriculum, as a response to real situations, and not as separate practice on grammar, punctuation, paragraph structure, and essay forms.

Dewey taught at several universities, but he did not discuss the teaching of writing at that level: The current/traditional paradigm flourishing in American colleges was no more the target of his reform efforts than was language arts instruction in American high schools. But he devoted much of his own teaching career to creating another level of writing instruction: for the advanced college and graduate student. At the University of Michigan, he taught basic and advanced undergraduate courses; at Chicago and Columbia, he worked primarily with graduate students in philosophy and education, offering seminars such as The Logic of Experience, The Logic of Ethics, Ethics and Educational Problems, and Social Life and the School Curriculum (Dykhuizen 123, 138). Although he advocated an active classroom for younger students, he taught his college classes by lecturing. He insisted, however, that students develop their own theories through their writing. As one of his students from the University of Michigan commented, "he wisely puts a much higher premium upon a single attempt at original, intelligent thought than upon the parrot-like repetition of whole volumes of other men's thoughts" ("John Dewey, Ph.D." 327–28). With undergraduates and graduates, he emphasized not classroom exercises or school papers but the careful investigation, logical development of theories, and practical applications needed for professional writing concerning philosophy and education.

Other Progressive educational experts whose discipline was English shared the same priorities: They concentrated on the education of primary-school students and advanced college students while tolerating—or at least not attacking—the current/traditional approach in the middle. Fred Newton Scott knew Dewey at the University of Michigan where Scott was first a member of the English department and then head of a separate Department of Rhetoric. In an 1894 article about Scott's promising career, Dewey predicted that his later work would be "marked by command of the resources available, by poise and facility of mind, by adaptation to the real currents of modern life" ("Fred Newton Scott" 122). Scott would make an impact on the discipline of English through his writing, his teaching, and his service as president of the Modern Language Association in 1907, the National Council of Teachers of English from 1911 to 1913, and the American Association of Teachers of Journalism in 1917.

In his early texts and writing, Scott objected to the traditional school curriculum of drill and memorization, but he espoused something very similar to it. In *The Teaching of English in the Elementary and Secondary School*, published in 1903, Scott and his co-authors George Carpenter and Franklin Baker maintained that teachers should "lead the pupil to learn something and to express it clearly, either orally or in writing" (123), with the aim being to communicate with others and the subject matter being personal experience, literature, and other school subjects. But along with that theoretical perspective, he offered curricula that he would rail against in his later writing. Students would work daily with spelling lists, grammar lessons, and paragraph formats, with frequent dictation of correct models. For the high school, he recommended study of description, narration, exposition, and argument, with time also given to writing about literature, paraphrasing, and summarizing.

In his later theoretical writings, he concentrated on the early years of education, speaking against the structured drill that he had advocated in his teacher's guide and bringing writing into the Progressive active curriculum more fully than had Dewey. He wrote of rule-based approaches to language as "untenable, both in theory and practice" because of the natural fluctuations of language and the impact of the changing culture, foreign citizens, and individual tastes ("The Standard of American Speech" 7). Not only was focusing on grammatical errors a waste of time, but it created a terrible conflict in the child. All children have a natural desire to communicate: "In infancy it is indeed the prevailing activity, supplying, next to food, the most urgent craving of the infant mind. It soon becomes a settled habit, with its roots buried deep in the subliminal consciousness" ("English Composition as a Mode of Behavior" 467). Children come to school with a language "adequate to the communication of their needs" which is "little conscious of itself": "It is a mode of behavior like leaping, running, or tossing the arms. Words to a child are wishes, commands, ways of securing what one wants, ways of piecing out gestures. It is a language of vivid sensory reactions" (467). Instead of allowing further natural communication development, Scott maintained, the school quickly "clamps the lid of linguistic ritual" and insists on school subjects and style (468). And thus students long for true communication or vacation as writing loses its real purpose. The student begins to write on empty school subjects in a quasi-academic voice, "a kind of scrambled language of his own, compounded of trite phrases and mangled idioms, which is neither fish nor flesh nor good red herring" (470).

An improved school system would allow children to continue language training, building upon their strong foundation of knowledge and interest by using language instead of by drilling on rules. Scott believed that students should be given ample opportunities to write and to react to writing, to address various audiences in natural communication. Then they would learn to combine abstractions with concrete images and speak in the "kindly, natural, unaffected" tone of the best English ("The Standard of American Speech" 9).

Although Scott frequently spoke and wrote about a new approach to writing, reversing his earlier dicta for the elementary school, he never extended this newer vision to the high school or the college freshman course. His textbook *Paragraph-Writing*, first published in 1891 with co-author Joseph V. Denney, used the paragraph as the basis of composition instruction in high school and introductory college classes. It discussed paragraphs as either *related* or *isolated* (the former being a special unit of a longer composition such as introductory, concluding, and transition paragraphs and the latter being a complete treatment of an idea) and then provided general laws for all paragraphs—unity, selection, proportion, sequence, and variety—using terminology like that found in textbooks by Alexander Bain, A. S. Hill, and Barrett Wendell. Under the isolated paragraph, Scott and Denney discussed placement of the topic sentence and means of development such as definition, contrast, explanation, and particulars. They next presented description, narration, exposition, and argumentation as paragraph and then as essay forms. This book appeared in two more editions in the 1890s and was again re-edited in 1909, without substantial change in its contents.

In *A Brief English Grammar*, published in 1905, Scott and co-author Gertrude Buck concentrated on the grammar rules that the current/traditional paradigm dictated for classroom instruction. They maintained that grammatical rules reflect current usage, not an unchanging system, and that children learn that usage "in a practical way" before coming to school (12). But they also claimed that high school and college students need systematic study, which they provided by explanations and definitions as well as exercises covering sentence types, parts of speech, clauses, prepositional phrases, the declension of nouns and pronouns, verb conjugations, and parsing. *Lessons in English*, which Scott co-authored in 1906 with Gordon A. Southworth, a school superintendent, for high school use, contained explanations and exercises on the parts of speech and mechanics followed by sections on three forms of discourse—narration, description, and explanation—and a chapter on paragraph types.

As head of the Department of Rhetoric at Michigan, Scott ran a required freshman curriculum sequence that involved the four forms and grammar drill: He argued against these methodologies for elementary students, but wrote the textbooks for high school and college and provided the administration for these courses at the college level. But

Scott also created a third level of instruction with completely different goals, separate from the free communication of the child's education and from the current/traditional paradigm of his curriculum for high school students and college freshmen.

In the rhetoric department, in addition to freshman composition courses, Scott and his colleagues created specialized professional education in writing for undergraduate and graduate students that could train them to become powerful members of their society. For creative writers, as the 1909–1910 university catalog indicates, Scott introduced a course in short story writing and an advanced seminar: "A limited number of advanced students who write with facility and are in the habit of writing" submitted their manuscripts for correction by the class and also studied principles of criticism and revision. Prospective journalists could take review writing, a course designed by Scott, who had worked on his college newspaper and for a Cleveland paper, "to give practice, under direction, in the writing of book-reviews for newspapers and magazines," and newspaper writing, a seminar involving theory as well as the editing and publishing of "several numbers of a daily paper" (57–58).

In 1909, the department began offering a program of study in journalism, which included the one journalism course, credit for work on student or university publications, and additional course work in rhetoric and the humanities. By 1920, as the 1919–1920 catalog indicates, the journalism curriculum involved 18 hours of journalism, 12 hours of rhetoric offerings, 10 hours in the English department, and courses in foreign languages, history, and political science. That year, the department added new courses in many genres: playwrighting, newspaper practice, a seminar on newspaper problems, newspaper feature writing, editorial writing, a seminar on editorial practice, and advertisement writing.

With Scott's urging, other academic units also began to offer advanced writing courses by 1920. Within the engineering college's separate department of English, Abraham Strauss and his colleagues offered scientific literature, commercial correspondence, technical journalism, technical exposition, and contracts (Russell 122). The Bachelor of Engineering required one of these courses; the Bachelor of Science in Engineering, which had a larger liberal arts component, required all of these one- or two-hour classes. The undergraduate program in business required no advanced writing instruction, but by 1920 students could elect to take two classes on business writing, covering advertising, commercial correspondence, and sales, that were offered by the rhetoric department.

According to Scott, the best elementary programs would teach free communication through group interaction, and the array of college courses would train skilled practitioners who could inform these active learners.

Sterling Leonard was another powerful advocate of change in the teaching of writing who concentrated on primary education and advanced college courses. He received a B.A. in 1908 and an M.A. in 1909 at the University of Michigan, where he studied with Fred Newton Scott. He taught at the University of Wisconsin as an instructor until 1910, and then at the Milwaukee State Normal School, the Danzig Gymnasium in Germany, and the Horace Mann School, the laboratory school of Teachers' College, Columbia University that was heavily imbued with Dewey's influence. He became an assistant professor at the University of Wisconsin in 1920 and stayed there until his death in 1931 in a boat accident with I. A. Richards (Brereton).

In *English Composition as a Social Problem*, Leonard followed Dewey, an indebtedness noted in the preface, in his conception of teaching writing for the development of both the child and society. He began by noting that children have a natural desire to express what interests them. Thus good subjects would come from "vital, realized experience" (2). In writing, children can also combine their own investigation and experimentation with borrowed ideas to create new productions adapted to an audience. Several active motives can drive this work: the storyteller or entertainer motive that may engender real or fanciful adventures, the teacher motive that leads children to investigate and explain to others, or the community-worker motive that encourages children to initiate useful projects and the writing necessary for completing them. Leonard stressed that children should write for each other and for groups in their community and beyond, using the class as a workshop for evaluating products and treating classmates "as cooperators and audience" (36).

Leonard spent most of the book outlining parts of the writing process. He believed that talking about writing in small groups, which can begin in grade three or four, gives the teacher an informal means of helping students with their speaking skills and paper topics. After this stage of writing, which he called "prevision," students would plan and draft their papers. Then they would read their work out loud in front of the class to receive criticism on organization, detail, and style and to evaluate for themselves where the work did and did not hold readers. In Leonard's view, these sessions, even with the youngest students, could lead to more systematic study of principles of criticism and thus to better written products.

Experience with planning, Leonard believed, had to reach beyond the paragraph to the complexities of longer themes. Students needed more work with grouping materials, beyond the too general beginning, middle, and end since "it is the 'Body' that must be grouped" (85): "They simply have not been taught the essentials of various types of organization, and particularly that of larger units than the single paragraph, about a central or topic sentence" (88). He suggested four basic organization types that could be combined to suit the purpose and audience: time order, emphasis, an order beginning with the basic things, and spatial order. In his teaching, there was no external rightness of any structure but only what worked—"the actual clearness and interest it produces in practice" (108). Thus the best experience would occur as the child tried various structures and realized that "a given form or mode of organization may prove valid and effective" in a given rhetorical situation (191).

For Leonard, grammar study should be approached as another method of making writing clear to readers; it should never dominate a writing course. He cited studies showing that a very large percentage of errors involved just a few rules; future investigation could establish the list of "actually national and reputable present usage" (120). Each child thus should work with a short list to truly master three to six of these essential rules each year, instead of struggling with "such a host of corrections that the child is unable even to remember them" (122). Students should then see the true usefulness of choosing the right forms, to participate in a larger community of writers and readers not to succeed with composition teachers.

But for Leonard this book was just the beginning of a research career. Although he criticized the forms of discourse, joining other teachers in English journals, he did not stay involved with freshman writing instruction. Instead he began to work with the teaching of literature and linguistics, in *The Atlantic Book of Modern Plays* (1921), *Poems of the War and the Peace* (1921), *Essential Principles of Teaching Reading and Literature in the Intermediate Grades and the High School* (1922), *The Doctrine of Correctness in English Usage, 1700–1800* (1929), and *Current English Usage*, completed after his death by an NCTE committee, in 1932. He helped advanced undergraduates and especially graduate students to pursue linguistic research through observations, mathematical calculations and models, and theoretical readings: Like Dewey, he was preparing advanced students to be specialists who could make an impact on their society. At Wisconsin, where writing instruction based on the forms of discourse and on grammar drills was thriving, Leonard thus focused not on reform of freshman composition but on a professional level of instruction.

The career choices of Dewey, Scott, and Leonard reflected the fate of writing courses during the Progressive era. Teachers were willing to consider an experience-based kindergarten. Elementary schools could easily incorporate active projects involving students working together on an experiment or observation and interpreting the results. Even though most lower schools retained some drilling in spelling, grammar, and vocabulary, the active classrooms of Pestalozzi, Froebel, Dewey, and Scott greatly affected these grades. But by the upper grades, which adopted the departmental structure of the university, "English" was becoming a separate daily hour, not the focal point of all learning. The separate English class was a place to achieve many discrete goals, such as study of literature, forms of discourse, and grammar, that might not be connected to the students' other course work and interests. Progressive theory did have some effect on high school courses, particularly by encouraging literary study situated in the students' experiences and creative writing. Between the wars, the Progressive emphasis on scientific investigation and social progress also led to new objective measurements, from IQ tests to grammar mastery sheets. But the current/traditional paradigm continued to dominate high school composition. Although Progressive critics might rail against this instructional model in journals, they did not devote their careers to changing it.

As was true of the high school, Progressive reformers had very little interest in basic college classes, which were viewed as a holdover from the earlier liberal arts degree, a temporary stopping place on the new route toward specialization. At this time, forward-looking college presidents created ever larger sections of the freshman requirements and began staffing them with graduate students or instructors, saving money to spend on what really mattered, advanced instruction and research. The university's emphasis would not be on basic instruction but on the last two years and on graduate work, on the specializations—engineering, agriculture, medicine, and business—that could create progress. Experts would conduct experiments and design new inventions; they would also form laws, serve on commissions, and monitor both business and government. Although, following Harvard's lead, many universities first adopted an elective system after abandoning the traditional liberal arts curriculum, by 1920 most universities had instituted specialized degree programs consisting of a major, general education requirements, and electives (Veysey 10). Students in professional programs spent a decreasing amount of time on general humanities study as career preparation dominated the curriculum.

Included among the new trained specialists would be writers who could educate and sway the populace. This group would be responsible to communicate regularly with the general population about political issues or the latest developments in their occupations. Like graduates of new programs in agriculture and science, they would have expert status—perhaps as the most important of all experts because writing and public speaking would be the primary vehicles through which leaders could reshape the nation. As Edward Bernays, a public relations specialist, commented in 1928 in *Propaganda*, a large Progressive democracy had mandated this ascension of communicators:

> The conscious and intelligent manipulation of the organized habits and opinions of the masses is an important element in democratic society. Those who manipulate this unseen mechanism of society constitute an invisible government which is the true ruling power of our country.... We are governed, our minds are molded, our tastes formed, our ideas suggested, largely by men we have never heard of. (9)

By 1910, Progressive universities would be providing these mind-molders, taste-formers, and idea-suggesters through specialized courses and majors: in journalism, public relations, advertising, public speaking, creative writing, film, and business and technical writing. The new genre offerings reflected the practical structures of other professional college majors as well as the development of American communication occurring, as Bernays commented, through "letters, the stage, the motion picture, the radio, the lecture platform, the magazine, the daily newspaper" (*Propaganda* 39). These classes designed to advance the ethics, professionalism, and public service of mass communications would expand both the university's influence and the media's power.

3

At Wisconsin: A Progressive Writing Curriculum for Advanced Students

The vision of a Progressive society posited a more powerful and active citizenry who would need information to pursue reform. To chart the future wisely, the populace would need guidance from trained communicators, not just from poorly trained newspaper printers or from college graduates who had taken one freshman composition course. At state universities, initially in the Midwest, college administrators and professors began developing new courses that would educate the specialists who would become important leaders of a new democracy.

The new form of advanced writing instruction was enacted first at the University of Wisconsin, during Bob La Follette's years in the governor's office and first terms in the U.S. Senate, from 1901 to World War I. These writing classes arose from the goals this politician shared with Charles Van Hise, his choice for president of the university, and with the first professional writing teachers, such as Willard Bleyer, that Van Hise hired. An influential model of instruction stemming from their vision of writing's role in a democracy soon spread throughout the Midwest and the nation, especially in states with Progressive governments. Although individual courses and teachers at Harvard University and the University of Michigan are studied more frequently, the programs at Wisconsin provided the fully developed, practical model for training communicators that other schools, especially state universities, soon followed.

LA FOLLETTE AS RHETOR

As a student and young politician, Bob La Follette realized that any shift in power in his state away from wealthy loggers, railroad owners, and the politicians they controlled would necessitate a well-informed populace able to understand complex information and choose good leaders. He envisioned himself as a true rhetor guiding the citizenry, thus fulfilling his own ambitions for a political career while creating a better society for all. As he pursued his career, he recognized that a new generation of well-trained, expert persuaders would be necessary to help him assert reform priorities in Wisconsin and throughout the nation.

This man who eventually instigated a new advanced writing curriculum received his training in the creed of public service and the power of rhetoric at the University of Wisconsin. La Follette entered the university's sub-first-year class to prepare for college and then became a first-year student in the general science major in 1875. His wife-to-be Belle Case from Barabou entered the modern classical major that same year. While he was a student, La Follette was influenced by President John Bascom's vision for the university, delivered both in the classroom and in Saturday addresses to the students. Bascom thought that the university could have a great impact on the state if its graduates used their learning to help others and not just themselves. The study of philosophy especially, he believed, would lead students toward a rational life of service. La Follette felt that Bascom's "addresses to the students on Sunday afternoons, together with his work in the classroom, were among the most important influences in [his] early life" (*La Follette's Autobiography* 27). Belle La Follette also appreciated Bascom's powerful rhetoric: "Again and again he would tell us what we owed the State and impress upon us our duty to serve the State in return" (La Follette and La Follette 38).

Even while he was an undergraduate, La Follette immersed himself in the writing profession. After his freshman year, he bought a semi-monthly college paper, the *University Press,* by borrowing money from a Madison lawyer. He published this paper with proceeds from about a thousand subscriptions and from advertisements, which he solicited himself, offering to take resellable merchandise in payment to encourage business. La Follette also wrote the editorials, gathered the college news, and set the type.

In college, La Follette also took every opportunity to improve his speaking skills. In his sophomore year, he acted in *Ici On Parle Francais,* playing a man who pretended to speak French to attract lodgers to his boarding house. He appeared as a villain in a play entitled *Waves* at the Burrows Opera House while taking private enunciation lessons. La Follette also participated in class declamations and orations, literary society orations, college rhetoricals (required orations that affected class standings), amateur dramatics and readings, and junior exhibitions at the capitol, at which he and Belle Case represented their literary societies. In the summers, he traveled with members of his literary society, giving performances in small towns for money. In 1879, he won the Inter-State Oratorical Contest in Iowa City, the first person from Wisconsin to do so, with a speech that analyzed the character of Iago. La Follette portrayed him in melodramatic fashion as an inhuman and conniving villain who preyed on Othello and Desdemona:

> This compound of wickedness and reason; this incarnation of intellect, this tartarean basilisk is the logical conclusion in a syllogism whose premises are "Hell and Night." He is a criminal climax: endow him with a single supernatural quality and he stands among the devils of fiction supreme. (qtd. in Burgchardt 157)

Upon his return home from the contest, La Follette was greeted by brass bands and crowds of students. The speech began his career as a Wisconsin orator, and it also secured his graduation. During this period, all faculty voted on each student's graduation; John Bascom broke the faculty tie on La Follette, arguing that his contributions in oration should override his poor grades. During his senior year, La Follette even considered a career as an actor, but, as he told Lincoln Steffens, "his debts chained him to the earth" (Steffens, *The Struggle for Self-Government* 81).

From the beginning of his political career, La Follette realized that his superior rhetorical skills would enable him to reach the public directly and thus to bypass traditional methods of gaining power and seeking patrons. In his first campaign for district attorney, La Follette stressed his achievements and abilities as a speaker, claiming that he would focus his skills on furthering the people's cause. As his political career developed, La Follette continued to rely on his speaking and writing skills, taking his message directly to citizens from the back of a wagon as they worked in their fields. As governor and as senator, he furthered his career with his stirring speeches and his ability to craft powerful legislation. Frequently, along with specific evidence, La Follette would present his legislation as involving contests between good and evil, using the melodramatic format of his Iago speech to enlist emotional support. When the Congress considered a tax on oleo margarine, a factory product whose success was harming the dairy farm, La Follette portrayed the new product as an evil demon:

> Here is a villainous device for making money lawlessly and subtly, eating the heart out of an industry which is to this Government what blood is to the body. It is not only striking prostrate the agricultural industry, but it accomplishes this by cheating and defrauding the balance of the people—the great

body of consumers—out of both money and health. It spares no one. (qtd. in Burgchardt 169)

In other speeches, railroads, monopolies, huge corporations, and party caucuses became La Follette's Iagos.

La Follette also recognized the power of journalism to further both his career and reform. When he first worked as an attorney, the *Madison Democrat* reported that in one trial his "argument to the jury was effective and eloquent and called forth the greatest praise from the bench and the bar." He often referred to this article in his first campaign for district attorney. When the Madison *Wisconsin State Journal* ran one of the first accounts of a La Follette political speech stating that he "closed with a glowing appeal to old soldiers and young men to reclaim the country," this reported success led to larger audiences of voters who wanted to hear more (qtd. in La Follette and La Follette 46, 48). The *Milwaukee Free Press* also supported La Follette's causes, enabling him to speak regularly to the state's largest urban audience and overcome the effects of the powerful Milwaukee *Sentinel*, which stood by the city's bosses and opposed railroad reform.

La Follette's local efforts were furthered by influential journalists outside of the state, one of whom was Lincoln Steffens. Before he went to *McClure's* as managing editor in 1901, Steffens worked at the *New York Evening Post* and the *Commercial Advertiser*, exposing the plight of immigrants in New York ghettos, the manipulations of Wall Street bankers, and the corruption of city police. He then began travelling to different states to expose governmental abuses. In *The Struggle for Self-Government* on state governments and *The Shame of the Cities* on mayors and city councils, Steffens bluntly reported results of his investigative interviews and observations. In his first piece, he described a Minneapolis cabal headed by Mayor Albert Ames as involving "loafers, saloon keepers, gamblers, criminals, and the thriftless poor of all nationalities" (*The Shame of the Cities* 43–44). After his re-election in 1901, Ames had "laid plans to turn the city over to outlaws who were to work under police direction for the profit of his administration" (47). In St. Louis, with power centered in a corrupt mayor and assembly, "the leading men began to devour their own city" (21). And Steffens was not easily impressed by claims of reform. He declared Philadelphia, where a new council promised change, to actually be the worst governed city: There the "city machine" backed by the "State boss" had initiated a few improvement projects only because city construction led to large kickbacks.

When he first heard of La Follette, Steffens, always skeptical, felt that the young governor must be "a charlatan and a crook." But when he went to Madison to expose this demagogue, he discovered "the story of the heroism it takes to fight in America for American ideals" (*Autobiography* 454, 463) which he recorded in "Wisconsin: Representative Government Restored," published in *McClure's* and *The Struggle for Self-Government*. He decided that La Follette's spellbinding oratory educated the people and that his well-run reform government deserved their support: "His long, hard fight has developed citizenship in Wisconsin—honest, reasonable, intelligent citizenship. And that is better than 'business'; that is what business and government are for—men" (*The Struggle for Self-Government* 118–19). La Follette felt very well served by Steffens' article: He referred to it in speeches frequently and knew that it had increased his national stature as a Progressive leader.

Having seen the power of Progressive publicity, La Follette began publishing *La Follette's Weekly Magazine* in 1909, contributing many of the articles on state and national politics himself. The magazine advertised itself as "an aggressive advocate of legitimate business, of clean government in the interest of the common good, of the ennobling of farm life, of better conditions for workingmen, and of social upliftment" in articles that would "not mince words or suppress facts" (2). Belle La Follette and Caroline L. Hunt's "Women and Education" section, its headnote in the first issue declared, would cover "health, children, home, education, life in Washington, and other topics of everyday interest to women, from the standpoint of personal observation and experience" (8). The Roll Call summarized votes in the House and Senate on important bills. The first issue featured an article on Progressive government by Lincoln Steffens entitled "The Mind of the State" and editorials on the protection of labor. Other magazine contributors included William Allen White, John R. Commons, Jane Addams, and Richard Ely, respected reformers whose contributions helped secure La Follette's position as a major leader of the reform movement.

VAN HISE, BLEYER, AND THE WISCONSIN IDEA

From his own career, La Follette recognized the crucial role of writing experts in the creation of a new society. He knew that superior training in writing as well as cultural studies could prepare young persuaders to further his causes nationally. As governor and then senator, he used his power to secure university training for these communication experts as well as for specialists in engineering, agriculture, sociology, economics, and other fields necessary for progress.

Soon after becoming governor in 1903, La Follette chose his classmate Charles Van Hise as the university's new president, over the objections of some regents, because both men shared a belief in the university's role in providing service to state residents: Belle La Follette later wrote that there were only two other men "for whom he cared so much or in whom he had such absolute confidence and trust as Charles Van Hise" (La Follette and La Follette 163). Van Hise's job was to implement La Follette's vision of a society in which citizens and experts united to work for progress and for the welfare of all, a goal that they labeled the "Wisconsin Idea."

Under Van Hise's leadership, to immediately extend the university's role in the state, university professors began to take on key roles in government. La Follette established a lunch club of professors and legislators that met each Saturday to discuss state problems. Professors sat on railroad and tax commissions and became government consultants, with 37 faculty holding such posts by 1910. Geologist Van Hise chaired the state board of forestry and the state conservation committee. Professor of political economy John R. Commons, a labor specialist who had studied with Richard Ely at Johns Hopkins, served on the Industrial Commission, which regulated factories and provided for the safety and health of workers. With help from his students, Commons drafted Wisconsin's civil service law in 1905, its public utility law in 1907, and its workmen's compensation act in 1911 while advising La Follette on taxation and railroads and creating the first multi-language public employment office in the country. Balthasar H. Meyer, also a professor of political economy, was one of the three members of Wisconsin's first railroad commission and was later appointed by President Taft to the Interstate Commerce Commission. Professor W. D. Pence, of the College of Engineering, served as chief engineer of the Wisconsin railroad commission and then as a member of the federal commission to fix the physical valuation of railroad property. For a 1913 *St. Louis Star* article, English professor Willard Bleyer remarked on the national influence of the well-worn path from Wisconsin to the federal government: "The 'Wisconsin Idea' is spreading from the state to the nation as the value of experts in government wins ever increasing recognition everywhere" ("The University That Is" 6).

As the university developed new programs, initiated research, and advised government officials, one of Van Hise's first concerns was to make these new roles known throughout the state. For Van Hise, the obvious answer was to hire a professional who could create an immediate public relations effort and then begin training future generations of public persuaders. In 1905, Van Hise switched Willard Bleyer from an instructorship to an assistant professorship in English so he could serve as a public relations specialist and teach journalism. They had begun working together on university business in 1903. Bleyer was born in Milwaukee in 1873, into a family of newspaper reporters and editors, and graduated from the University of Wisconsin in 1896. As a student at the University of Wisconsin, he edited three student publications and served as president of the University Press Club, advocating university training in journalism in several newspaper and newsletter columns (D. Ross 9). From 1892 to 1898, he worked for his father and uncle at the *Milwaukee Sentinel*; in 1898, he received a master's degree in English from Wisconsin; he then taught English for two years at East Side High School in Milwaukee and received the PhD in English at Wisconsin in 1904.

Van Hise chose a journalist for his public relations specialist because a massive publicity effort would require the cooperation of newspapers, the best means of reaching the most citizens. In an address that Bleyer wrote for Van Hise to deliver at the Wisconsin Press Association in February of 1905, they made the press's importance to the university clear:

> The question now arises, how can the press assist the University ? . . . The press can assist the University by giving to the people full information concerning the University . . . . This is not advertising in the ordinary sense; for the University does not exist for itself, but for your constituents. ("The Relations of" 3)

In this speech, Van Hise and Bleyer acknowledged the potential of university pamphlets and meetings as publicity vehicles, but asserted that because of the large circulation "it is to the newspapers of the state therefore that the University feels it must look for its support in the effort which it is making to reach all the people" (3).

Van Hise and Bleyer's primary medium for getting the right information to newspapers was their press bulletin. Beginning in 1905 as one of the first such organs in the country, the bulletin was a mimeographed sheet about the work of the agricultural college only, but it developed into several 8 1/2 x 11-inch pages about the entire university with features, summaries of articles, lists of accomplishments, discussions of faculty and student travel, course and conference announcements, and legislative news. The bulletin's Progressive goals, as Bleyer summarized them in a 1918 report to Van Hise, were three: to educate citizens concerning the university's research and investigations, to inform them of the university's programs, and to furnish accurate reports on official news of the university. In different versions for different constituencies, the bulletin was sent to Wisconsin's daily and weekly papers, to state agricultural and dairy papers, to metropolitan dailies in all states, to national news bureaus, and to educational magazines. By 1918, 239 Wisconsin dailies received bulletins of about 1,000 words, usually containing four news articles and a few notices, once or twice per week. A special agricultural bulletin of about 1,500 words went to 239 Wisconsin weeklies and 36 agricultural weekly and monthly periodicals. Bleyer, along with editorial assistants and student aides, handled the news collection and the writing or rewriting of submissions as well as the typewriting, mimeo-graphing, addressing, and mailing. In the press bulletins for 1905, for example, Bleyer called farmers' attention to the agricultural experiment station's research on dairy production and feeding, indicating that further information could be obtained by post card request. He also publicized lectures given by the English department and short courses in meteorology offered by the university's weather bureau.

Besides reaching the newspapers, Bleyer built the school's reputation and service through informational bulletins. In 1906 for this series, Bleyer wrote a pamphlet entitled *The High School Course in English*, which was publicized through notices in the press bulletin and the *Wisconsin Journal of Education*, sent out to high school teachers and principals, and mailed by request to teachers and administrators in other states. Because of the overwhelming response, the bulletin was reprinted and marketed by Post Publishing in Appleton, Wisconsin. Its success led to a series of pamphlets dealing with problems in lower-school education.

Representatives from other universities and from companies wrote to Bleyer frequently for information on these public relations campaigns. In 1913, 120 visitors, including mayors, editors, college presidents, school superintendents, and teachers from Pennsylvania, New Jersey, Massachu-setts, and New York, met in Madison to learn about the Wisconsin Idea and the public relations effort that sustained it. After four days of presentations, including a lecture by Van Hise, they especially praised the "statewide dissemination of the vast accumulations of knowledge in a form accessible to the public" (Bleyer, "The University That Is" 2). Their trip would enable them to plan for effective publicity in their own states.

As a further means of reaching the citizenry, Van Hise and Bleyer sponsored public relations events through the alumni association, beginning in June of 1904 with a campus showcase, the Jubilee Celebration, at the opening of which Van Hise discussed the Wisconsin Idea. Bleyer also introduced specialized alumni clubs, like the Alumni Teachers Club, which he addressed at its inaugural meeting in Milwaukee in 1906. In 1910, Bleyer helped Van Hise to organize and host an alumni reunion for which they prepared an illustrated guide to the university as a souvenir.

Another major educational and public relations effort sponsored by Van Hise and Bleyer was the University's Extension Division, conceived of as a crucial component of a Progressive university, a direct link to the citizenry for providing more instruction than could occur through newspaper articles and individual bulletins. Extension courses and information packages could improve farm production, city government, and cultural life and introduce citizens to Progressive theories of economics and politics. These courses could thus produce the well-prepared readers and thinkers who would work together in their communities to ensure progress. Special foundations at the Lowell Institute in Boston, the Cooper Institute in New York, and the Peabody Institute in Baltimore as well as the Chautauqua Movement had been doing extension work; extension programs were also well established at Oxford and Cambridge. But the University of Wisconsin was the first American university to establish its own extension department, to help citizens and improve the university's image.

To further promote the university, one group that the extension department immediately began serving was newspaper reporters. In August of 1912, the department sponsored the first National Newspaper Conference where Governor McGovern talked about Wisconsin's reform movement and the head of the Board of Regents, James E. Trottman, spoke of the ties between the state, the university, and newspapers. Bleyer had urged Van Hise in a letter from May 3, 1911, to sponsor such an event and offered to take care of the arrangements. This conference, he asserted, could be a public relations coup: The journalists' exposure to the university could "prevent in the future much of the criticism, particularly by editors of weekly papers who do not realize the size of the university or the magnitude of its work." His letter offered this example of better communication and its positive effects:

As an illustration of the effect of getting weekly newspaper editors to come to the university and see its work may be cited W. H. Bridgman, editor of the Stanley Republican and President this year of the Wisconsin Press Association, whom, at my suggestion, the authorities of the college of agriculture secured as the principal speaker on "The Relation of Weekly Newspapers to Rural Uplift" at the recent county life conference. Mr. Bridgman has always been inclined to criticize the university, although not as an enemy. Since he was down here, he has taken on several occasions a decided stand for the university and now proposes to send four persons to the ten day courses [journalism seminars] next winter, as you will see from the accompanying copy of the Stanley Republican.

Bleyer believed that if, like Bridgman, other critics came to subsequent conferences, they too would leave singing the university's praises.

Another part of the extension division, called the package library department, sent out packets of newspaper clippings, magazine articles, reports, and pamphlets "to anyone, anytime, any where, for the mere asking," generally on current issues about which the books in public libraries provided little assistance (Bleyer, "University of Wisconsin Extension" 5). In 1912, according to director Almere L. Scott, the department lent 2,450 packages containing over 98,000 articles to 315 places in the state: authors' clubs, literary societies, men's clubs, social centers, working girls' clubs, normal schools, trade and high schools, equal suffrage associations, farmers' clubs and Grange meetings, and temperance organizations. The most popular packages concerned Progressive social and political issues: women's suffrage, income tax, immigration, presidential election, tariffs, election of senators, commission government for cities, the minimum wage, and government ownership of railroads.

The extension division also established a Legislative Reference Library at the state capitol, called the "bill mill," for use by state legislators. Its head, Dr. Charles McCarthy, a political science professor, offered to collect information and create first drafts of bills, following models provided by legislation from other states and nations. Other professors and their students, from political economy, political science, law, and sociology, aided McCarthy in his work. This collaboration epitomized La Follette and Van Hise's vision of the university serving its state.

BLEYER AS JOURNALISM PROFESSOR

From the time that he secured Van Hise's appointment as university president in 1903, La Follette advocated immediate efforts not only at informing the citizenry and improving the state, but also at training a new generation of professional rhetors who would be able to join him in carrying the Progressive message to the people. His experiences as an undergraduate, a struggling young politician, and a respected state and national leader all convinced him that one of the new professions for a modern democracy had to be persuasion. Like La Follette, Van Hise recognized that writing would be one of the key modern specialties because it could deliver knowledge to citizens and argue for the best leaders and best routes to progress. As he did in developing other specialized course sequences—in agriculture, medicine, science, engineering, and business—Van Hise focused on advanced, professional training in writing that combined research, theory, and practice. Instead of covering general skills, he focused on professional genres like public relations, journalism, creative writing, business writing, technical writing, and speech. La Follette and Van Hise believed that the reporting and interpreting of social change should not be left in the hands of poorly trained journalists bereft of a vision for the nation's future, without college degrees and specialized writing training. Instead, by combining journalism instruction with thorough study of social problems, they planned to prepare students to continue the state's efforts at governmental reform and progress. Bleyer's clear vision of an advanced curriculum, and his indefatigable efforts to achieve it, led to a fully developed journalism major at Wisconsin before World War I.

In developing this curriculum requested by La Follette and Van Hise, Willard Bleyer portrayed the ironic combination of priorities found in La Follette's career and in Progressivism generally. Bleyer wanted to train students so that they could have a powerful impact on their society, to not only write correctly but to evaluate their culture, educate the populace, and thus change the world. But like La Follette, Bleyer found in this new vision of democracy a seat for his own ambitions. Within journalism, he could be the chief enabler or teacher, or "Daddy" as students called him, creating his own empire and insisting on his own vision of instruction even as he opposed the power of America's political bosses. Although he advocated greater power for the people through free speech, Bleyer trained only the brightest college students and restricted others from access to writing careers. In the Progressive search for experts generally, in engineering, law, and other fields as well as in writing, such exclusivity reigned: Only the brightest and best trained should help the people.

From the beginning, Bleyer and Van Hise carefully defined their goals and curriculum as tied to the need for experts in the new democracy. In "The

Relations of the University to the Press," an address that Bleyer wrote for Van Hise to deliver before the Wisconsin Press Association in 1905, they announced that this program would teach students "to interpret present conditions in the light of past history" and provide "a fair, unbiased view of the great subject of government and administration." To achieve those goals, students would study American history, the history of political thought, contemporary politics, diplomacy, state and federal administration, public finance, modern sociological thought, municipal government, and agricultural industries. In these courses as well as writing courses, students would learn "a high sense of responsibility to the public," so that they would not cater to "debased taste" but would instead "raise the level of material, intellectual, and spiritual living" (Bleyer, "Relations of ").

Wisconsin's new classes on reporting were the beginning of a new college specialty. Earlier journalism instruction at other colleges had focused on printing skills. In 1869, along with programs in law, engineering, and business, Robert E. Lee instituted college instruction in newspaper printing at Washington College (later Washington and Lee) to help revitalize the South and publicize its progress. Kansas State College of Agriculture and Applied Science began teaching printing in 1873. Cornell, Denver University, and the University of Missouri also hired local printers to offer this practical training.

In his constantly developing array of writing courses, combined with social studies requirements, Bleyer focused on training influential writers, not printers. Thus his 1905 course entitled Newspaper Writing was labeled by his colleague Grant Milnor Hyde as "the first course of journalistic instruction which has continued without a break. . . 'the journalistic year one'" ("Taking Stock" 8). The next year, to extend the students' control over influential newspaper genres, Bleyer established a second course that covered editorial writing, special feature and magazine work, and the history of journalism. By 1911, Bleyer had further increased the number of writing courses, adding Newspaper Reporting and Correspondence, Newspaper Editing, Editorial Writing, and Special Feature and Magazine Writing. Bleyer also offered additional "seminaries" in journalism each year, on different topics such as special articles for magazines and the history of journalism, as well as Technique of Printing and Publishing and Technical and Trade Journalism. In 1911, the Department of Political Science began offering the senior-level Current Political Topics, a course for journalism students on interpreting and writing about various types of documents, as well as The Law of the Press, which covered copyright, literary property libel, and privileged publications. In 1913, Bleyer added a requirement for seniors to write a thesis.

Bleyer also advocated the institution of advertising courses because he knew that, as newspapers became big businesses, he could not simply teach writing and editing and assume that students would be prepared for leadership roles in journalism. As he noted in a 1918 book, advertising had gone from filling one third of the 8 to 12 pages of the 1890 newspaper to one half to two thirds of the contemporary 24- to 60-page newspaper, and it contributed from two-thirds to three fourths of each paper's budget (*The Profession of Journalism* 19). By studying this monolith, Bleyer believed, journalism students would never underestimate the causal chains existing among advertising, newspaper readership, and newspaper content. The first advertising course, Methods of Farm Advertising, was offered in the College of Agriculture in 1910, and philosophy professors contributed Principles of Advertising in 1911. In 1915, the Department of Political Economy was also offering Newspaper Advertising.

After 1915, Bleyer added many more professional courses: on German and French newspapers, free hand and applied drawing, typography and makeup, women's departments and women's features, national advertising campaigns, country weeklies, newspaper management, marketing methods, social service and educational publicity, the relation of the press to the public, and newspaper administration. In 1929, he established four separate tracks—on general newspaper writing, community journalism, advertising, and the teaching of journalism. Along with the increased number of journalism courses, he maintained extensive social science requirements, one fourth of the degree program as in 1905.

As he extended his course offerings, Bleyer also began professionalizing his syllabi to create complete instruction for activist professionals. When he first taught reporting, Bleyer handed out lists of facts for students to write stories from as practice work. Soon students began doing fewer of these "make believe" exercises, which could not teach them about "gathering news, judging news values, developing initiative and imagination." Instead, students were given assignments by editors of Madison's *State Journal* and *Capital Times* and the student newspaper, the *Cardinal.* In the first term reporting class, the city newspapers phoned in a variety of work—"city hall, capitol, court house, meetings, interviews, fact articles, feature stories." To help students prepare their articles, Bleyer acted as city editor and fellow students acted as proofreaders. In the second semester, students had regular city beats—and thus found their own story topics—but they still met with their teacher/editor to assess results. In courses on engineering and agricultural journalism, students worked on the *Wisconsin Engineer*, a quarterly published by the College of Engineering, and the *Student Farmer*, a monthly sponsored by the College of Agriculture that was renamed the *Wisconsin Country Magazine* in 1910 (Bleyer, Digest of Talk).

As the journalism curriculum developed, the early meetings with teacher/editors grew into a sophisticated workshop method. In Women's Features in 1922, for example, Professor Ruby Black taught a thorough process for each article type the course covered: interviews, personality sketches, achievement stories, feature stories, articles on politics, the women's editorial, and the long creative article or series of articles. First her students researched the freelance market for each piece and studied similar published articles. They next reported these findings to the instructor and classmates, decided on their own topics, and began their research, providing daily updates on their progress. As they wrote, they discussed their rough drafts and subsequent revisions in class sessions and in conferences with the instructor; classmates then worked together on marketing their completed articles ("Teaching Women's Features").

In beginning and advanced reporting courses, however, instruction never focused solely on this practical training; it also prepared students to evaluate their profession and culture. Class sessions covered the history of the news story and the changing ethics of reporting. Additionally, students analyzed news sources, like press releases and wire services, to decide how fully they covered events and whether this coverage revealed any biases. Next students considered the news stories that various papers assembled from these reports to judge the papers' readership and editorial policies. They learned to further analyze a newspaper by evaluating the space and positioning of various features, including comics and ads. Students also studied the organization and practical workings of municipal, county, state, and federal government agencies as well as courts, industry, banks, schools, churches, and clubs, a detailed project for which they used Madison as an example (Bleyer "What Schools of Journalism").

While taking these reporting classes, students could join several press clubs where they further analyzed the power and ethics of their profession. The University Press Club, for men, organized in 1892, held monthly dinners where professionals spoke. The Women's Press Club, including university and Madison women, held bi-weekly meetings with speakers. By 1910 the journalism program also sponsored Cubs' Club for first- and second-year journalism students, a journalism fraternity for juniors, seniors, and graduates, a journalism sorority for junior and senior women, and an advertising club.

Bleyer also helped form national journalism honorary societies for students so that they could begin functioning as working colleagues. A Wisconsin affiliate of a women's honors society, Theta Sigma Phi, began in 1909 with Bleyer as sponsor; he received from the national group the only lifetime membership ever given to a man. Sigma Delta Chi, a national honorary fraternity for men and women, began that same year. Bleyer lobbied at national meetings over the next seven years for its membership to be restricted to journalism majors with high grades, a battle he finally won. The fraternity's second annual convention was held in Madison in 1914, with the principal address given by Hamlin Garland and the opening address by Joseph M. Davies, the federal Commissioner of Corporations. Students came from 14 universities: Wisconsin, Michigan, Washington, Iowa, Illinois, Kansas, Missouri, Denver, Virginia, Pennsylvania, Oregon, Ohio State, DePauw, and Purdue.

Along with undergraduate study, Bleyer quickly developed a graduate program in journalism, the first in the nation. Candidates for this master of arts degree took eight hours in journalism and eight hours in English. They also undertook independent projects in journalism history. The university offered its first graduate fellowship in journalism to Louis P. Lochner, a University of Wisconsin graduate who would win a Pulitzer Prize for meritorious service in journalism. Graduate students could also apply for an alumni fellowship of $400, from money raised through the alumni magazine. By the 1920s, Bleyer also offered a minor in journalism that students could pursue as they completed their PhD requirements in other fields, usually in the social sciences. Ralph D. Casey, who became director of the University of Minnesota's school of journalism, was the first to be awarded this minor in 1929, along with a PhD in political science.

For Bleyer, graduate study offered the chance to foster reform of journalism standards by involving teachers and students in evaluating the profession's past and its ethics. An avid researcher of journalism history, Bleyer visited Europe and Asia to study early newspapers. At the British Museum in the summer of 1923, he discovered 15 of the first 16 issues of Ben Franklin's paper, the *New England Courant*, and then published an article concerning its contributors and their criticism of the church ("The Beginning of"). He also researched the *Ladies' Home Journal*'s answers to correspondents and compared them with similar ethics columns in seventeenth- and eighteenth-century English periodicals ("Answers to Correspondents"). He shared these archival materials and his research methods with his students because, as he explained in a 1918 report to his dean, "instruction relative to the influence of the press on the social and political life of the state and the nation must be based on carefully ascertained facts" ("Report of the Chairman"). Careful study of the media's influence seemed especially critical to him as a world war was being waged on battlefields and championed by the press.

In doggedly crafting a curriculum at the undergraduate and graduate level, Bleyer was establishing a powerful force for the future: His graduates could lead the country. Because of that possible influence, he wanted only the best students to enter his program and move on to writing careers. Strict entrance standards would also increase journalism's professional status, as Bleyer's colleague, Grant Milnor Hyde, who was hired in 1910, declared: "Only the law school and engineering college have similar standards. This is as it should be, since journalism is a professional course" ("Raising the Quality" 18).

To achieve their goals, Bleyer and Hyde also enforced stringent requirements for students after they had been admitted to the journalism degree. They were required to enter the program during their first year and remain there: They could not transfer in as sophomores or juniors without starting over and doing the complete four years' work. Instead of judging beginners through an entrance or psychological test, Bleyer and Hyde used the first two years, with careful evaluation at the end of each semester, as a required pre-journalism program designed to help students see if the career was right for them and to help professors decide if the students were right for journalism, a process Hyde called weeding out the "unfit," the "deadwood," and the "browsers." Hyde maintained that this arrangement was unique to Wisconsin: Instead of making decisions about the students' aptitude for the career at the freshman year without enough information or at the senior year without enough strictness, his staff insured that students were judged fairly but rigorously ("Raising the Quality" 17). Those students who remained took the advanced courses in journalism and advertising together: No other undergraduates could enroll. In the last two years, these journalism students had to maintain an 83 average, "high fair," although the university required only a 77 average. In expecting students to take an extensive social sciences component as well as the journalism courses, Bleyer really asked them to commit to an additional semester or year. He maintained in 1931 that he had continuing faith in this combination's results:

Personally, I would be willing to pit the average journalism graduate against the average liberal arts graduate, not on the basis of his fitness to enter upon a journalistic career, but on the basis of his ability to think straight and to apply what he has learned to present-day social, political, and economic problems. That, after all, is the final test of the value of a college education, and that is a test that I believe the average school of journalism graduate is ready to meet. ("What Schools of Journalism," *Journalism Quarterly* 44)

Because he wanted to build a state and national reputation, Bleyer worked diligently at preparing students for their careers. Besides their work on campus and city papers, he wanted them to form contacts at other regional newspapers. To gain further experience, students went to various locations around the state each year to operate local newspapers for a week, taking over the editorial, advertising, and business departments for a "University of Wisconsin edition." Bleyer also arranged for students to take trips, with their classes or clubs, to large-city papers. In April of 1913, for example, students went with him by train to Chicago where, in one day, they visited the Western Newspaper Union, the American Press Association, the Barnes-Crosby Engraving Company, the Associated Press, the City News Bureau, the *Chicago American*, and the *Chicago Tribune*. By using his professional contacts and relying on his own graduates, he helped students move from school to their first jobs ("Outline for Analysis of News Report").

Although he provided opportunities and guidance, Bleyer intended for students to follow the program and not diverge. He was loyal and good-natured, a man who liked jokes and who liked students. The preface to Bleyer's *Journalism* described his special relationship with the majors waiting for their advising appointments:

They are waiting to see a Dr. Bleyer who has shown himself a friend. He has helped one to get a summer job, another an exceptionally good newspaper assignment; through encouragement and suggestion he has helped a third to sell a special feature article. . . . To them Dr. Bleyer is not only author and authority but a wise counselor, a professor of sound judgment and fair mind, and a man who knows more about your ability than you know yourself. (7—8)

But "Daddy," as he encouraged students to call him, also expected students to learn his facts and heed his counsel. They could not alter their curriculum, argue over assignments or grades, or question his control of the *Cardinal*. He was not regarded as a stirring teacher; in fact he was "dry as dust" according to Curtis D. MacDougall, his student who later taught at Northwestern. As Dan Mich, who became editor of the *Wisconsin State Journal* and later editor of *Look*, stated, "It was ever his misfortune that he could not bring to his classroom lectures the informal sparkle which characterized his private conversations." As Walter Monfried of the *Wisconsin State Journal* noted, Bleyers assigned readings and his lectures often failed to engage students (qtd. in Nelson 5).

Bleyer encouraged women to prepare for newspaper careers, but only within certain limits. He and Hyde felt the need to sidetrack them into courses on the women's section of the paper or on teaching journalism in the high school and thus keep them away from hard news, a male dominion:

> Although not every woman is fitted for newspaper work, she may be fitted for some other branch of journalism. Such a broadening of the field has saved us from the embarrassment incidental to the persistent influx of women students into journalism courses. (Hyde,"Raising the Quality" 21)

Bleyer was willing to write a textbook with an instructor from the English department, Margaret Ashmun, but when she insisted that her name be placed first on the cover because she had done most of the work, he withdrew from the project. His 1910 letter to Reading Publishers declared that he had expected his name to appear first because of "masculine superiority." Women were welcomed on the faculty, but discouraged from teaching courses other than those concerning the women's page; newer hires such as Ruby Black and Helen Patterson, however, did move into some reporting courses in the 1920s.

As he built his own curriculum and molded students, Bleyer also continuously sought separate departmental status and control, combatting with the Dean of Arts and Sciences, biologist Edward Birge, who opposed the entrance of new professional programs into his college. Having been hired by John Bascom, Birge endorsed the view that the university would best serve the state by developing the traditional arts and sciences and he disliked "cheap political tricks" by faculty who wanted to deter the college from his goals (Curti and Carstensen, *The University of Wisconsin* II 303). In 1907 Bleyer began his quest by asking the dean to make him advisor to all students who wanted to pursue the interdisciplinary Courses Preparatory to Journalism, a major involving the few writing courses and social science requirements. In the catalog for 1908-09, Bleyer appeared as an Assistant Professor of Journalism, both at the beginning of an expanded list of journalistic writing courses within the English department and at the head of a section on the Course in Journalism. He had requested this change in the program's title, replacing Courses Preparatory to Journalism, from the Board of Regents to reflect his stress on the theory and practice of actual newspaper work; the new title appeared in the catalog before the board approved it on February 23, 1909.

Although new labels were an improvement, his ultimate goal, which he kept masked when necessary, was a separate administrative unit. On January 9, 1909, Bleyer wrote to Van Hise to call his attention "to the desirability of organizing a department of journalism in the university," arguing that his courses did not fit into the English department's curriculum. Dean Birge, however, still planned to maintain the existing situation: He did not want a new power base or budget unit in his college. On January 21, 1909, Bleyer wrote to Dean Birge to protest his decision to keep journalism within the English department and offer a comparison to the new Department of Public Speaking, formed in 1906 from the rhetoric and oratory courses that had been housed in English. He here stated his goals in a less strident form than with the more supportive Van Hise: "While not urging departmental organization for journalism, I would, of course, prefer that form to the grouping which you suggested [an interdisciplinary major only]."

But, even as he reassured Birge, Bleyer continued to lobby Van Hise; the chair of the English department, John Cunliffe; and members of the Board of Regents for separate departmental status. In a June 27, 1910, letter, having been informed of this ongoing effort, Birge complained to Bleyer that

> I have been placed in a wholly false position with the Regents and find myself now in a somewhat humiliating position, since I am compelled to take back entirely the assurances which I gave them only a little more than a year ago [that no further positions or schools would be needed].

In a letter on June 28, Bleyer assured Birge that he was not planning expansions, and here he honestly if coyly maintained that he was not fighting for the "school" that Birge had mentioned, but he had instead been trying to obtain a separate department: "No one, so far as I know, has ever advocated the establishment of a school of journalism at Wisconsin. I do not believe that such a school is necessary or desirable, now or in the future."

By 1915–16, Bleyer was listed as chairman and associate professor of journalism under the Course in Journalism, which was still not a separate department, but he and Hyde were no longer members of the English department: the result of a compromise between Birge and Bleyer. In 1919, he finally formed a separate department and was made professor of journalism. He achieved the ultimate goal of director of a new school of journalism, offering a BA and MA, in 1927. This ultimate decision occurred after the Twentieth Anniversary Journalism Reunion sponsored by the Journalism Alumni Association on June 20, 1925, at which with Bleyer's encouragement all participants signed a petition for a separate school, a move that would increase the reputation of "the oldest and largest professional course of study in journalism in the world" ("Wisconsin Alumni Want School" 12).

Bleyer also had difficulty getting Birge's approval for advertising courses, which seemed too vocational for the college. The first advertising course, Methods of Farm Advertising, was offered in the College of Agriculture in 1910, but Birge and the English department were not willing to crosslist it for journalism students. In January of 1911, Bleyer maintained to Birge that a separate, more theoretical advertising course offered through the journalism program might become a requirement in commerce, agriculture, and engineering and that it would extend the journalism students' ability to persuade the public. Bleyer informed Birge that R. T. Carver, from the Associated Advertising Clubs of America, and A. M. Candee, president of the Milwaukee Advertising Club, would be in town to address the Students' Advertising Club on the need for university instruction. He pressed Birge to approve the course immediately and thus avoid antagonistic meetings with club members who would be stringently supporting this addition to the curriculum (no doubt at Bleyer's request). This piece of persuasion led to advertising courses taught in the philosophy and political economy departments.

For both the journalism and advertising courses, Bleyer also appealed to Dean Birge for space where he could emulate a professional environment. In 1910, he got his frequently requested "lab" located next to his office, which he soon filled with six typewriters, several thousand clippings from newspapers and magazines, instruction sheets on biographical, descriptive and statistical stories, illustration files, and reference books. By 1915, Bleyer added a reading room and a seminary room.

Another Bleyer acquisition for his select group of students was the campus newspaper. In 1909, as he explained in a letter to Franklin Scott of the University of Illinois, he had begun to "take charge of" the student-run *Daily Cardinal*, requiring first-year journalism students to act as sub-reporters, sophomores as reporters, and upper-class students as editors and business managers. Other Wisconsin undergraduates were no longer able to participate. To secure the paper as a laboratory for only his students, Bleyer assured its board of directors, including Charles Van Hise, that he was not attempting to control editorial policy or to censure the news, but to offer practical experience to journalism students enrolled in a coherent sequence of courses on writing and editing. He argued that the few nonmajor participants did not need this professional experience (Letter to George E. Vincent).

As Bleyer and Hyde formed their professional program to train communicators, they also sought a greater influence throughout the region and country. Bleyer worked to form the American Association of Teachers of Journalism (AATJ), which held its formative meetings between 1910 and 1912. When the organization became officially established in Chicago in 1912, Bleyer was elected its first president. The 1913 meeting in Madison was attended by 24 teachers from 17 schools, primarily in the Midwest: Wisconsin, Beloit, DePauw, Illinois, Indiana, Iowa State, Kansas, Marquette, Minnesota, Michigan, Missouri, Notre Dame, New York, Oregon, Louisiana, Columbia, and Pittsburgh (Hyde, "Taking Stock" 9). Discussion focused on improving professional practices and reaching a larger public. Papers concerned teaching techniques, agricultural journalism, advertising, the college and city paper as possible laboratories for students, and printing plants. Dean Birge participated in a panel discussion on journalism's place in the university curriculum; J. W. Cunliffe gave a talk on the journalist's social responsibility. Cunliffe was by then teaching at Columbia as professor of English and associate director of the School of Journalism, a job for which years of coping with Willard Bleyer had provided preparation (Final Programme).

Bleyer later recalled that at these first meetings professional journalism instruction was still on trial—with both newspapers and universities—and so attention had to be given to its validity and basic methodologies. In an address at the 1921 meeting, however, he declared that the association was ready to move beyond these fundamentals and focus on larger issues, such as the quality of American journalism and the role of the press in a democracy. Bleyer wanted AATJ meetings to become scholarly gatherings that would guide the teaching of journalism and ultimately journalism itself ("A Constructive Program"). For the 1923 conference, he spoke on research issues that needed thorough investigation, such as the effect of form and typography on rapidity of reading; the space and prominence given to news, scandal, trivia, editorials, illustrations, and ads; the newspaper's impact on a nation's ideals; the publicity and propaganda in newspapers; and advertising's effect on readers. He also introduced mathematical formulas for analyzing a newspaper's priorities by the location and size of the headlines, body, and pictures ("Research Problems and Newspaper Analysis"). Public relations pioneers Ivy Lee and Edward Bernays were invited speakers at the convention who discussed the newspaper's role in forming public opinion. (Programs for the 1923).

Bleyer and Hyde's early organizational work, strong presentations, and large alumni group gave Wisconsin an especially strong presence within the society and among the profession's leaders. At each convention, Bleyer was said to ceremoniously get a program, check over the names of Wisconsin graduates participating, hand the program to Hyde, and remark, "Another Wisconsin show." Bleyer's first cousin, Mrs. John L. Meyer, said that when the heads of schools of journalism met in the early 1930s, all but one had been Bleyer's students. Among his alumni were such well-known teachers and administrators as Ralph Casey of Minnesota, Curtis D. MacDougall of Northwestern, Blair Converse of Iowa State, and Roy L. French of Southern California. Bleyer felt that this spreading influence would create support around the nation for rigorous professional and social science training—and would aid his students in the job search.

To provide necessary materials for courses at Wisconsin and at other universities, and to thus further promulgate their curricular priorities, Wisconsin's faculty led the nation in writing journalism textbooks. In 1925, Grant Milnor Hyde claimed that "some one must always pioneer. I feel that we at Wisconsin, with nine pioneer books to the credit or discredit of the school, have almost done our share" ("Journalism in the High School" 3). By 1927, department members had produced 14 books with additional ones appearing throughout the 1930s (Hyde, "Raising the Quality" 21). These first textbooks stressed that Wisconsin was not teaching more general reading or composition, but instead a professional skill and art by which graduates could explain social change and politics to the public. At the beginning of *Types of News Writing* (1916), Bleyer stated that news stories could incorporate narration, description, exposition, or a combination of them, but he didn't mention those school forms of discourse again. Instead he considered stories on police news and crime, criminal and civil courts, politics and elections, labor trouble and strikes, and other subjects, with discussion of their purpose and audience presented along with examples from various newspapers. His *Newspaper Writing and Editing* (1913) and *How to Write Special Feature Articles* (1919) more thoroughly introduced students to the genres that could explain politics and involve citizens in their nation, states, and cities.

In 1921, Hyde published the first *Handbook for Newspaper Workers*, with his intentions stated in the preface: to move students beyond the stilted tone of their school work to the stronger voices needed to communicate with urban and rural residents. He may have intended this text, in part, as a rebuttal to Edwin Woolley's popular *Handbook of Composition* (1907).

Woolley relied on an extensive grammatical vocabulary, giving directions like "a predicate substantive completing a finite verb should be in the nominative case" (35). Hyde also used grammar terminology, but, unlike Woolley, he provided explanations of these terms: After the term "present participle," for example, he included in parentheses "the verb form ending in *ing*" (10). Hyde also gave reasons for correct usages by referring to their effect on readers: Whereas Woolley merely stated that "*there is* should be followed by a singular noun; *there are*, by a plural noun or nouns" (30), Hyde explained that "*there* as a sentence beginning is to be avoided because it lacks emphasis and wastes space" (20). Woolley cautioned students to avoid the improprieties found in newspapers:

> Newspaper usage does not establish an expression as good English. The best newspapers set high standards, and oblige their writers to study 'style books' similar to this Handbook, in order to avoid offenses against good English. But many newspapers have no such standards, and employ provincial and vulgar language. (2)

He also warned against "hackneyed newspaper mannerisms" that have "arisen through the effort of writers to adorn their style where no ornament was needed, or to introduce a forced humor, or to avoid repetition of the same word" (16–17). Unlike Woolley, Hyde defended the modern newspaper and noted the exaggerations of its detractors: "Critics of American newspapers are wont to speak of newspaper writing with a sneer and to brand it with the terms, 'journalese' or 'newspaper English,' while they point to incorrect usage, bad diction, and careless English in the press" (66). Hyde wanted students to respect the profession and feel motivated to contribute their best work to it.

While forming their own program and influencing practices at other schools, Bleyer and Hyde also worked with high school teachers and students because they feared that new journalism curricula at that level could undermine the success of university programs. In a 1925 article, Hyde wrote that teachers at Wisconsin had recognized six years earlier that journalism courses were rapidly spreading to the high school. These courses, many of which focused on practical techniques and employed college textbooks, might encourage students to feel that they didn't need additional training—an ominous possibility because college teachers had only recently convinced newspaper and periodical editors to endorse university training. Hyde instead urged that high school courses concentrate on general skills of reading and writing and the role of the press in society ("Journalism in

the High School"). In 1920, Bleyer and Hyde set up the Central Interscho-
lastic Press Association for high school students. Its membership went from
a handful that year to 800 in 1925 ("Journalism in the High School" 1–2).
Through its meetings and contests, Bleyer and Hyde reinforced the idea
that publication work should be an extracurricular activity in high school
to provide students with a creative outlet, not to prepare them for careers.
In the preface to his own high school text, A Course in Journalistic Writing
(1922), Hyde again stated that professional instruction should be delegated
to the university. His book covered the literary magazine, the student
newspaper, newspaper reading, and journalism's importance as "non-voca-
tional training for citizenship" (vii). When he reviewed a new high school
text in 1925, Hyde criticized its vocational sections and argued that high
school teachers had already accepted other priorities: "They realize that they
will injure the newspaper profession as well as their students if they allow
their work to imitate professional training" ("What of the High School
Class?" 22).

From 1905 until his death in 1935, Willard Bleyer labored to create
writing courses in which students learned professional research methods and
formats, worked together as colleagues, and sought publication regularly.
He intended for these classes to create graduates who would become
journalism's leaders, furthering their own careers as well as the status of
college degree programs, as did indeed occur. He wanted not only competent
writers and managers but social critics, formed through their journalism and
social science courses to become careful evaluators of American society and
champions of democracy. Through his associations and textbooks, he
transferred this vision of journalism's potential and power from his own
university to the Midwest and to the nation.

OTHER ADVANCED WRITING COURSES

As Van Hise and Bleyer realized, professional journalism and advertising
would be essential to a Progressive society. Although Van Hise invested most
heavily in journalism, he recognized that real growth and progress would
also require clear scientific and agricultural writing, good communication
between businesses and their clients, effective public speaking, and the
poetry, short stories, and plays that could engage audiences and inspire them
to desire a better future. His curricular plans, therefore, involved not just
journalism but a full array of professional genre courses.

Agricultural Journalism

In the 1908–09 catalog description of the Course in Preparation for Journalism, Bleyer noted that a combination of journalism, agricultural journalism, and agriculture courses could be an excellent preparation for the trade journalist as well as the agricultural researcher or agent. In Wisconsin and the nation, improvement in agricultural methods was crucial to prosperity. Farmers, whose political power had been demonstrated through the Grange and Populist parties, could create progress through informed voting and implementation of new farming methods. They would need expert communicators to put them on the right path.

Wisconsin's College of Agriculture began offering Agricultural Journalism in 1908. The lectures—covering the agricultural press, types of agricultural writing, reporting of fairs, stock, and corn shows, technical description, and photography—focused on requirements of popular and scholarly journals and of technical reports. The teacher, John Marquis, editor of agricultural publications for the university, provided practice with conducting interviews, writing various article types, editing, proofreading, and reviewing. Like Bleyer, he initiated further training opportunities, by requiring students to work with university publications and with bulletins produced by the U.S. Weather Bureau station housed at the university. By 1910, the college offered a Seminar in Practical Editing that covered editing and publishing, circulation, and advertising, with practice supplied by the *Student Farmer*, as well as Methods of Farm Advertising, on principles and methods of advertising new products to farmers. Further practical experience could be gained through the Hoard Press Club, established in 1908 for agricultural students.

By creating a specialty in agricultural journalism, Van Hise, Bleyer, and Marquis were acknowledging the future power of not only newspapers and journals aimed at the general public, but of the trade publications by which a profession forms its own standards and reaches its own constituency. Through its course work in agricultural journalism, the university recognized the role of professionals who could speak to researchers, practitioners, and the public and ultimately determine how new advances and policies would be perceived by all three groups. In the Midwest at the beginning of the century, agriculture was a crucial part of the economy that trained persuaders could promote; engineering would come next.

CHAPTER 3

Technical Writing

As early as the late 1870s, the English faculty experimented with special first-year composition classes for engineering majors: In 1876–77, civil and mechanical engineering sophomores took Rhetoric and Crystallography; in 1877–78 and in 1878–79, they enrolled in Rhetoric and Mechanics. Both courses covered essay forms, paragraphing, and sentence structure, with readings and assignments on engineering. In 1894, first-year engineering students again took a separate rhetoric and composition course, with stress on technical description and exposition. In 1900, the text was Spencer's *Philosophy of Style*, augmented with exercises on describing structures and machines.

After Van Hise became president, science students again took the regular freshman composition, and the focus shifted to advanced writing training that would prepare scientists to explain innovations to each other and to the public. In 1908–09, the English department began offering Technical Writing for students in engineering and other technical or scientific majors. The teacher, Thomas Dickinson, an assistant professor of English, structured the class by lectures, class exercises, and frequent conferences. It was also crosslisted by Bleyer as an appropriate English course for journalism students who wanted to specialize in scientific journalism. This class covered the newsletter, newspaper, and report writing. Beginning in 1911–12, an additional English course, Technical Composition, featured imitation of trade journal articles and speeches and of strategies for addressing fellow engineers. It was required of juniors in electrical engineering and was an elective for other science students who had finished freshman composition.

Another advanced technical-writing elective, begun in 1911, had a cultural emphasis, with readings geared to helping engineering students see the relationship of science to society. This course was taught by Karl Young, who also wrote textbooks on freshman composition and conducted research on medieval drama. Students in his class read engineering reports, scientific articles, and popular essays and considered important social questions: What is the difference between a trade and a profession? Is the function of the engineer in this new era of the manufacture of power that of hired expert or leader and advisor? What is the aim of engineering education? What is the relation between pure science and applied?

By developing a curriculum in technical writing, Van Hise, Bleyer, Karl Young, and others applied a model from agricultural journalism to engineering, another key specialty in their developing region. They planned for two graduate types: journalism majors who had taken some science as well as technical communication and engineering students who would specialize in professional writing. With this combination, the university could train persuaders who would be influential both with their colleagues and with the public.

Business Writing

In 1859, Madison's two-year-old Bacon Commercial College became part of the university, offering a separate business curriculum of five classes that students could take to qualify for the "mercantile" profession. The third course was on business penmanship and the fourth on commercial forms and correspondence, with instruction covering invoices, accounts, promissory notes, orders, checks, articles of co-partnership, and business letters. David H. Tullis held the instructorship established by the Board of Regents for these courses. In 1866–67, this program and Tullis were gone, but notice was given in the University of Wisconsin catalog thatstudents could study bookkeeping or other business skills at the Madison Business College for two thirds of its regular fee.

In 1901, the university began offering a bachelor of commercial science degree in its School of Economic History, Geography, and Commerce, which had also initiated the track in Courses Preparatory to Journalism. This Progressive business curriculum included courses on the manufacturing industries of the United States, railroad and water transportation, economic crises, rights of labor, and corporate finance and securities, which together formed a thorough exposition of modern capitalism. In 1903, the program moved to a separate School of Commerce. Students took first-year English and sophomore composition as their required English courses; then they took advanced writing classes to teach them to promote new products and communicate with clients effectively.

In 1905, assistant professor Edward Hall Gardner from the English department taught Commercial Correspondence, an elective crosslisted in the commerce degree and taken by students from various disciplines including journalism, but not for credit by students majoring in English. With this course, Wisconsin was one of the first universities to offer business writing, here with a progressive emphasis on communicating with the public and establishing good business practices. By 1911–12, the department offered Commercial Correspondence and Advanced Commercial Correspondence: The first one considered principles and formats; the second provided work with additional genres and more practice. Both courses were intended to encourage business professionals to follow ethical principles while presenting their case to a sophisticated audience of consumers.

Gardner's *Effective Business Letters* (1915), the first college-level business writing textbook, provided specific instruction for this real writing, as did Wisconsin's journalism texts. He began by considering various purposes, audiences, and general organizational principles and then discussed letters intended to give information, order goods, give notice of shipments, sell products, and collect debts, focusing on specific situations and the formats they engender: the "you ought to buy" argument, the "consider what this means to you" argument, the predicament to remedy argument, and resemblance (of one accepted service to a new one; of the actions of one clientele to another). He also stressed the efficacy of testimonials from customers, experts, and national figures in persuading various readers about various subjects.

In an article in 1919, Gardner indicated that, like Bleyer, he believed in shaping instruction through ongoing research. His commitment to reform business practice led him to analyze 5,000 letters, drawn from his ten-year collection and from collections of business executives. He asked these executives to judge letters they had written and received, determining those that produced the best results and those that did not achieve their goals. His conclusion was that the best letters were well structured. "No study is nearly so essential as the study of logical plan," he asserted, using the analogy that a train may pass great scenery but it also must stay on its rails ("What Makes a" 56). He also discussed the audience's reactions to his organization types: In the general to particular order, he argued, the proof provides a point of meeting between writer and reader. Testimonials are most convincing when they come from people who might be perceived as neighbors: Experts are given less credence in the United States when they appear removed from or unconcerned with the common people.

Gardner later moved to the business school where he taught marketing and the economics of business advertising as well as business writing. His courses applied advanced techniques and ethics to another key specialty of the future, another site where Progressives could use trained rhetors to inform and persuade the public. Journalism or business majors who took some combination of reporting, advertising, and business writing could become that necessary link between corporations and a newly empowered citizenry.

Speech

As Bleyer and Hyde developed their journalism program and their colleagues such as Karl Young and Edward Hall Gardner experimented with technical and business writing, other English professors created a full curriculum in speech. In the 1880s, all first-year students studied elocution once a week, and students in the other years could elect to continue their lessons. For seniors, elective elocution work included reciting speeches, writing orations for characters from *Macbeth* and *Othello*, making chapel-stage orations, and participating in class debates. By 1900, however, these courses were offered infrequently because students were devoting more time to their majors and to newer elective choices.

Under Van Hise's leadership, many of these older electives were dropped as the university turned its attention to developing a complete speech curriculum that would enable leaders to inform and persuade their constituencies, just as La Follette had furthered the Progressive cause through his many addresses to Wisconsin's citizens. By 1904, the array of courses on voice training, persuasion, and dramatic presentation included Phonetics, concerning proper speech sounds and voice articulation; Elocution, with lectures on vocal physiology, proper use and care of the voice, reading, and gesture; Oratorical Delivery, an advanced offering in speaking techniques; Oral Rhetoric, a course in argument and persuasion with debate practice; Dramatic Reading, featuring declamations from *Macbeth, Othello, Merchant of Venice,* and *Hamlet*; and Declamation, covering oral interpretation of literature. The university also offered Elocution and Oratory, a law school elective that provided voice training, lectures and exercises on gesture, practice in reading statutes and other documents, practice in extemporaneous speaking, and class discussions on "the questions which interest the lawyer as a public speaker" (*Catalog 1904–05,* 154). By 1906, Forms of Public Address was added to offer training in set forms of public speaking: the argument, eulogy, political speech, commemorative address, and after-dinner speech. Practical Public Speaking was a second law school course. Elocution, a new elective for engineers, covered voice training and the plain reading and speaking required in the profession.

In 1906, public speaking left the English department to become a separate unit led by David B. Frankenburger and Rollo Lyman. In creating this major in speech, Van Hise and these professors transformed one of the university's oldest curricular features, oral training, into one of the new communication specialties. In speech courses, whether their ultimate goals involved politics, law, business, or theatre, students could acquire the rhetorical skills with which to succeed.

Creative Writing

Also included in La Follette, Van Hise, and Bleyer's conception of powerful rhetoric that could reach the populace was creative writing, the stories that describe American myths, moral imperatives, and visions for the future.

In 1904–05, the English department began offering Narration, the study of representative forms of the story, with exercises on plot structure and criticism. In 1911, Margaret Ashmun, Bleyer's erstwhile co-writer, taught this course, and Thomas Dickinson taught Dramatic Writing, a course in the theory and practice of writing plays, for which students had to submit a portfolio to gain admission. In Special Feature and Magazine Writing, offered by Bleyer as a journalism course, students could gain additional training in writing articles and short stories for publication.

For additional writing practice and for technical experience with publishing, students were encouraged to participate in the university's literary publications: the *Sphinx* (later the *Awk*), an illustrated humor bi-weekly run by students, and the *Wisconsin Literary Magazine*, a monthly devoted to short stories, verse, and essays. For the literary magazine, Willard Bleyer appointed a student editor and sponsored a cash prize of fifty dollars for the best short story under 1,500 words.

In 1910, the Wisconsin Drama Society, involving students, professors, and local citizens, began performing original plays in Madison and Milwaukee and on tour throughout the Midwest. The group's Progressive purpose was "to provide for the section [of the country] in which we live the impulse of the practice of an art as a corrective of human standards" (Dickinson, *Wisconsin Plays* x). This experimental program, sponsored by the university so that it would be free from commercial considerations, aimed to train actors, encourage the study, criticism, and writing of plays, and foster dialogue on social reform. The organization sponsored the publication of *Wisconsin Plays* in 1914, an anthology of original one-act plays from their repertory, edited by Thomas Dickinson and reprinted seven times by 1930.

Through its playwrighting and acting courses and the drama society, the university, as dramatist Percy MacKaye commented in *La Follette's Weekly Magazine* in 1912, was offering the developing American theatre "an educated ideal, an ideal formed of a perspective of the past, an interest in the future and the freedom to think" (7). Creative writing perhaps could convey the Progressive message even more effectively than journalism or public speaking by enacting it in lifelike situations and with characters accessible to everyone: "It deals with the same masses as does politics and touches millions more than the university ever reaches." The theatre thus provided the university with an opportunity "to influence national life" (7). For Dickinson, writing in 1915, drama was the essential "democratic art": "It is laid upon drama by the conditions of its substance that it shall promote that social solidarity of which it is itself the outgrowth and the completest expression in art" (*The Case of* 70).

Through all of the advanced writing courses, Wisconsin professors were creating college-trained experts who would be able to reach the citizenry with data and emotional appeals, with both exposition of facts and persuasive interpretations of them. Progressive communication could enable citizens to become the well-informed and active populace necessary for a Progressive future. This desire to create the rhetors of a democracy, however, was accompanied by a type of elitism: Only the best need apply. The goal was clearly to empower the citizens at secondhand, by training those experts who would address them, not encouraging everyone to speak and write. And in offering the advanced course work, albeit with thorough grounding in ethics, these teachers were releasing into business, politics, and the media highly trained practitioners of mass persuasion who could be used to fulfill any goals, not just the Progressive vision. These course types—advertising, journalism, public speaking, business and technical writing, and creative writing—soon began appearing at other schools across the country, at first especially in midwestern states like Kansas, Michigan, and Illinois where Progressive ideals flourished. But La Follette, Van Hise, and Bleyer could not control what goals these courses would serve or what these graduates would do with their expert skills.

4

Professional Writing Instruction Crosses the Country

While the University of Wisconsin developed a professional writing curriculum, other schools also began to experiment with advanced courses for Progressive rhetors. As chapter 1 indicated, the first generation of advanced electives, from the late nineteenth century, stressed forms of discourse along with creative genres that reflected individual teachers' interests, providing more general skills training for the liberal arts graduate. But the second wave of advanced courses, developed between 1890 and World War I, stemmed from a new source and inspiration affecting higher education: the belief in specialization and reform originating in Progressivism. New offerings moved writing into the realm of a vocation, appropriate to the land-grant school, a professional subject like agriculture, home economics, or pharmacy taught through workshops and lab experiences, with instruction provided by practitioners rather than traditional academics. These new courses trained writing specialists, an elite class that could serve democracy by persuading the citizenry to accept modern governmental and scientific developments. Writing courses in Kansas, Nebraska, Minnesota, Iowa, and Illinois exemplify this growing Progressive influence. Similar offerings spread out from the midwestern states to other regions of the country. As happens with any curricular trend, however, these writing courses appeared in modified versions in various states and universities, suited to local political situations and to the institutions' goals. Certainly not every program administrator and advanced writing teacher shared the vision of a new democracy promulgated by Bob La Follette. In fact, advanced writing courses soon encountered a paradoxical influence. State administrators in Florida, Texas, and Montana sought new legislation that would control business and industry, but they also wanted the prosperity that could only be achieved by business growth. A writing form that combined facts with persuasion could be effectively used to achieve both corporate reform and corporate might.

IN KANSAS

In Kansas, the writing programs developed at two state universities arose from a political climate of dissent. Political reformers offered to support the university only when its programs appeared to be meeting the immediate needs of the populace. Thus advanced writing instruction, and the new departments that it engendered, came to seem more important than literature study in the English department. Like the University of Wisconsin, both the University of Kansas and Kansas State focused their attention on writing as a profession for the future.

In the 1880s and 1890s, Kansas legislators began initiating Populist reforms, such as grain inspection and stockyard regulation. College researchers, farm agents, and engineers turned their attention to new irrigation systems, new crops like hard winter wheat, dry farming, ranching, and natural-gas exploration—and they were anxious to get the word out about their innovations to the small farms that extended westward. For their part, farmers wanted a voice in railroad-line extensions and rates, especially on the powerful Santa Fe Railroad, and they sought state and local candidates who could give them that voice.

Populist officials, endeavoring to improve the economic lot of farmers, supported higher education when it seemed to offer benefits to the common citizen. The 1862 Morrill Act funding, through which the federal government authorized the selling of federal land to support higher education in technical fields, was used in 1863 to establish a university at Lawrence, an agricultural college at Manhattan, and a normal school at Emporia, to serve students across the state and settle the squabbling among these towns over access to federal grants. In 1893, the Populist-controlled legislature, led by Governor Lorenzo D. Lewelling of Wichita, voted funding for the University of Kansas in Lawrence to build a library, a new physics and electrical engineering building, and a chancellor's residence, doubling the amount of buildings on campus and thus treating the school better than had any previous legislature. But many reformers thought the school, primarily a liberal arts institution, gave inadequate service to the state and its citizens. They agreed with the Lawrence *Jeffersonian* when in 1894 it declared that the university suffered from "aristocracy and seclusiveness"; its professors, who were "puffed up" on their own importance, the newspaper charged, just worked on their own research projects and on teaching the elite (qtd. in Griffin 186). In 1897, following the lead of Populist governor John W. Leedy, the legislature responded to criticisms by refusing to grant further assistance, voting against buildings for a museum and the chemistry department and cutting the university's general appropriation.

When Frank Strong of the University of Oregon became chancellor in 1902, he hoped to cement the relationship between the university and citizens by demonstrating the university's relevance to their lives. Using the Wisconsin Idea as his model, he declared in his inaugural address that "the whole modern movement is away from extreme individualism and toward social unity." The liberal arts university should train men and women to a "sense of moral responsibility in government; for unselfish collective action for the good of the community; for self-denial for the collective honor of the State" (qtd. in Griffin 225). In 1910 in his biennial report to the board and legislature, Strong argued that under his leadership the university's main purposes were no longer just to teach individuals and foster faculty research:

> A university like the University of Kansas must be a universal institution, to contain in its plan of life all of the activities known to the civilization that it serves, and there is no man so humble that the University ought to disregard him, and no community within the confines of the commonwealth so far removed that the University should not send its men and women to serve it. (qtd. in Griffin 243)

In asserting this redefinition of the university, Strong committed himself to a massive communications effort: Like La Follette and Van Hise in Wisconsin, he would have to create in Kansas both an immediate publicity effort and training for future rhetors who could continue the persuasion process.

Strong, like Charles Van Hise, initiated a publicity campaign that encouraged citizens to view the university as a servant to the commonwealth. Upon his arrival, he developed a press bulletin, reinvigorated the alumni association, and began an alumni magazine, edited by R. D. O'Leary of the Department of English. He also formed a Committee on Publicity to systematize these efforts and began investigating the feasibility of a journalism school, "one of whose main tasks [would be] preparation and dissemination of publicity" (qtd. in Griffin 228). With this effort underway, he then, again like Van Hise, turned his attention to thorough professional training for the writers of the future.

In 1894, Edwin M. Hopkins, a Princeton graduate who chaired the English department, had offered what he called a "highly experimental" course on newspaper writing for freshmen to replace their usual dose of grammar and composition. He planned for students to investigate social forces and the power of the press in shaping modern thought, noble goals for a Populist area, but he only enrolled three students (O'Dell 35–36, 49). In 1904, with Strong's encouragement, Hopkins introduced a second news writing course in which freshmen studied social trends but also wrote articles for campus publications as though they were a functioning city desk:

> In the fall of 1904 a volunteer section of freshman rhetoric was organized into a group of reporters, and the newspaper class proper into a corps of editors; beats were assigned, and edited. Matter was sent to the local papers including the *University Daily Kansan*. (O'Dell 49)

In these two courses, Hopkins and Strong began to establish what they, like Willard Bleyer, wanted a new journalism major to be: a combination of cultural study and practical training.

With Hopkins' help, Strong began organizing a journalism major in 1904, his first departure from the liberal arts curriculum. Intended to provide service to the state, his interdisciplinary major involved journalism study as well as courses in economics, history, sociology, and modern languages and noncredit lectures by Kansas newspaper editors. In 1905, Charles Harger of the Abilene *Reflector* became the program's director; he visited once a month to review curricular plans and made arrangements with the Kansas City, Missouri *Star* to provide large quantities of unused, unedited copy on which students could practice their skills. All of the members of the new advanced class in newspaper writing—14 in the fall of 1906—served as cub reporters for either the student *Kansan* or one of the Lawrence papers. Through this combination of on- and off-campus work, Strong, Hopkins, and Harger hoped to form practically trained journalists who would bring a cultural and historical perspective to their work.

In October 1909, the Regents agreed to a separate department of journalism, with Harger as chair and Leon Flint, editor of the alumni magazine, as his resident assistant. In 1911, Strong hired Merle Thorpe of the Department of Journalism at the University of Washington as a full-time resident chair who immediately began to sharpen the program's professional focus. In 1910, the department had six courses of its own: two each in reporting and editing, and one each in advertising and the history of journalism. By 1912–13, as the catalog indicates, there were 17, including additional courses in advertising and editing, and new offerings on the short story, the mechanics of printing, and comparative journalism. Majors still took three quarters of their work in history, political science, economics, and literature to sharpen their knowledge of their culture.

With Thorpe as the program's director, part of the regular work, in class and as an extracurricular requirement, occurred at the college publicity bureau where students helped foster the school's image while preparing for their own careers. In Thorpe's first year, he and his students divided the state's 690 newspapers into four categories based on their attitude toward the university and sent each one an appropriate letter explaining the journalism department's attempts to represent the university to the public. Thorpe himself went to visit those editors who were the most unfriendly to the university while students contacted other editors. The department then began sending out a daily newsletter about the faculty, students, programs, and alumni to the state's 70 dailies and a six-column news bulletin to the weeklies. From 40 to 50 special articles also went out each week to those papers that were the most opposed to furthering the university's reputation and its role in reform efforts but would print articles about hometown students. At the same time, Thorpe and his students worked with the Lawrence commercial clubs to bring pressure on anti-university papers, like the *Jeffersonian*, to alter their editorial bias (Griffin 227–28). By recruiting William Allen White, influential editor of the Emporia *Gazette*, for the State Commission of Higher Education, Strong and Thorpe secured a powerful champion of an activist university and of journalism training. As they interacted with influential leaders like White and assumed the role of persuader with newspaper editors, students were being prepared to view themselves as leaders who would control papers across the state (Griffin 343).

With help from Hopkins who remained as chair of the Department of English, Strong also participated in the development of additional writing courses that could train the states' rhetors. By 1915–16, according to the catalog, the English department had a course in versification and a literary magazine, which Professors Arthur Richmond Marsh and William Carruth viewed as evidence of a vital, democratic literature forming in the West. In an additional creative writing class, Technic and Theory of the Drama, students worked on dramatic dialogue, diction, characterization, and stage presentation. In a new Department of Public Speaking, additional public communication courses included two on acting as well as debating, extemporaneous speaking, and advanced public speaking, in which students prepared for public lectures and debates. In all these courses, Hopkins and Strong hoped to train students who could reach citizens through the imagination and passions as well as through their reason.

Under Populist and then Republican legislators, Strong's new programs and building projects received wide support. This power base enabled the

University of Kansas, like the University of Wisconsin, to initiate extension courses, correspondence study, library packages, summer school, and scientific and technical assistance programs that could further extend the university's services to the state. In 1911, Republican governor Walter Roscoe Stubbs proposed that Strong and the Board of Regents journey to Wisconsin to examine Van Hise's programs; the group visited Madison in the latter part of October. But Strong felt that the greatest university service was not the direct support programs such as extension and correspondence courses. Instead, after 1912, he concentrated the service efforts, through his public rhetoric and his expenditures, on training the university's undergraduate and graduate students, such as those studying journalism, creative writing, and public speaking, to insure a future of progress.

At the state's agricultural university, writing also became a key specialty, a priority of presidents supported by Populist and Republican reformers. Following the donation of land and buildings from the Methodist Bluemont Central College in Manhattan and a legislative guarantee of land grant funding, Kansas State Agricultural College opened in 1863, with a much larger enrollment in its preparatory classes than in the college itself. Debate ensued immediately about this school's responsibility to offer practical agricultural training and not just more liberal arts. When in 1887, Reverend John A. Anderson became president, he eliminated study of Latin and Greek and advanced humanities courses and instituted blacksmithing, stone cutting, woodworking, and farming methods. In 1897, another Populist choice for president, Thomas E. Will, a Harvard graduate and professor of political economy, extended the agricultural classes, strengthened the work of the agricultural experimental station, and gave greater attention to the study of economic principles governing the distribution of wealth, expressed by the Regents in their minutes of April 1894 as a "healthy inquiry among the people into the causes that depress industry and paralyze agriculture" (qtd. in Carey 70). By expanding requirements in only the politically relevant liberal arts (history, economics, and civics), he attempted to provide the education for citizenship deemed necessary by Populists for the preservation of free institutions. C. B. Hoffman, the Populist leader of the Regents, spoke at a student assembly to argue that the college should also offer instruction in marketing, transportation, taxation, and public finance to change the system of distribution and thus raise the living standards of the nation's producing classes. But, in 1898, as Republicans elected the governor and took control of the legislature, they first rescinded Will's invitation to William Jennings Bryan to give the commencement address in June 1899 and then removed Will and his chief allies. His replacement, Ernest R. Nichols, built on Will's goal of extending those programs that clearly offered service to the state, but without Will's social science emphasis. When the next president, Progressive Republican Henry Jackson Waters, gave his inaugural address, he called for the university to offer an education balanced enough "to fit men for efficient service in their several professions and pursuits of life, and at the same time liberal enough to prepare them for the highest service as citizens" (Carey 114).

Whatever educational balance these presidents sought, they all agreed to the primacy of training public rhetors. As compared to the University of Kansas, this agricultural and mechanical school more strongly emphasized the practical writing skills that could transform the world of work. In journalism, Kansas State focused on training the newspaper printer and owner, the people who controlled small town and industrial papers. In 1874, the year after Anderson became president, the university catalog first announced printing courses and the regents purchased a printing press. Besides offering advanced technical training on printing and producing a paper, Anderson instituted an introductory printing course for students lacking proficiency in basic English composition. This course, which provided training in typesetting, also covered spelling, grammar, and punctuation, a practical alternative to traditional rhetoric requirements. Thomas E. Will hired new printing teachers and enlarged the student's course work to include study of the printer as a member of society, an influential Populist citizen.

It was Henry Jackson Waters, however, who most fully appreciated the positive impact of a full journalism curriculum on reform efforts. In 1911, he instituted a four-year program in journalism within the English department, and in 1915 he established a separate Department of Industrial Journalism. Although legislators questioned these developments as duplicating curricula at the University of Kansas, Waters convinced them of the need to prepare students to work at technical journals in industrial fields as well as at local newspapers (Carey 119). The new department, according to the 1915–16 catalog, covered printing skills in courses like Typography I and II and Platen Presswork I and II. Along with basic reporting, students could take Industrial Writing, on principles of journalism as applied to agriculture, engineering, home economics, and scientific research. Agricultural Journalism covered writing for newspapers and farm journals; Industrial Feature Writing I concentrated on developing agricultural and other industrial subjects for newspapers, farm journals, and magazines; Industrial Feature Writing II concerned agricultural, trade, and other highly specialized journals, with a course requirement of submitting work for publication. This course also covered the makeup, editorial, illustrative, and management work required of an editor. Other classes were Principles of Advertising; Circulation and Advertising Promotion, dealing with the business management of a newspaper and especially with advertising agencies, rates, and circulation; Magazine Features; and Column Conducting, involving study of various journals and of humor writing.

By 1915, Waters had also encouraged the English department to form courses that would enable graduates to explain new scientific developments and urge citizens to participate in the state's industrial and governmental progress. That year's catalog lists two courses in oral English that covered selling and other business talks, travel talks, introductions, announcements, presentations, and speeches for various occasions. The English department also offered an advanced course entitled Engineering English to teach letters, technical manuscripts, and reports, with Homer Watt's *The Composition of Technical Papers* and Frank Aydelotte's *English and Engineering* as texts. Watt's book included chapters on correspondence and reports as well as technical description, exposition of processes, and exposition of ideas. Aydelotte's text provided pieces by Ruskin, Carlyle, Emerson, Whitman, and other authors to help students examine the effects of technology and progress on modern society. In Business English I, with Edward Hall Gardner's *Effective Business Letters* as the text, students studied the business and sales letters of the commercial world. Business English II continued that instruction and also covered sales talks. Advertising English, with Samuel R. Hall's *Writing an Advertisement* as the text, covered principles as well as practice for writing and producing advertising copy and campaigns. The department also offered Agricultural English covering the business communication of the modern farm manager, county agent, and high school teacher, including correspondence, bulletin writing, business talks, and farm advertising. A separate course, Farm Advertising, taught methods of advertising all kinds of produce and thus securing regular customers. The course focused on display ads, story ads, and handbills along with a study of markets and marketing. The course Farm Bulletins taught the simple, direct style needed for agricultural bulletins; students used facts from their agriculture courses as the content of their articles. The department also offered Technical Writing with Watt's *The Composition of Technical Papers* as the text.

Additional English department courses focused on creative writing, with emphasis on community theatre. Community English, with Bates' *Pageants and Pageantry* as the text, covered pageantry's role in the education of rural citizens. After playwright Percy MacKaye staged *Masque of the Golden Bowl* in New Hampshire in 1905, emulating an English performance, American towns became engulfed in a twenty-year enthusiasm for pageants, which furthered Progressive goals of forming a better educated and more involved citizenry. With participation from clubs and schools, many town governments created outdoor spectacles on historical themes, involving large casts and elaborate costumes, often with interludes of dance and parading. Towns hired pageant directors and writers, such as Hazel MacKaye, Percy's sister, to direct these efforts. Clubwomen also presented their own pageants, concerning suffrage and peace as well as more traditional historical and literary themes. College courses on writing and directing pageants, common at state universities, thus prepared students for specific professional work in a more democratic and participatory United States (K. Blair 118–42). As Thomas Dickinson, drama professor at the University of Wisconsin, commented in 1915, for Progressive reformers these pageants were a "potent instrument in the social programme," through which professionally trained dramatists could awaken "social spirit and community cooperation" (*The Case of* 147).

THROUGHOUT THE MIDWEST

As in Kansas, other midwestern schools quickly developed similar arrays of courses to publicize the university and its role in reform and to train rhetors for the future.

After he was hired in 1891, president James H. Canfield of the University of Nebraska immediately pressed for a reform curriculum that included advanced writing programs. When he taught literature and history at the University of Kansas, he published *Taxation: A Plain Talk for Plain People* (1883), arguing that government's sole role was to provide security for its laborers and protesting the "arbitrary rulers, commercial politicians, and self-asserting placeseekers" of the Congress (Griffin 94). After coming to Nebraska, he traveled across the state at least 10,000 miles annually discussing the university as an extension of the lower schools, bringing education to all and thus ministering "to the needs of the greatest number." As he said, "I may not know the University from Alpha to Omega, but I know it from Arapahoe to Omaha" (Manley 114). After one year, an influential newspaper editor remarked concerning Canfield's impact on the university's reputation:

> The new interest taken by all the people, the increased mention in the state press, the kindlier feeling on every side as the helpfulness of the institution is felt, the hearty support given by all industrial and agricultural associations, the good words spoken by the most prominent men in the state, and last and best the swarm of students that is even now settling down on the campus; all this shows that the work is not in vain. (Manley 114–15)

But, like Charles Van Hise and Frank Strong, Canfield realized that he could not press a reform agenda solely by his own speaking efforts: He also needed to train rhetors who could further the effort.

Like his colleagues in other states, therefore, Canfield immediately turned his attention to advanced writing instruction. In 1894, Will Owen Jones, a university alumnus and managing editor of the Lincoln *State Journal*, taught a journalism class on the newspaper's influence and on specific practices, the beginning of a complete journalism curriculum that was soon housed in a separate school. Canfield convinced the Regents to establish a publications fund and chose English professor Lucius A. Sherman as university editor, a job he did with regular assistance from journalism students. In a separate department of rhetoric by 1915–16, according to the catalog, the university offered two graduate classes in play construction, with study of writing principles, workshop sessions, and stage presentation. Such creative writing courses were intended to enable students to tell the region's stories.

In Minnesota, forest fires that killed hundreds of residents in the 1890s led to interest in conservation and environmental controls; vast iron-ore deposits discovered in the 1890s brought about new questions of land management as did a diversifying agricultural economy and farm laborers who wanted better working conditions and a larger share of profit. At the University of Minnesota, chartered in 1851 with engineering and forestry as its leading programs, Joseph Thomas, who had been a colleague of Fred Newton Scott's at Michigan until 1909, offered technical writing for future farmers, ranchers, and loggers in a rhetoric department located within the College of Agriculture. There Charles Washburn Nichols also offered a half-year course in which agriculture and engineering students studied four Shakespeare plays, along with technical reports and articles, to broaden their understanding of human motivations, a "professional need" because engineers in a democratic society had to understand the general public's interests and priorities:

The typical engineering Freshman has an interesting, active mind, but a very narrow one. His eye has been so steadily fixed on his future profession that he has failed to see the need, even the professional need, of a broad contact with life, of a sympathetic knowledge of human nature. Literature, and particularly dramatic literature, where character is unfolded in action, gives any student a contact with life. (366)

Nichols noted that the engineering student especially enjoyed studying plot because "he likes to see how things are put together" (367). The university also offered a complete journalism curriculum; 10% of the students in these classes were engineering, forestry, and agriculture majors who planned to choose communication careers.

Although midwestern schools generally emphasized journalism and advertising, that was not always the case. The University of Iowa, for example, instituted a thorough curriculum in creative writing as well as journalism (Wilbers). With farm mechanization in the late nineteenth century and with increased trade, Iowa began to develop a large urban population: Iowa City was thought of as the "Athens of the Midwest." The city sponsored museums and theatrical productions as well as literary and debate clubs, which formed around 1890 to provide a place where students, faculty, and townspeople could read their own work and receive criticism while also discussing modern poetry and social change. As an extension of these societies, the University of Iowa began offering creative writing courses before 1900. In 1897, Verse-Making Class had the following catalog description:

Practice in metrical composition in the fixed forms of verse such as the heroic couplet, Spenserian stanza, ode, rondeau, sonnet, ballad, and song. Analysis of the best examples of these forms in English poetry. Informal discussions of artistic questions (*University of Iowa, Catalogue* 1895–96 38).

The instructor, George Cram ("Jig") Cook, had started college at Iowa and then spent his senior year at Harvard in 1893 studying with Barrett Wendell.

Another poetry writing teacher at Iowa was Edwin Ford Piper, who had participated in writing workshops at the University of Nebraska. His collections of poetry—*Barbed Wire and Other Poems* (1917), *Barbed Wire and Wayfarers* (1924), and *Paintrock Road* (1927)—reveal his commitment to regional themes that could stimulate pride in the region and empower its citizens. An avid collector of ballads and broadsides, he was known as the "singing professor," as one student remembered: "Reading 'Zebra Dun,' he was a cowboy talking to his horse. When he said 'whoa,' it was not as a professor reading to class members for their souls' edification, but as a top-hand who cajoled his pinto or mustang" (Wallace 1). Besides conducting these "singings," Piper discussed regional authors in class and urged students to emulate them so that they could influence their regional audience.

At the University of Chicago, creative writing was also a priority, reflecting the school's evangelical calling in a difficult political environment. The Haymarket Riot in 1886 and the Pullman strike in 1894 signaled a crisis in the relations between labor and capital. Further clashes occurred with the established power of utility companies, the streetcar system, municipal contractors, and packing houses, causing Lincoln Steffens to declare in 1903 in a *McClure's* article title that the city was "half free and fighting on." After Jane Addams opened Hull House, Chicago also became the focus of a national settlement movement, pioneering social, economic, and political reform through programs for the poor.

One response to social upheaval was higher education that would focus on service to the community. With the support of John D. Rockefeller, the American Baptist Education Society established the University of Chicago, picking William Rainey Harper, a biblical specialist at Yale, as its president, to combine Progressive service with Protestant evangelism. The new university chose as its motto, "service for mankind wherever mankind is, whether within scholastic walls or without those walls and in the world at large" (Storr 59). The university's plan called for a union of scholarship and outreach, of a spreading of divine truth through the university's three divisions: the University Proper, University Extension, and University Publication Work. Harper began a journalism program in 1899 because, like Strong and Van Hise, he believed that well-trained teachers and their students should guide the university's publicity efforts and its reform agenda.

For Harper, another key part of the university's service mission was teaching young people to express themselves through imaginative writing and thus to communicate the best ideas to others. In 1893, he hired Robert Herrick, a student of Barrett Wendell at Harvard, who began his career at MIT teaching composition and literature. His friend at Harvard, Robert Morss Lovett, who had served as editor of the *Harvard Monthly*, also came to the university that fall. In courses on the short story and on poetry, Lovett wanted not to assign set formats but to help each student "to find his own best material, advising him as to form, and sometimes putting him in the way of publication" (*All Our Years* 123), a professional focus that Lovett thought distinguished this program from Harvard's:

> We had in common our job—to develop writing at the university. In Herrick's view this implied writing ourselves and stimulating our young colleagues and students to write for professional publication. This was in marked contrast to the tendency at Harvard, where the *Monthly* and the *Advocate* were the goals. (*All Our Years* 96)

Through stories and poetry as well as journalism, Harper believed, Chicago graduates could bring to fellow citizens a vision of a better life and the strength to deal with tribulation.

Following these evangelical goals for writing, Lovett encouraged students to convey social messages. As Lovett asserted to Gertrude Stein on her visit to the university, all literature (including the Bible, Greek tragedy, Dante, and Milton) was to some extent propaganda. In classes, he strove to make students aware of the experience they controlled and of the vision of society they might produce (*All Our Years* 94–95). He encouraged his student Margaret Wilson, for example, to write on the plight of women in India for the *Atlantic Monthly* and then to portray in a novel the strength and endurance of her Iowa farm family. Lovett commented on her achievements:

> She attempted a big novel of three generations about her ancestors in Iowa, which I tried to whip into shape in the conviction that here was the great American novel, but the canvas was too vast. Cut down to a single episode, it won the Pulitzer prize as *The Able McLaughlins*. Later, as wife of the governor of prisoners in England, she wrote *The Crime of Punishment* and *One Came Out*, which made me an active supporter of the League to Abolish Capital Punishment. (*All Our Years* 125)

Herrick also felt that new ideals for writers were needed "in a country whose imaginative writing is so sloppily sentimental and romantic as is the case with ours" (Nevius 41). He eschewed the nostalgia of older regionalist stories for a greater realism concerning the plight of the working class, in his teaching of writing and in his own novels, such as *The Common Lot* (1904), *The Memoirs of an American Citizen* (1905), and *A Life for a Life* (1910).

In 1916, Lovett decided that Chicago's courses on versification did not give poetry students adequate time to craft their work, so he started the Poetry Club along with student Harold Van Kirk. The club began as a meeting among four male students and *Poetry* editor Harriet Monroe at Lovett's home: "After dinner the poets read their verses, which Miss Monroe pronounced deplorable" (Lovett 122). The next year the larger number of members included Gladys Campbell, Elizabeth Madox Roberts, Janet Lewis, and Jessica North, all of whom achieved literary distinction with tales of struggling families and workers.

Besides creative writing courses, as the catalog from 1915–16 indicates, these colleagues had also developed a course on writing historical monographs; one on writing literary criticism, in which students studied works by Chicago faculty and by Wilhelm Scherer, Matthew Arnold, and James Russell Lowell to learn to write literary criticism; a seminar on the history of rhetoric; and a course in rhetoric and composition for teachers, in which the students wrote each day and studied textbooks, teaching methods, and theme criticism. These courses were also taught by William Wilkinson and Edwin H. Lewis, author of a study of the English paragraph. Lewis also offered business writing and business journalism as extension courses.

No matter whether the emphasis was on journalism, advertising, creative writing, or technical writing, these courses at midwestern universities were intended to train professional communicators. Though each university tailored its curriculum to meet the needs of its citizenry and fulfill its own priorities, universities in the Midwest generally followed the lead of the University of Wisconsin in connecting advanced writing courses with the university's immediate public relations efforts and with long-range reform efforts. To train influential rhetors, these schools placed their emphasis on practical instruction in specific genres and the social science education. In creating a Department of Rhetoric in 1903 and a curriculum in journalism, creative writing, and technical writing, Fred Newton Scott of the University of Michigan was reflecting a well-established trend. Although Donald Stewart, James Berlin, and other scholars have considered Scott to be an alternative voice, he was not that. He was an academic leader and well-trained authority on rhetoric, but in the courses he created, Scott joined his colleagues at many other schools in representing his region's Progressive politics and commitment to training professional persuaders.

AND THROUGHOUT THE COUNTRY

Before World War I, these professional writing courses spread out from the Midwest to universities in other regions although with varying purposes. Progressivism had its strongest site in the thoroughly settled Midwest, an established area rebelling against eastern controls. In the South, seeking redevelopment after the Civil War, and on the western frontier, the new stress on "progress" had a different meaning. Reformers in these states worked to secure the rights of workers, particularly white ones, but they also sought new railroad lines, business ventures, and crop markets. In these developing regions, as can be seen by examining university catalogs from 1915–16 as an example, advanced writing courses thrived for slightly different reasons than at the University of Wisconsin: They could serve the growing power of business as well as protest it.

The South especially found itself in disarray after the Civil War. A revival of its economic stability became the focus of its Populist and then Progressive reform movements, with growth coming from new industries, new agricultural practices, and tourism. As elsewhere, reformers attempted to regulate railroads and banks and to provide better city services. But at the same time, these politicians saw the need for Northern investments and thus wanted to court businesses as well as to control them.

One of the richest states before the war, Louisiana became one of the poorest in its aftermath, with commerce at a standstill. The state and its businesses sought a revival involving diversification of agriculture, increased railroad business, and new services for citizens. Louisiana State University, founded in 1870 and named Louisiana State University and Agricultural and Mechanical College after its 1877 merger with a technical college in New Orleans, became a key participant in that revival. By 1910, the journalism department had eight courses, including Publicity, a class on planning and executing campaigns, with practice working for the university and for local businesses. Although public relations specialist Edward Bernays often claimed that his 1923 course at New York University was the first one in public relations, it was only the first one with that specific title. By 1915–16, besides the news and editing courses, the Louisiana State journalism department also offered Newspaper Advertising, on soliciting, writing, and laying out advertising, with campus and city papers furnishing a laboratory. The School of Agriculture provided further courses in agricultural journalism and agricultural English. The Department of Public Speaking had 20 courses, many aimed at improving business communications, including Forensic Oratory, Popular Addresses, Eulogies and After-Dinner Speeches, and Extemporaneous Speeches. Although this university offered the writing practice of the midwestern colleges, students were not expected to take the social sciences courses in which their counterparts studied the rights of labor. And this more practical curriculum in writing did not as thoroughly analyze the role of journalism or advertising in society. While Louisiana State, like midwestern schools, was training skilled, responsible communicators, the emphasis was more on progress than reform.

In the Progressive period, Florida was achieving its transformation from a frontier wilderness into a growing state through the tourism encouraged by Henry Flagler's east-coast railroad, chain of hotels, and steamship line, publicized widely in the North as creating a "winter playground." Henry B. Plant developed the Gulf coast, with the Plant Railroad System stretching to Tampa flanked by grand tourist hotels. Phosphate, cigars, lumber, and shipbuilding as well as improved orange and vegetable growing also propelled a new economy. The necessary involvement of state residents in these agricultural and industrial developments helped shape the curriculum of the University of Florida, founded in 1905 after a merger of several state academies. To supplement offerings in technical fields, the university offered a six-hour course in agricultural journalism within its agriculture college (Drewry 37–39). By 1915–16, the English department's Engineering Exposition provided special training for engineering students on the writing of their profession; in workshop sessions, students critiqued papers assigned in other engineering courses. The English department also offered Newspaper Writing, Expression and Public Speaking, and two-semester sequences on poetry and the short story. As in Louisiana, these courses trained public rhetors, but they were not part of any initiative to cast the university as a leader in service. Without a tie to a "Wisconsin Idea" model of reform and publicity, rhetoric did not receive the attention devoted to agriculture and engineering.

In Texas, unsettled areas became settled as Indian resistance was broken and cattle ranching spread throughout the state. Texas entered the twentieth century with a fairly strong economy, led by the cotton market and an oil boom. But the fourfold rise in population between the Civil War and 1900 also led to unstable economic conditions and an agrarian protest movement. The Farmers' Alliance, a Populist organization like the Grange, created the People's Party, which elected a number of legislators who fought against the power of banks and corporations.

At the University of Texas, founded in 1883, writing courses reflected increasing professional specialization and stressed techniques for informing and persuading, here again with the stress not on social critique but on practical methods of communication. In a developing state, both business and Populist groups could make use of the techniques taught. By 1915–16, the Department of Journalism and the Department of Business Administration crosslisted Selling Problems, which stressed advertising as a factor in selling. The School of Business Administration also offered an advanced course in Business Correspondence. The Department of Journalism had Principles of Technique of Advertising, in which students learned about the psychology of advertising and applied theory to practice by writing copy, selling advertising, and planning publicity campaigns. The department also offered Agricultural Journalism, a class in which students prepared articles for the agricultural press, and Educational Journalism, covering the writing of news, editorials, and feature stories for educational publications. Class Publications concerned article writing for religious, scientific, and other specialized journals.

In the West, expansion and reform again led to advanced writing courses that could train both reformers and business executives. Populists secured the election of some reformist officials, such as Governor Robert Smith of Montana, as well as legislation for change. A major debate concerned free coinage of silver, an issue dating back to 1873 when the federal government discontinued the release of silver dollars and established gold as the only coinage standard (Smith 151). Especially after the Panic of 1893, when banks and businesses closed, farmers and mine workers fought for railroad regulation, monopoly control, the rights of labor, stable crop prices, and free silver (R. W. Larson 11). But even though these citizens sought inde-pendence and control, they realized that mining and other industries had to be capitalized, new railroad lines had to be laid, and new crops and farm markets had to be found. As the tense interdependence between Populism and big business continued, the universities responded by creating writing courses that could serve both.

In Montana, completion of the Northern Pacific Railway in 1883 gave impetus to increased farming and stock raising as well as to the copper and silver industry, whose power controlled state government although farmers continually protested mining's influence and its unreasonably low taxation. Reformers joined together in 1890 in the Independent Labor Party and the Farmers Alliance to press for railroad regulation, eight-hour work days, and the abolition of child labor along with the opening of new mines and railroad routes (Larson 89). Much of their platform passed after 1900 as reform Republicans recognized the need to make concessions to workers as well as to the business owners who could further develop the state.

The University of Montana, founded in 1894, quickly instituted a writing curriculum that would enable persuaders to inform the populace of new advancements and policies and thus to forcefully influence public decisions. In the business and forestry programs, advanced writing courses became degree requirements. By 1915–16, the Department of English offered Ranger School English, a required course on letters and reports for forestry students. The department also offered Business Composition, required of sophomores in the School of Business Administration. The Department of

Fine Arts provided Advertising, a course on the practical use of art in creating persuasive posters, folders, and booklets that was required of seniors in Merchandising in the School of Business Administration. Students in business also took Advertising and Selling, which covered advertising media, finances, recent ad campaigns, and psychological principles.

To train the rhetors who could influence citizens through stories and pageants, the university also created a specialization in creative writing through a prerequisite system. The English department offered Story Writing, practice in writing narrative and intensive study of representative short stories; Writing of Dramatic Sketches, for students who had taken Story Writing, on telling a story in play form; and Creative Writing, covering all literary genres, with one of the first two courses as a prerequisite. The department's ordered sequence in public speaking included Story Telling, Dramatic Presentation, and Pageantry. With this full set of courses, along with those in Ranger English, advertising, and sales, the university sought to empower both citizens and the state's industries.

As at the University of Montana, the University of California and the University of Southern California developed the writing courses suited to promoting the state's resources as well as the citizens' rights. In the 1870s, when California's farmers and other workers were challenging established wealth and authority, many found the university too elitist to serve the needs of the common people. The Mechanics' Deliberative Assembly, an early labor organization, and Grange societies in rural portions of the state argued for education in farming, building, and manufacturing. Many reform politicians also wanted a fuller business and technical education to support railroad construction, diversified agriculture, the citrus industry, irrigation, oil exploration, real estate development, and tourism. When Benjamin Ide Wheeler from Cornell became president of the University of California in 1899, he attempted to improve the university's reputation in the state by emphasizing its key role in creating a new, prosperous land of promise.

During the twenty years of his presidency, the university began offering new courses in technical writing and journalism as well as in creative writing and persuasive speaking to publicize the state and sell a myth of California to eastern residents and developers. By 1915–16, the Department of Economics taught Advertising, Commercial Reviews and Trade Journals, and a public relations course called Industrial Goodwill, another one that preceded Bernay's. Along with reporting and editing, journalism students took English in Business Practice, an English department course in business correspondence. The English department also offered English in Engineering Practice, Short Story Writing, English Verse Composition, and Play Construction. Wheeler intended these courses to create the story tellers, promoters, and business communicators needed to promote the state.

In Washington, complete degree programs in writing supported the state's growth. The first railroad that came to Washington state in 1883 started rapid development of the state. The discovery of gold in Alaska and the Yukon Territory in 1896 led to Seattle serving as an important embarkation point. The city's population tripled in a decade at a time when the state was also developing its agriculture and horticulture. The University of Washington in Seattle, which opened in 1861 as the oldest state supported school on the West coast, opened a degree program in advertising within the College of Business Administration requiring Economics of Advertising, Principles of Advertising, Advertising Campaigns, Research in Advertising and Marketing, Typography of Advertising, and Business Correspondence. The Department of Dramatic Art offered Play-Acting and Play-Producing as well as Play-Writing. The Department of Journalism offered The Short Story, The Sporting Page, Critical Writing, Function of Newspaper Advertising, Display Advertising, Advertising Typography, Editorial Writing, Trade Journalism, and General Publicity.

At Washington as at other schools outside the Midwest, advanced writing courses developed in journalism, advertising, business communication, creative writing, and other genres to promote the region as well as to reform its legislative and business practices. Perhaps more than in the Midwest, these schools witnessed the complexity of the era's vision of progress. Experts became trained to inform the public concerning new advances in science and industry, but also to increase the profits of businesses and the growth of the region. Educated in these college classes, students could fight the establishment or cause it to prosper.

THE ADVANCED WRITING IDENTITY

Across the country, although titles and purposes varied, the new courses shared similar characteristics related to their goal of creating trained persuaders. Their originators wanted this training to be completely separate from freshman composition, with any formats introduced being professional ones and the teachers being experienced writers. Whereas such aspirations did engender thorough training in the theory and practice of real genres, these goals also led to classes offering little more than unguided practice sessions or newspaper grunt work.

Because writing entered the university as one of the new practical disciplines, its identity came from its relation to actual writing practice. Thus instruction substituted actual genres for school forms of discourse although students might still be learning a set of rules for a format without gaining a clear understanding of the principles involved. In *Types of News Writing* (1916), Willard Bleyer presented a possible syllabus of news stories: on fires and accidents, crime, criminal and civil courts, weather, sports, and society. In *News Writing* (1917), Matthew Lyle Spencer of Lawrence College dealt with audience analysis, effective leads, and story structures before turning to court, accident, crime, sports, and society reporting. To illustrate the formats and various writing techniques, these books presented examples from published news articles, usually with introductory sentences explaining the features being illustrated, such as "The following is a typical football story," and "Note the suspensive effect of the following leads" (Spencer, *News Writing* 171, 200, 230). Wisconsin professor Edward Hall Gardner's *Effective Business Letters* from 1915 also contained instruction and examples about specific genre types: letters intended to give information, order goods, give notice of shipments, sell products, and collect debts. Walter Kay Smart, of Armour Institute of Technology and Northwestern University, wrote *How to Write Business Letters That Win* (1916), which provided formats for applications, inquiries, orders, adjustments, collections, sales, and other types of letters. Early poetry writing texts also concentrated on professional forms. In *Verse Writing* (1917), William Herbert Carruth, who taught at Kansas and then Stanford, provided assignments such as the following, with 15 of these paired exercises suggested as a semester's work:

> Write two pieces of four stanzas each, iambic tetrameters, with masculine endings (same as Exercise I) but with rhymes a: a, b: b (couplets), the one on The Trees of the Santa Clara Valley, The Engineer, or My Dearest Hope; the other on an optional theme. (76)

In *The Art of the Short Story* (1913), Carl Grabo helped students with generating ideas for stories that emphasized theme, plot, or character.

As quickly as possible, most advanced writing programs began trying to involve students not just in genre exercises but in the real profession, making the classroom resemble the work place. Like agriculture or engineering students, writing students were considered as participants or interns, ready to take on the challenges of real situations, and thus to spend their time on the minutiae of publication as well as on general training. At the University of Missouri in 1908, *The University Missourian* provided a laboratory for students, who covered news and features of interest to the community, edited copy, secured advertising, and circulated the paper in town. Each day in reporting courses, class sessions combined lectures with production:

> The bell in the tower of Switzler Hall rings for eight o'clock classes; the day's work begins. In one room a professor lectures on the writing of editorials . . . in the news room a group of students gather for work on the *University Missourian*. The work is divided into hours according to the general University program. At nine o'clock come other lectures—advertising in one room, the history and principles of journalism in another—and other student reporters assemble for assignments. . . . After ten o'clock virtually all the work of the School is of a practical nature, the formal lectures having been given in the first two hours. Pencils scratch busily, typewriters click, the telephone rings. This is the "laboratory" of the School of Journalism. (Williams 29–30).

Many universities also moved into relationships with local or regional publications to give students more firsthand opportunities. At the University of Iowa, for example, "once a year the class in community weekly goes to a nearby town, gathers and writes all the news and editorials, designs, writes and sells all the advertising for a 24-page community weekly" (Lazell, "Weeding Out the Unfit" 29).

Like their colleagues in journalism, creative writing teachers involved students in an environment that duplicated the professional roles of writers and editors, and they helped students seek professional publication. In his text, William Carruth suggested that creative workshops convene during a class period of at least two hours to allow time for reading and discussing the students' poetic exercises for that day or their revisions from the day before as well as professional samples. He recommended an informal class structure:

> A classroom with straight rows of seats does not afford in any case the most congenial conditions for the enjoyment of poetry. It is especially unfavorable to verse writing and mutual criticism. If possible a verse-writing course should meet out-of-doors, or at least in a private study and around a table. Stiffness and conventionality must be dispelled. So far as may be, the class should be like a club of friends gathered for common enjoyment and helpful suggestion and criticism. In such surroundings it is easier to draw out the real thought and the serious consideration of even the shy members. (54)

For his workshops, Iowa's Edwin Ford Piper created the type of informal atmosphere that Carruth recommended, which his student John Frederick described in an essay about Piper:

> Attendance is optional, but there are few of us who fail to find our way in the late afternoon to Mr. Piper's basement office, where we sit in nooks between bookcases or even share a table with heaps of papers and magazines, and read the stories and poems and essays we have written for the comments of one another and of our leader. In that group, as rarely elsewhere in my experience, there was practiced by Mr. Piper the principle of criticism which I believe to be the only right one for dealing with student work: "Something to praise, something to blame." (83)

In classes and clubs where students studied playwriting and produced their own work, drama was also presented as the professional genre functioned. Many state schools also offered courses on pageantry, in which students learned to stage local parades and patriotic plays.

For the creative writer, this seriousness of immediate purpose also provided the opportunity to study current American authors, something rarely done in literature courses at that time. In Newcomb College's The Short Story, introduced in 1908, students read Poe, Hawthorne, Bret Harte, George Cable, Lafcadio Hearn, and Edith Wharton. In Lovett's and Herrick's short story writing classes at the University of Chicago, the syllabi included works by George Washington Cable, Joel Chandler Harris, Bret Harte, William Dean Howells, Brander Matthews, Arthur Conan Doyle, Octave Thanet, and Mary E. Wilkins. This opportunity to study current published writing was also found in journalism, technical writing, and advertising courses.

Although the new advanced writing offerings stressed practical experience and current models, they also generally had historical and psychological content intended to fully form writers as influential leaders. This emphasis stemmed from the Progressive desire to use professional genres to persuade citizens: Writers would need to understand the world they lived in, not just how to write a headline or slogan. As in Wisconsin's journalism program, writing students at many schools were not allowed to take professional writing courses until they gained a solid background in economics, history, and political science.

Within the writing courses themselves, students considered the history and ethical codes of their field as well as theories of consumer psychology.

Spencer's *Editorial Writing* (1924), for example, described the superficiality of American readers:

> Readers in the mass are not philosophers or deep students of any school of political thought. They are a practical working host, concerned with only the most pressing realities of life, craving to be amused, to be made to laugh or cry over passing occurrences, but not to be made to think too hard over any subject that does not concern them vitally. (68)

According to Spencer, editorialists must carefully examine the desires of these readers: "The underlying motive that inspires everybody to read is self-interest." Thus a subject must be presented "in such a way that readers would see its application to themselves and their own affairs" (61–62). Spencer also understood, however, that editorials would not, and should not, always reach the entire newspaper audience; some might influence a "thoughtful minority" (69).

Audience psychology and the ethics of persuasion were also frequently featured in advertising texts and courses. Warren B. Dygert's *Advertising Principles and Practice* (1936) reviewed the needs of consumers, as established by a social scientist: "A native want might be man's craving for emotional excitement; an acquired want, his wish to attend motion picture shows" (53). Both native and acquired wants involve human motives, such as appetite, health, love, safety, and control, that can be analyzed by their relative strengths at different ages and incomes. Thus the advertiser will succeed by first using surveys and other tests to examine a certain consumer group and by then relating a product to these key motives. This strategy combined the product's best attributes with the consumer's needs, an effective form of persuasion also judged as the most ethical advertising. Brewster and Palmer's *Introduction to Advertising* (1924) discussed the lack of truthfulness in earlier ads, such as those for patent medicines, as a bad memory from "the Stone Age," but they recognized that some politicians and business owners continued to employ unethical persuasive strategies (425).

To reinforce the vision of advanced writing instruction as preparation for the "real world," most universities hired writing teachers who had professional experience. Especially when journalism programs began, however, the new hires' background might be minimal—and more might seem suspect to other English or liberal arts faculty. Herbert L. Creek studied shorthand and typing, failed to prosper in a business job, worked as a school teacher, and then entered graduate school so that he could get a college teaching job; he was asked to teach business writing at the University of Illinois because "somebody remembered that I had once been a stenographer" ("How I Became" 6). Harrison McJohnston came to Illinois in 1913 after teaching economics at Ohio State and working as a copywriter, sales correspondent, and editor at *System Magazine* and *Printer's Ink*.

In journalism the ideal candidate was a experienced reporter with an academic background, at least a college degree, and perhaps some teaching experience. Such rare breeds were often charged with planning new courses and departments. Joseph French Johnson graduated from Harvard in 1878, studied political economy in Germany, worked for the *Springfield Republican* and *The Chicago Tribune*, and founded *The Spokane Spokesman* before he accepted the position of professor in charge of journalism at the University of Pennsylvania's Wharton School of Business in 1893. Walter Williams, first president of the American Association of Schools and Departments of Journalism, had a high school degree, training in printing, and editorial experience at five newspapers when he became dean of the new School of Journalism and professor of history and principles of journalism at the University of Missouri in 1908.

The first teachers of creative writing, like Piper and Cook at Iowa, were generally literature teachers who published their own poems or stories, but by the 1920s, professional writers also began coming to campus through writer-in-residence programs. Miami University of Ohio made playwright Percy MacKaye, who had studied with George Pierce Baker at Harvard and was largely responsible for the American pageant movement, a writer-in-residence in 1920, building him a much publicized studio and giving him a reduced course load (Thompson and Winnick 263). Robert Frost was a professor of English at Amherst for parts of 1917 to 1920, and then went to the University of Michigan during 1921–22 as a poet-in-residence with no instructional responsibilities. Thomas Wolfe served in a less glamorous capacity as a composition instructor at New York University from 1922 to 1930.

From 1900 to 1917, the number of advanced writing classes and professors teaching them increased tremendously. Advanced writing courses had achieved a clear identity, involving professional genres and work environments, practically trained teachers, historical and ethical information, and psychological analyses of audiences. But by then, growing pains were evident. Professors argued about the proper mix of practical and theoretical training, about the appropriateness, for example, of journalism students spending so much of their time producing college newspapers. English professors opposed new colleagues who seemed inappropriate for membership in a liberal arts department; and teachers began to leave the English department, entering schools and departments of journalism, advertising, communications, business, and speech, where practical professional training might find better homes. These advanced courses had been instituted in Wisconsin and other midwestern states to serve reform movements, to awaken the public through a combination of explanation and persuasion. As they spread across the country, however, they came to serve other, often paradoxical goals, of furthering progress as well as guarding against its most dangerous excesses. Even though their purposes and components varied, these curricula were well established by World War I and were shaping American public discourse before 1920.

5

University-Trained Persuaders Sell
Reform, Consumerism, and War

Between 1890 and World War I, as we have seen, colleges throughout the country began teaching public persuasion. Although these courses emerged from reform initiatives, they began to involve proponents of business growth as well as business oversight, of states' rights and other political agenda as well as of a stronger democracy. As increasing numbers of teachers studied mass persuasion, its potential for controlling public opinion became increasingly clear, beginning during the presidency of Theodore Roosevelt, whose rhetoric was shaped with direct help from the advanced curriculum's originators, Bob La Follette and Charles Van Hise. Business and scientific leaders also began taking advantage of the media's new potential, with guidance from college teachers and graduates. Then the great power of the persuasion professions was thoroughly demonstrated by World War I, a war sold to a skeptical American public through words. Advanced writing courses developed within this circularity of influence: The media's goals, techniques, and ethics both shaped college courses and were shaped by them.

ROOSEVELT'S PROGRESSIVE POLITICS
AND THE MEDIA

After Theodore Roosevelt arrived at the White House in 1901, he revolutionized the relationship between the media and the president, exploiting college-trained writers to reach a growing nation and achieve his Progressive vision. Like Bob La Follette, he realized that a Progressive platform could only succeed through constant interaction with a newly powerful public. He frequently consulted with La Follette and Charles Van Hise on the progress of the Wisconsin Idea and the role of the media in bringing that vision to the public. When Roosevelt spoke in Madison in 1911 on the success the university had achieved in ten years, he recognized the media's role in this progress ("Wisconsin: An Object Lesson"). With La Follette's guidance, Roosevelt retained Gifford Pinchot as chief of the forestry service and asked him to also serve as a public relations specialist. Pinchot had studied forestry in Europe but, like La Follette, he had concentrated on writing and speaking in his undergraduate curriculum, at Yale. He had won a medal in a speaking contest in his senior year and had been much praised for his theme "Education for Citizenship," concerning the political responsibility of the college educated, who should guide the masses and thus curtail the power of tyrants like Boss Tweed in New York.

Just as La Follette courted Wisconsin newspaper writers and national spokesmen like Lincoln Steffens, Roosevelt and Pinchot nurtured relationships with magazine and newspaper owners and with individual reporters, allowing them exclusive interviews and access to information. Roosevelt provided the press their first quarters in the White House and met with five or six reporters during his afternoon shave each day. He dispatched news, ordered investigations, and uttered denunciations dramatically so as to keep his active leadership before the public. He often chose to release news on Sunday so that it would make the first page on news-slow Monday. To undercut opposition from Congress, he frequently leaked strategic information to preferred members of the press. In 1905, for example, he told them that he planned to call a special session on tariffs because he wanted to keep the issue alive in the Senate. By leaking possible decisions, he could judge public reaction before attaching his name to any new plan (Cornwell 15–23). In many fights with Congress, Roosevelt counted on his press ties to produce favorable copy: When he was fighting for railroad legislation, for example, his favored Progressive journalists wrote essays on the sins of the railroads for McClure's, The Outlook, and The World's Work. For Roosevelt, as he wrote in his autobiography, these techniques were not undue manipulation of the people but exploitation of the available means of getting a message to them. According to political scientist Elmer E. Cornwell, Jr., in dominating the press and public, Roosevelt demonstrated a new, stronger role for the presidency: "a kind of 'model' for future executive exploitation of the mass media for opinion leadership. To the general outlines of this model his successors added surprisingly little" (14).

Besides manipulating daily coverage, Roosevelt made frequent trips throughout his presidency to stir up press and public interest. As Pinchot wrote in his autobiography: "Action is the best advertisement. The most effective way to get your cause before the public is to do something the papers will have to tell about" (329). In August 1902, Roosevelt conducted a speaking tour in New England and the Midwest, and the next year he went to the west coast. In the fall of 1905, following his triumphant reelection, he began a lengthy tour of the South: "Vast numbers heard Roosevelt's speeches and absorbed, by listening, ideas which they never would have read" (Pringle 258). For the battle in the Senate over the Hepburn Act, which would increase railroad regulation, he campaigned across the country for 18 months in 1905 and 1906.

In addition to seeking support for trade and railroad legislation, Roosevelt needed help in his fight for land conservation, a controversial idea to Americans still accustomed to spreading into new territory and using the land for farms, cattle ranching, mining, and logging with few restrictions. Gifford Pinchot realized the key role of publicity in changing public opinion about the appropriate uses of land and sought help from conservationist Bob La Follette, who supported these efforts although he objected to older, agricultural lands being included in government protection plans. In 1909 in his magazine, La Follette spoke of "the untiring efforts of Mr. Pinchot to safeguard public interest," siding with him in a conflict with Richard Ballinger, Secretary of the Interior, whom the magazine labeled an obstructionist and accused of making personal profits from coal lands ("Pinchot or Ballinger" 3). Responding to a telegram request from La Follette in 1910, Pinchot helped him campaign for his reelection to the Senate and was especially happy about the outcome. "Your splendid victory," he wired La Follette, "will help every man who stands for right things throughout the United States" (qtd. in W. Johnson 194). In 1911, they worked together toward blocking a coal and oil bill. At La Follette's suggestion, Pinchot also sought advice from Charles Van Hise who, as a geologist and successful publicist of the University of Wisconsin, was uniquely qualified to help with a massive public relations effort for the environment. The connection between Pinchot and La Follette would remain solid until Roosevelt decided to pursue the presidential nomination against La Follette in 1912.

Like Van Hise and Bleyer at the University of Wisconsin, Pinchot used press bulletins and pamphlets to manage the press and to influence public opinion. He declared in a 1903 letter, "Nothing permanent can be accomplished in this country unless it is backed by sound public sentiment" (qtd. in Ponder 97). By the end of the nineteenth century, the Department of Agriculture had begun publishing technical advisories and the popular *Agricultural Yearbook*, mailed to citizens by their Congressman. Between 1898 and 1910, Pinchot greatly increased the number of these publications, sending out pamphlets, advisories, bulletins, and reports to citizens and to newspapers and journals, reaching a monthly audience of nine million readers (Ponder 97). His press bulletins summarized speeches and research findings to preach the doctrine of conservation while also providing information on farming innovations. The bulletins also included Roosevelt's Congressional speeches on natural resources, which were usually written by Pinchot.

Pinchot also recognized the potential of film to send a powerful visual message to the citizenry. The Department of Agriculture established its own production facilities in 1908; by 1914 practically every government agency used publicity films. Pinchot equipped special cars to travel across the country, stopping to exhibit short films on animal husbandry, farm marketing, and conservation. Any organization could ask to be sent educational shorts on Care of Babies, Handling of Milk, The Street Beautiful, and other subjects. The Office of Public Roads used films and slides of road building in France to organize efforts for rural improvement.

Following the model of La Follette's state commissions, Pinchot persuaded Roosevelt to create a series of Presidential commissions between 1903 and 1909 to dramatize the need for conservation: Their meetings would "inspire" press coverage. Like Van Hise and La Follette, Roosevelt would thus bring in experts to participate in government decision making. Of particular importance were the Inland Waterways Commission, the National Conservation Commission, Civil Service Commission, the Commission on Public Lands, the Commission on Inland Waterways, the Commission on Country Life, and the Commission on National Conservation, all of which involved University of Wisconsin experts who had served on state commissions (Roosevelt, An Autobiography 401–02). These groups gained publicity through the American Forest Congress held in Washington in 1905, Roosevelt's cruise down the Mississippi for the Inland Waterways Commission in 1907, and the White House Conference on Conservation in 1908, a national conference of governors that launched the National Conservation Commission.

Roosevelt appointed the Inland Waterways Commission, including Congressmen and scientists, on March 14, 1907, to emphasize the role played by water, coal, iron, soil, and forests in natural resource problems. Like La Follette's lunch club and other joint meetings in Madison, this commission created a very favorable public bond between government and academic experts. In October 1907, Roosevelt's trip down the Mississippi River with these commissioners gave their work, as he wrote, "a new standing in public estimation" (An Autobiography 445). On the trip, the commission's chair and secretary asked the President to hold a conference of governors on national resources: He announced his decision to do so to a large audience awaiting the boat in Memphis. As Van Hise noted in a publicity booklet for the commission, it later grew to include governors, members of the Cabinet, Supreme Court justices, Congressmen, heads of scientific bureaus, representatives of educational societies, reporters, and notable citizens (6). In Roosevelt's opening address for the first commission meeting, according to Charles Van Hise, the President "was able, although not a man of science, to present most effectively and in wonderful proportion the views which the scientific men had been developing through the past twenty-five years with reference to conservation" (7). Following this opening were addresses by scientists and governors and discussion sessions that led to state conservation commissions. As Van Hise wrote, "for the first time in the history of the country the governors were assembled to consider a great national question" (7). No newspaper could ignore such an event: Even William Randolph Hearst, a staunch opponent of the President, placed a picture of a group of delegates across the front page of his New York *American* with the headline "President, Vice President, the Governors and Guests—Probably the Most Notable Group of United States Statesmen Ever Photographed" (qtd. in Ponder 99). Once again, the media were crucial to selling national policy to the public.

In the fall of 1909, Pinchot and Roosevelt organized the National Conservation Association to be the "center of a great propaganda for conservation," an education effort like Wisconsin's extension courses (Van Hise 12). They chose Charles Eliot as honorary president, Pinchot as president, and one representative from each state and territory as a board of managers. Each state also created its own committee to initiate a campaign, in the universities and then in secondary and primary schools, "to advocate and support adoption by the people themselves and by their representatives" of the governors' principles for protecting waters, regulating lands, planning for waterway improvement, preventing forest fires, preserving soil fertility, and retaining titles to lands with mineral reserves (qtd. in Van Hise 394). Van Hise immediately recognized this educational effort's importance and planned for the University of Wisconsin's participation in it: "Since it seems to me that the universities should take part in this movement for the advancement of the nation as they have in others, this course of lectures is given at Wisconsin" (13). His 20 lectures, which Willard Bleyer helped him to write and revise, were used in seminars on campus and reprinted to create a handbook of essential information on conservation for

all citizens. In these lectures, Van Hise discussed the Progressive President
and his cause:

> I believe that what he did to forward this movement and to bring it into the
> foreground of the consciousness of the people will place him not only as one
> of the greatest statesmen of this nation but one of the greatest statesmen of
> any nation of any time. (10)

By first involving Wisconsin students in conservation, Van Hise could
support Roosevelt's publicity efforts while extending the university's role in
progress and thus its national status.

Although Congressmen did attend Roosevelt's conservation conferences, they were beginning to debate the growing power of Pinchot and of
"Pinchotism," of governmental agencies exerting undue persuasive influence on the public they supposedly served. Representative Franklin Mon-
dell, speaking for western timber interests, accused the Forest Service of
great extravagance in sending out self-laudatory bulletins at a cost of
$87,000 a year. Unwilling to undertake the entire communications issue,
the Congress voted, in March 1908, that the Department of Agriculture
could not pay for favorable newspaper and magazine articles, a practice that
seemed more questionable than the endless stream of informational bulletins (Herold 15).

Pinchot's power eclipsed with the election of William Howard Taft, who
took office in 1909 and fired Pinchot in 1910. In 1912, Congress appointed
a committee to inquire into the duties of the various press bureaus. This
committee's attempts to rein in Pinchot's counterparts at other agencies,
including the State Department, the Bureau of Public Roads, the Smith-
sonian Institute, and the Post Office Department, finally culminated in a
1913 vote to forbid the federal hiring of "publicity experts." The bill had
originated in reaction to an announcement for a "publicity expert, men
only," by the Office of Public Roads. In 1919, Congress added the prohibition that agencies could not hire lobbyists to pressure Congress (Herold 15).
This legislation, however, did not end or even slow the hiring of public
relations employees; it only led to varied job titles and disguised activities.

By manipulating all the available means of good public relations, as La
Follette and Van Hise had done on the state level, Roosevelt helped create
modern discourse. For the first time, a national audience was assaulted by
a combination of genres—newspaper coverage, public speeches, public
relations events, scientific pamphlets, advertisements, and university instruction—in the service of a cause. Because of the close ties between

university and government in the Progressive era, knowledge of persuasion grew in both quarters, with college representatives like Van Hise helping governmental officials and thus recognizing new possibilities for publicizing their universities and states and for educating professional writers. Through this circularity of influence, professional mass persuasion became an essential tool of the successful political leader.

NEWSPAPERS AND MAGAZINES

As politicians such as La Follette and Roosevelt and their staffs mined the potential of modern political rhetoric, a new generation of college-trained journalists formed the twentieth-century newspaper. During the Progressive era, this influential medium became more professional, and aggressively persuasive when the cause was right.

Before the Civil War, the daily or weekly paper was manufactured essentially by hand from expensive materials to serve a small market. Newspapers were often organs of a particular party, faction, or candidate. Andrew Jackson, for example, received consistently favorable press from Amos Kendall, who ran the *Argus of Western America*. John Quincy Adams said of Jackson and Martin Van Buren, "Both . . . have been for twelve years the tool of Amos Kendall, the ruling mind of their dominion" (qtd. in Emery and Emery 114).

The lack of reportorial staff meant that many news reports came from involved parties, often from rumors circulating near a scene. In August 1831, for example, the Washington *National Intelligencer* reported Nat Turner's slave revolt in this fashion:

> The number of the insurgents has been variously estimated at from 150 to 400, acting in detached parties. From twenty-five to thirty families are said to have fallen to their ferocity. We are happy to say that the latest intelligence from the scene of disorder assures us that the further progress of the wretches has been arrested, that they are seeking shelter in the swamps and that they are by this time surrounded by the militia and volunteers. The letter which we give below, written by a highly intelligent and respectable gentleman of this town, is the latest account received here, and relieves us from the necessity of detailing the various rumors in circulation.

In that same issue, the paper had to rescind election results that had been brought in by a faulty source: "Yesterday we stated, on authority which we could not doubt, that Mr. Chilton had been elected over Mr. Hawes. To-day we find it our duty to announce Mr. Chilton's defeat by a majority of thirteen votes." Papers also included unsubstantiated stories from other American and from European newspapers. The same *Intelligencer* issue, for example, provided reprinted news on the House of Commons, the Polish war, and the following paragraph from the *Edinburgh Evening Post*: "We have just heard from good authority that Sir Walter Scott is very ill, and in great danger" (Emery, Schuneman, and Emery 28).

The technology and purpose of the nineteenth-century paper complimented each other: Limited circulation and slow, costly manufacture favored highly partisan journals of opinion with small audiences. National and international news could be reprinted; the editor collected local items from eyewitnesses and wrote political editorials that would attract a small but faithful audience who could pay the high price. The profession of "reporter" was thus not a widespread one.

The newspaper would change drastically by the beginning of the twentieth century, a change caused in large part by new technology. This technical revolution began with steam-powered presses in the 1830s and continued with folder-cutters in the 1870s and electric presses in the 1890s. The evolution of typesetting involved stereotyping in the 1860s, Linotype in the late 1880s and 1890s, and the monotype process shortly thereafter. The telegraph made possible the beginnings of wire service in the 1840s; the telephone in the 1870s and the typewriter in the 1880s also helped speed the reporting process. Large newspaper illustrations became possible when photoengraving was developed in the 1880s. Declining costs followed each new mechanization as well as the change from rag paper to wood pulp, which dropped the price of newsprint from 12 cents a pound in 1872 to less than two cents in 1897 (Mott, *American Journalism* 601).

All of this machinery made the newspaper increasingly more efficient to operate, but much greater capitalization was needed to begin operation. To reach a larger public, newspapers began charging lower prices and covering a wider variety of news, not simply the political philosophy of one group. The resulting "penny daily" attracted a new working-class audience with a cheaper price, more lively and local subject matter, and fewer articles on political philosophies.

The livelier subject matter was usually some form of sensationalism. Hearst's New York *Journal*, for example, flourished with adventure, sex, and crime, as in the many issues from 1910 that on the front page featured an ongoing series of clues to solve a murder, accompanied by lurid photos of the headless, limbless victim. The front page of the March 10, 1911, *San Francisco Chronicle* provided reports on war with Mexico as well as more sensational headlines: "Treadwell Mining Town in Grip of Flames," "Train Saved by a Nervy Engineer," and "Special Policeman Shot Down by One of Trio of Desperate Footpads—Wound Will Prove Fatal!" In the New York *World* from June 29, 1914, war in Europe shared the front page with "Keeper Shot Down by Mad Convict Trying to Escape," "All Ablaze, She Leaps Out of Second-Story Window," and "Pig's Eye Fails in Child" (Emery, Schuneman, and Emery 57–58).

While sensationalism was beginning to make newspapers attractive to a larger audience, the Spanish-American War demonstrated the real power that could lie behind exciting and persuasive stories. Hearst's New York *Journal* and Pulitzer's *World* competed in printing fiery denunciations of Spain for its atrocities in Cuba, cruel actions against American citizens, and the *Maine* disaster. Together these newspapers created war fervor that overcame President McKinley and even swept over last minute capitulations by Spain, leading to a declaration of war. On the day after the *Maine* sunk in Havana Harbor, Hearst offered a $50,000 award for "the detection of the perpetrator of the *Maine* outrage." One of the headlines on the full page given to the story declared "Officers and Men Tell Thrilling Stories of Being Blown Into the Air Amid a Mass of Shattered Steel and Exploding Shells." Hearst left no doubt that the Spanish were responsible although this cause had not been verified: "Captain Sigsbee, of the Maine, and Consul-General Lee both urge that public opinion be suspended until they have completed their investigation. They are taking the course of tactful men who are convinced there has been treachery" (*New York Journal* February 17, 1898). The New York *World* got the scoop on Dewey's successful attack on the Phillipines, printed with a headline focusing on the newspaper's own victory in getting the story: "Dewey's Marvelous Naval Achievement—The World's Splendid News Victory" (*World* May 8, 1898). As many as 500 writers and photographers, including Stephen Crane and Frank Norris, gathered at Florida staging camps, covered activities of the blockading fleet in Santiago Harbor, followed Major General William Shafter into Cuba, and sailed with Dewey to Manila. Without censorship, newspapers freely reported movements of the navy and army and made their own statements about Amrican glories (Emery, Schuneman, and Emery 52–53).

Along with war coverage and crime stories, Progressive investigations of those institutions that seemed to prey on the lower classes—such as Wall Street brokerage firms, banks, and corporate trusts—sold the new, cheaper papers. Throughout this era, newspapers offered detailed news that broke down the citizens' isolation from ongoing events and created the awareness essential to reform efforts. On July 7, 1892, for example, Pulitzer's New York *World* derided the Carnegies' handling of a mill riot with the headline, "First Fruit of the Ironmaster's Resolve to Crush His Men." The *Evening Post* battled Tammany in 1894; the New York *Press* published a series of exposés on government briberies in 1898–99. The *World* campaigned against insurance company mismanagement in 1905 and 1906. This paper also secured an injunction to prevent a gas-franchise deal, fought graft in the Brooklyn trolley franchise and the electric-light franchise, and investigated delays in paving construction on Fifth Avenue. With aggressive newspapers increasingly available to a more literate populace, circulation rose astronomically. In 1892, only 10 papers in four cities counted over 100,000 circulation; this number had increased to 30 papers in 12 cities by 1914. The number of dailies increased by one third during that same period, and their average circulation doubled (Mott, *American Journalism* 547).

Many college journalism graduates, a new generation of skilled professionals, involved themselves in the efforts to reform politics through investigations and persuasive articles. Riley Harris Allen, a student at the University of Washington and University of Chicago, promoted education, suffrage, self-governance, and the crusade for statehood at the *Honolulu Evening Bulletin*, where he became editor in 1912. Howard Walter Blakeslee was expelled in 1901 in his senior year at the University of Michigan because his reporting on campus policies in the *Michigan Student* angered the administration. He became a science writer and able critic of brutal new war tactics and later of atomic energy. Raymond Clapper, who studied journalism at the University of Kansas, edited the university newspaper, and was a campus correspondent for the Kansas City *Star*, became a political analyst for the United Press and then the *Washington Post*. Genevieve Forbes Herrick graduated from Northwestern in 1916 after serving as the first woman editor of the school newspaper; she began doing exposé work for the *Chicago Tribune* after receiving an M.A. in English at the University of Chicago. Donald Ring Mellett, who graduated from Indiana University in 1914 where as editor of the *Indiana Student* he waged campaigns to reform the campus Greek system and to improve the water supply to the university, went on to write for newspapers in Columbus and Canton. At the *Canton Daily News*, he wrote 243 editorials against corrupt politicians and organized crime before hired thugs murdered him in 1926. Robert S. Abbott, a son of former slaves, studied printing at the Hampton Institute, worked in several Chicago printing shops, and then in 1905 began his *Defender*, a four-page paper of handbill size with the motto "American race prejudice must be destroyed." This paper regularly contained editorials on inequality of opportunity, unjust legislation, the Klan, and lynchings. It gained a 230,000 readership in a decade.

Magazines, where longer research articles had their home, provided another medium for Progressive reformist writing. Journals of the 1890s, like *Harper's, Scribner's, The Century,* and *The Atlantic Monthly,* were primarily literary, appealing at high prices to cultivated readers. When S. S. McClure formed *McClure's Magazine* in 1893, he started an era of cheap mass-circulation periodicals that extended the Progressive investigations begun by newspapers. His first issue sold at 15 cents, in comparison to 25 or 35 cents for the older periodicals. By 1900, his circulation totaled 370,000; by 1907, it was close to a million (Mott, *A History of American Magazines* 596–99).

Magazine articles against fraudulent patent medicines and food adulteration provided the ongoing pressure leading to the Pure Food and Drug Act of 1906 and thus ended one dangerous form of corruption and victimization. The advertising agency N. W. Ayer & Son had in the 1870s touted Compound Oxygen and Dr. Case's Liver Remedy and Blood Purifier as curing almost all illnesses, and Kennedy's Ivory Tooth Cement as making "Everyone his own dentist!" (Howar 44). Dr. Williams' Pink Pills for Pale People and Paine's Celery Compound were sold imaginatively in the 1890s through invented testimonies and false data on cures (Howar 92). But by 1900, magazines were beginning to expose these frauds. A series in the *Ladies' Home Journal* included titles like "Babies Killed by Patent Medicines," "Diabolical Patent-Medicine Story," and "Inside Story of a Sham." Stories on food adulteration and dishonest labeling appeared frequently in *World's Work, Nation, Outlook, Ladies' Home Journal,* and other Progressive magazines. Harvey Wiley, chief chemist of the Department of Agriculture, contributed a book to the food and medicine reform effort as well as well-substantiated periodical articles. He credited Upton Sinclair's *The Jungle* (1906), however, as being the most persuasive argument for federal controls.

Reformist magazines like *McClure's* attracted writers who were college graduates with training in journalism and literature. McClure and his colleague John Sanborn Phillips, who founded *The American Magazine* in 1906, had both attended Knox College in Galesburg, Illinois, where they worked on student publications, studied writing, and began planning for careers in journalism. Their staff at *McClure's* included Ray Stannard Baker, who studied journalism at Michigan; Willa Cather, who had taken advanced writing classes at the University of Nebraska and worked for the university's journalism professor, Will Owen Jones, at the *Nebraska State Journal*; and Will Irwin, a Stanford graduate who had won prizes there for his stories and poetry, participated in debate and theatre, and edited the student newspaper. These students had the background in literature, journalism, history, and the social sciences necessary for interpreting politics and American culture for *McClure's* readers.

In this development of professional news operations with persuasive goals, college-trained writers were an essential element. Graduates entering newspaper jobs had studied investigative reporting, the political editorial, and the critical essay as well as taking social science requirements like labor problems and legislation, party government, financial history of the United States, public utilities, and city planning. They had generally learned about business management and advertising, run university newspapers, and attended professional meetings to gain further practical training. Then, with their professors' help, they went to work for expanding newpapers and magazines, reinforcing the media's reformist goals. Before World War I, as writing programs developed, newspapers and magazines with large compliments of well-trained college graduates became modern businesses with a very powerful social voice. In this transformation, college training was both cause and effect.

NOVELS AND FILM

As the new century began, college-trained creative writers joined journalists in heralding the Progressive cause. Within a few years of 1890 came the deaths of Emerson, Longfellow, Melville, Lowell, Whitman, Whittier, and Holmes, perceived by then as representatives of an older established order, part of an idealized past of esthete intellectual pursuits and privilege. During the Progressive period, American creative writing would undergo changes similar to those occurring in journalism and other genres. Novels and poets were increasingly inclined to discuss the power of established business and the organization of workers and reformers against it.

Many writers of the time believed that art's purpose was to reveal corruption and elevate the working classes, goals of Progressivism. In 1895, when he was in his fifties, William Dean Howells' reading of Tolstoy led to a reorientation of his art: "The supreme art in literature had its highest effect in making me set art forever below humanity" (258). To fulfill his new social purposes, he began to realistically portray urban poverty and injustice. In *A Traveler from Altruria*, for example, a visitor's stay at a resort hotel revealed the reality of American social classes: The rights of individuals mattered only if they were property holders. Howells' young protégé, Hamlin Garland, depicted the hopelessness of farmers caught in a capitalistic trap in *A Member of the Third House* and *A Spoil of Office*. Frank Norris' *The Octopus* detailed South Pacific Railroad's domination of California politics, with the octopus serving as a metaphor for the railroad's multiple means of getting a stranglehold on the state, and *The Pit* showed grain speculators taking control of the grain market. David Graham Phillips, who wrote the magazine piece to which Roosevelt objected in "The Man with a Muckrake," dealt with evil politicians in *The Plum Tree* and the corrupting power of money in *Great God Success* and *The Second Generation*. His *Susan Lenox* analyzed the social forces that led a country girl into prostitution. Zona Gale's novel and then play adaptation, *Miss Lulu Bett*, offered a realistic portrayal of women's domestic servitude, their lack of legal rights, and the tyranny of "reputation."

In *The Jungle*, Upton Sinclair portrayed the plight of a poor immigrant working in the stockyards: his victimization by employers, landlords, thieves, police, politicians, and the justice system. Robert Herrick questioned the ethics of the meat packing industry in *The Memoirs of an American Citizen*. In Theodore Dreiser's trilogy—*The Financier, The Titan*, and *The Stoic* (posthumously published in 1947)—Cowperwood began as a vital man of great ambitions who had been wronged by political bosses and unfairly imprisoned, but he was shaped into a malicious business force capable of any deal or offense. William Allen White's *A Certain Rich Man* also attacked predatory wealth. Even though these artists varied in their views of whether degredation and oppression could be ameliorated, they all made the public aware of the tyrannies of capitalism.

Although the first films portrayed an optimistic, sentimental world where inner goodness brought just desserts, this medium was also affected by the Progressive spirit. In the independent 1913 production *Why?*, a mob of laborers was shot at by the army and then burnt the Woolworth building: What they built they could destroy. In *The Lost Paradise* (1914), laborers began to strike and riot while also collecting proof that the factory owner stole a poor inventor's ideas to make his fortune. In films from 1915 and 1916, like *The Man with an Iron Heart* and *The Money*

Master, the reformation of a cruel and greedy owner led to a happy ending. In *Dust*, a story of bad factory conditions, the reformed heroine used her fortune to improve the workers' lives (C. W. Campbell 10–11).

This creation of an American literature and cinema of Progressivism was part of an extended interaction involving the university, journalists, and creative writers. After participating in the *Harvard Monthly*, Frank Norris became a war correspondent in South Africa for the *San Francisco Chronicle* and then associate editor of *The Wave*, a Progressive magazine in San Francisco. Theodore Dreiser worked for newspapers in Chicago, St. Louis, Pittsburgh, and New York City. He later held editorial positions at *McClure's*, *Century*, and *Cosmopolitan*. Robert Herrick wrote a textbook on short story writing and taught creative writing at the University of Chicago while writing novels on the plight of the poor. Zona Gale, who had taken advanced writing courses at the University of Wisconsin, began her career by writing romantic stories about small-town life, but then she became involved with Bob La Follette's reform program in Wisconsin and his campaigns for the presidency, and she organized women's clubs to study child labor laws, women's suffrage, and women in industry, a program for change that she discussed in *La Follette's Weekly Magazine* in August of 1909 ("Civic Problems"). She also worked in the Wisconsin Dramatic Society with Thomas Dickinson, teaching students about playwriting and production and contributing her one-act play *The Neighbors* to its repertoire. With earnings from her novel *Miss Lulu Bett*, Gale established the Zona Gale Scholarship for the best writing students at the University of Wisconsin.

Like programs in journalism, creative writing courses reflected the power of an influential form of public persuasion. As professional writers entered the university and trained students through individual courses, and later through undergraduate and graduate majors, they were making creative writing another modern profession, not just a pastime of academicians or literary clubs. As new members of a modern business, students were encouraged to start campus journals, get experience with acting and with theatre management, send writing out for publication, and take jobs with publishers and at theatres. The workshop pedagogy emphasized professional work habits and writing's immediate effect on real audiences. Like journalists, creative writers were being trained to offer a service to the people, by portraying hardships and questioning established powers.

PUBLIC RELATIONS

As the Progressive era revealed, politicians needed the carefully planned press releases and events that could be provided by effective public relations strategists like Charles Van Hise, Willard Bleyer, and Gifford Pinchot. Because journalistic muckraking and political speeches made businesses vulnerable to attack, corporate leaders began to rely on similar tactics to state their case. As Eric Goldman has written:

> The muckrakers used publicity as an anti-business weapon and industry, in direct reply to the muckrakers, began to feel that if publicity could be used against them, it could also be used for them. Hence the birth of the whole public relations industry. (qtd. in Weinberg and Weinberg, xxi)

Like modern journalism and fiction, public relations emerged during the Progressive period, in response to muckraking, but more directly in response to the Progressive view of the populace—as a powerful body to be persuaded and organized but never ignored. The Progressive political system "legitimized the power of public opinion in an extraordinary fashion" (Raucher 19); many businesses quickly responded to that message.

Nineteenth-century "public relations" mostly promoted circuses and entertainers, with P.T. Barnum being the best known self-promoter. In 1835, he exhibited a slave named Joice Heth, claiming that she had nursed George Washington 100 years earlier. He also kept the midget general Tom Thumb and the original Siamese twins, Chang and Eng, in the news. A few businesses also hired specialists to improve their image. George Westinghouse, for example, created a publicity department in 1889 to promote his revolutionary alternating-current system of electricity, which the Edison General Electric Company had labeled as unsafe.

But before 1900, the common business attitude was that such campaigns were superfluous: Americans would buy the necessary goods available at local stores and labor faithfully for their employers without any attention being paid to them. Henry Clay Frick had crushed a labor union riot in the Carnegie Frick Steel Company in Homestead, Pennsylvania, in 1892, using his own security force and the Pennsylvania state militia to beat and kill protesters. During this pitched battle, Carnegie remained sequestered in his Scottish castle. When in 1882 a reporter asked William Henry Vanderbilt, head of the New York Central Railroad, if he had placed a new fast train on the New York to Chicago line for the public's benefit, he was widely quoted as replying, "The public be damned!" (Butterfield 234).

Vanderbilt's hauteur was no longer possible, however, in the era of the Progressives. The citizen had more information and more clout, exercised through voting, choosing goods, and fighting through unions against employers. Steffens, Sinclair, and other muckrakers were making well known the abuses of American business, informing a public with a right to know and with a new political power that made persuading them worth the effort. Railroads, utilities, and oil companies, which were hit by bad publicity from Progressive legislation and muckrakers, especially felt the need to hire press agents who could make their case persuasively. In 1911, the AT&T annual report summarized the company's extensive public relations campaign; most large firms hired agents by 1913. A writer in the *Saturday Evening Post* in 1909 said that more than 10,000 press agents were working in New York City alone (Pimlott 5). The Progressive era was thus leading to better treatment of citizens—and to more effective methods of manipulating them.

In 1900 the nation's first publicity firm, The Publicity Bureau, was established with Harvard University as its sole client. College officials wanted the bureau to publicize the university and transform its image as an effete college inconsequential to an industrializing nation. Public relations expert Edward Bernays recognized the lack of respect for academia in the modern United States and thus the problem universities had in soliciting support from business:

> Men who, by the commonly accepted standards, are failures or very moderately successful in our American world (the pedagogues) seek to convince the outstanding successes (the business men) that they should give their money to ideals which they do not pursue. Men who, through a sense of inferiority, despise money, seek to win the good will of men who love money. (126)

Harvard later created its own office of public relations, employing Bernays among others. It operated under a Secretary of Information to avoid the "public relations" label, which had been criticized by Congress (Bernays 131).

Although The Publicity Bureau began with publicizing one university's service record, its professionals soon turned to other causes. This firm helped railroads to fight Roosevelt's regulatory regulations, opening offices in New York, Chicago, Washington, St. Louis, and Topeka and employing agents at other sites to respond to railroad clients. In each region, agents visited newspaper editors to gather information. They then sent out newspaper articles and informative pamphlets for a certain town or group of towns, often about free trade and land use but with propaganda for the lines: These texts did not mention that the railroads employed these writers. Then agents watched the results carefully to gauge the railroad's reputation in each location. If an editor was anti-railroad and would not publish the free stories sent to him, agents spoke with local business leaders and stirred up public opinion to force a change of attitude. The offices also sent out pamphlets and books tailored for professors, farmers, lawyers, clergy, and other groups without any indication of their sponsorship. One popular pamphlet was a 206-page book for lawyers discussing the legal aspects of railroads with summaries of relevant court decisions (R. S. Baker). Using methods similar to those by which Frank Strong and Charles Van Hise publicized their universities and Pinchot sold Roosevelt's conservation efforts, this agency made opposition to powerful railroads difficult.

Although firms such as The Publicity Bureau pursued newspaper reporters to foster a better image for their clients, they also realized that a good event would bring these writers and the citizenry to them, lessons learned from Roosevelt and La Follette. The biggest mail-order firms, Montgomery Ward and Sears, Roebuck, presented themselves through their catalogs as champions of consumers and enemies of overpriced mill stores. They launched fairs and special programs, such as seminars on modern farming methods, to benefit rural areas where they did the most business: creating good will and trust and thus regular purchasers. Henry Ford sold cars through auto-racing events and car owner clubs. J. C. Penney began a campaign stressing honesty and good service: All employees had to do regular community service, a highly publicized requirement (Raucher 22–23). Other businesses like the Illinois Central Railroad and the Metropolitan Life Company also sold their positive role in the community through ongoing community service projects as public relations began to be viewed as a continuous effort and not just as a response to a crisis.

In the Progressive period, businesses also quickly realized that the new medium of film could bring their message to the people. In 1914, a time when feature films were becoming common, the American Steel and Wire Company produced *Through the Mill to the Farmer*, an informative program shown at farmer institutes and hardware conventions. By that time companies like Postum Cereal, Du Pont Powder, Northern Pacific Railway, Old Taylor Whiskey, and Ford Auto had publicity shorts showing at theatres. Westinghouse created Mrs. Thrifty to speak for electrical cooking and new appliances while Kellogg produced a short on the cereal-making process. In

1915, Edison made two reels for Ford showing how this philanthropic company helped immigrants to become solid citizens (C. W. Campbell 5).

In this time of new techniques and influence, public relations specialists developed ethics codes aimed at further establishing acceptance and trust. Ivy Ledbetter Lee, who opened a publicity office in 1904 after working as a journalist for the New York *World*, issued an influential "Declaration of Principles" that geared public relations to informing citizens— and thus to public service:

> In brief, our plan is, frankly and openly, on behalf of business concerns and public institutions, to supply to the press and public of the United States prompt and accurate information concerning subjects which it is of value and interest to the public to know about. (qtd. in Goldman 8)

Regardless of theory, Lee actually provided the public with information he wanted them to have and with symbolic action, as he did when the Pennsylvania Railroad had an accident in Gap, Pennsylvania: The railroad paid for reporters to travel there, set up facilities for them, and issued Lee's news releases to them regularly. In 1913 Lee enabled the actor Richard Bennett to secure funding for a controversial play about syphilis, *Damaged Goods*, by creating a "Sociological Fund" and convincing prominent people to contribute to it and thus back the play. For the Rockefellers in 1913–14, during a coal strike in Ludlow, Colorado, an incident later known as the Ludlow Massacre because the owners' brutal response resulted in the death of 20 workers, Lee sent out accounts that portrayed strikers as the violent participants and pictured John D. Rockefeller, Jr., as the working man's friend. As Lee's clientele grew, he hired many employees, often graduates of the Columbia School of Journalism (Hiebert 154). When Harvard hired Lee to undertake a funding campaign in the mid-twenties, Deane Malott of the business school worked with him and later joined his firm.

Journalists became the first public relations professionals because they knew how to inform and persuade. Spiraling production costs and the rapid growth of chains and wire services made for an insufficient amount of jobs for the large number of journalism majors. Hearst and Scripps–Howard established efficient national chains, which involved 55 papers by 1929. As Bleyer noted in his study of the profession, "Instead of a large number of papers, each having a limited circulation and struggling to make both ends meet, we have strong successful ones, with large circulations. Larger and larger units in newspaper circulation have come to be the rule" (*Journalism* 17). In this period, many journalists abandoned newspaper careers and instead took advantage of opportunities in public relations, at independent firms like Ivy Lee's, in advertising agencies that began extending their services, and in public relations divisions of large corporations.

Charles P. Johnson, for example, attended the University of Colorado from 1920 to 1923, worked as a reporter for the *Rocky Mountain News* and *Pittsburgh Press*, began as a public relations writer for the lamp division at Westinghouse, and then opened his own public relations firm in San Francisco. John Wiley Hill studied at Indiana University, wrote for the *Cleveland News*, the *Iron Trade Review*, and *Daily Metal Trade*, began doing public relations work for corporations in 1927, and opened a firm with Don S. Knowlton in 1933. Walter Talmadge Arendt graduated from the University of Wisconsin and began a career as reporter for the *New York Sun* and then as political editor for the *New York Evening Post*, but in 1913 he became secretary and publicist for the Municipal Government Association, a Progressive political group, and then began doing public relations work for the Committee on Training Camp Activities during World War I. Peggy Neubauer Phillips studied journalism at the University of Missouri, worked for many different newspapers in Missouri and West Virginia in the 1920s and 1930s, and then became director of the news bureau for Stephens College in Columbia, Missouri. Nicholas Popa studied journalism at Columbia, became a statehouse reporter in Lincoln, Nebraska, and then, after military service from 1942 to 1945, entered the public relations division of the Byer and Bowman Advertising Agency in New York.

As the profession grew, with its own ethics codes and accepted techniques, a few state universities began to offer public relations courses in colleges of journalism or business although separate programs or majors did not appear until the 1940s. The new courses, often taught by practitioners, featured practical campaign experience. Like the other Progressive genres, this one entered the university in its best light, as helpful communication between business or government and the consumer, thus as another public service. The discipline's growth as well as the university course work was a response to other powerful Progressive genres, which made all sides need their own advocates.

ADVERTISING

Advertising, like other genres, was completely transformed during the Progressive era. Advertising was certainly not new: Ancient Romans encountered signboards, public criers, and tablets set in walls. Medieval

English merchants used handbills, criers, and signs to identify their business types although not to sell competitively since the guilds discouraged competition. Posters and printed pamphlets, intended to extend the good image of a corporation, such as the East India Corporation and the Virginia Company, became popular in the Elizabethan period. The small English newspapers of the seventeenth century contained advertisements for goods that mentioned their special features, often through testimonials. The first American newspaper, the *Boston Newsletter* of 1704, carried a notice that "all persons who may have any houses, lands, tenements, farms, shops, vessels, goods, wares, or merchandise, etc., to be sold or let, or servants run away, or goods stoll or lost may have the same inserted at a reasonable rate" (qtd. in Brewster and Palmer 8). Even by the 1870s, the country's premier advertising agency, N. W. Ayer & Son, specialized in small, local ads in newspapers: "legal notices, boys wanted, dogs lost, offers of board and lodging, secondhand furniture for sale, and the like" (Howar 44).

With the Industrial Revolution, larger quantities of more commodities could be transported over greater distances. Successful industries could reach any city's local customers, but customers had to be convinced to want the newly available goods and to choose one specific brand. Many corporations had relied on teams of salesmen, but this older means of selling was becoming prohibitively expensive as the territory became the entire country. Magazines and newspapers offered a better means of reaching large audiences as did direct mail, posters and bulletin boards, streetcar cards, and window displays. As advertising text author George Burton Hotchkiss commented, "The increase in the amount and elaborateness of advertising since the beginning of the twentieth century has been so enormous, particularly in the United States, that its earlier forms and uses seem insignificant by comparison" (3). Just from 1892 to 1914, newspaper advertising multiplied three and a half times (Mott, *American Journalism* 593).

Along with increasing in frequency, the ads themselves changed greatly during the Progressive period. The few small advertising firms operating before 1900 simply contracted with businesses and newspapers to arrange for space and rates. Businesses wrote their own ads, usually a list of a product's features or a testimonial. But the many agencies in 1900 provided copywriting, art work, and market research as well as ad placements. The impact of well-trained professionals at work, on attractive copy that reflected psychological principles and market surveys, was widely felt before World War I. Ads for bicycles, stressing independence and fun, motivated one in seven people to buy one; the first wave of car ads, featuring sleek automobiles and happy riders, led to a doubling of production in two years. "Aunt Jemima" and "Sunny Jim" sold new breakfast cereals by proffering folksy wisdom on health and success. Department stores regularly placed half- and full-page ads to make their goods appealing to women, who would look better and be happier in their new clothes (Fox 13–39). By World War I, advertisers were realizing that their job was not just to explain the product, but to create a persuasive image of who consumers could be if they bought it.

Magazines and newspapers eagerly courted this new advertising revenue because they needed the income to meet production costs and survive in a competitive arena. Because of newspapers' intensive local coverage (94% of families by 1924) and their timeliness, they created the major market for advertising although magazines were also used to reach specialized audiences (Brewster and Palmer 272). By 1914, newspaper circulation receipts were only half as much as the revenue from advertising (Mott, *American Journalism* 597). During this period, both newspapers and magazines allowed for a much greater percentage of advertising space than had been common earlier: In the December 6, 1929, *Saturday Evening Post*, for example, 168 of 272 pages were advertising (Hotchkiss 59). A definition of *medium* in a 1924 textbook, *Introduction to Advertising*, reveals the advertiser's view of the modern newspaper or magazine as simply a conduit for his messages:

> A medium is something that goes between the advertiser and the person he wishes to reach with his message. The word "medium" is used in advertising to denote any sort of publication, poster board, painted sign, gift specialty, program, or in fact anything that carries an advertising message from the advertiser to the one who sees it. (Brewster and Palmer 245)

The result of failing to attract advertising revenue could be fatal. During 1890, Joseph Pulitzer's daily, the New York *World*, did not secure adequate advertisement revenue and even though the paper had 300,000 readers, it ceased publication.

To get the advertiser's business, editors frequently agreed to blur the line between news and ads. Newspapers began to place advertisements next to reading matter instead of in separate sections as was the earlier custom. They also agreed to mention products in news and feature articles in exchange for ad contracts. A 1915 text *The Principles of Advertising* discusses this sales technique:

> People who wish to influence public opinion are continually attempting to
> secure space in the news or editorial columns of newspapers and in special
> articles in magazines in order to present their propositions under the guise of
> news and information. Hundreds of thousands of dollars have been spent in
> this way. (Tipper et al. 378)

This book cynically claims that such indirect advertising had been limited
by only the newspaper's need for profits: although newspapers charged for
this service, they could charge more for standard advertisements.

Many larger daily newspapers also offered valuable merchandising and
public relations service to attract regular advertising revenue. The *Okla-
homa City Times*, for example, prepared campaign portfolios and introductory letters for use by retail salesmen. This paper also published a local
merchandising monthly to notify merchants of new sales campaigns,
supplied sales agents with maps to the city and retail route lists, sent the
paper's own sales staff out to help retailers, booked dates for their window
displays, distributed window or counter cards, and conducted surveys to
check on sales and product distribution: "Any other cooperation not
mentioned above but which is essential to the success of a campaign,"
the paper announced, "will be given special consideration" (Brewster and
Palmer 275–76). The magazine *Delineator* published photographs of re-
decorated rooms fitted with furniture, rugs, and other merchandise of
their advertisers. The magazine's agents encouraged retail stores to
create similar rooms in their stores to feature these products.

The advertisers' clear need to persuade often caused enmity between
advertisers and journalists although each depended on the other to reach
its public. Whereas newspapers survived on income from advertising,
they began to object to the ads' most outrageous claims. E. W. Scripps in
1903 appointed editor Robert F. Paine as advertising censor of all
Scripps–McRae papers. The Philadelphia *North American* in 1909 began a
campaign to inform its readers about impure foods and labeled products
that it advertised as "Honest Foods." The New York Globe and other
papers soon followed similar evaluative procedures. The New York *World*
campaigned against the advertising and selling of impure drugs in 1911.

Like public relations professionals and journalists, advertisers were
caught between two Progressive views of the public: as a respected group to
inform and as a powerful group to persuade. The Associated Advertising
Clubs of America organized in 1905 to campaign for "Truth in Advertising"
and adopted an ethics code in 1914. A statute devised in 1911 by the *Printer's
Ink*, the chief journal for the profession, made "untruthful, deceptive, or

misleading statements" by an advertiser a misdemeanor. This law was adopted by 22 states in the next decade, and, with modifications, by 15 more (Pope 204–06). But the profession still had to make people need a product and buy it, a manipulative purpose often at odds with ethics codes.

Although the fields of journalism and advertising sometimes conflicted, many advertisers came from journalism schools and jobs, finding advertising to involve similar skills and perhaps to offer more opportunity. Bruce F. Barton, for example, graduated from Amherst College and then served as managing editor of *Home Herald*, a small religious newspaper that failed in 1909. In 1910 he obtained a similar post at *Housekeeper* magazine, which failed the following year. In 1912 he moved to New York and to a position at the muckraking *McClure's* where he wrote advertising copy, most successfully for the Harvard Classics. He then became editor of *Every Week*, collaborated with Norman Rockwell on a campaign for Edison Mazda Light Bulbs, wrote inspirational editorials for Redbook, and then in 1918 formed his own advertising firm, later called BBDO, with other professionals he had met doing publicity work for the war effort. His colleague Alex F. Osborn attended Hamilton College where he worked for the school newspaper and organized a drama club. He then began as a cub reporter for the *Buffalo Times* and police reporter for the *Buffalo Express* while also publishing poems and essays under a pen name. At the advertising agency E. P. Remington in Buffalo in 1913, Osborn wrote ads for patent medicines and created a baking contest for General Baking Company. After working with Bruce Barton for the United War Work Campaign, he joined his friend in forming BBDO. At their agency in 1932, 69 of 196 members had worked in journalism and 57 had worked in sales (Applegate 123).

Other journalists opted for careers not in private agencies but with manufacturers and other businesses. Leo Noble Burnett, for example, graduated in journalism at the University of Michigan in 1914 and worked as a printer's assistant and cub reporter for the *Peoria Journal*. In 1917 he went to General Motors in Detroit to begin marketing cars, not through claims about features or benefits but through images that portrayed consumers' happier lives in the car and their close relationship with the car company. Bernice Bowles Fitz-Gibbon graduated in English from the University of Wisconsin in 1918, became a society reporter and advertising assistant for the *Rockford* (Illinois) *Register-Gazette*, and then went into department store advertising in New York, at Wanamaker's and Macy's

(Applegate). Thus the distinction between journalist and advertiser was becoming blurred.

The growth of advertising was reflected in and furthered by curricula at American universities, by courses that emphasized ethics, psychological principles, and professional techniques, taught in colleges of business or journalism. Teachers with professional experience emphasized practical work on campaigns and in administration so that students would be prepared for influential jobs involving writing, marketing, and management. These courses extended the vision of advertising as a "public service" that, like public relations and journalism, helped citizens to obtain essential products and services even as it shaped their wants and needs.

PROFESSIONAL WRITING'S PROGRESS: THE FIRST WORLD WAR

In the first decade of the century, the new powerful public discourse moved out from the government to the private sector, with leadership from college writing programs and their teachers and graduates. The strength of these genres—alone and in combination, within and outside of their new ethics codes—was fully established before World War I. At the beginning of the conflict, Americans did not believe that a European disagreement should cause them to abandon their policy of isolationism and risk American lives. They were not even sure, as they examined a complicated scenario of European rivalries and past offenses, that one side was clearly in the right. German Americans in Wisconsin and other midwestern states even held bake sales in 1914 and 1915 to raise money for German troops.

In 1917, Wilson drafted George Creel, who had been active in both his 1912 and 1916 campaigns, to form the Committee on Public Information (CPI) and use every possible rhetorical technique to sell the United States on war. His methods very closely resembled La Follette, Van Hise, and Bleyer's publicity campaign in Wisconsin, Roosevelt and Pinchot's efforts for conservation, and the advertising and public relations programs of many American businesses. The war would clearly reveal both the power of public rhetoric and its dangers. When serving a cause, the different genres could join together under the banner of public service and be intensely forceful, as ironically they were in the assault on passivist Bob La Follette in 1917 and 1918. Many writers gained experience with new discourse types during the all-out propaganda campaign for war, altering their own careers and extending their spheres of influence.

Creel began his career as a muckraking journalist who protested the unfair manipulations of both politicians and publicists. In 1899 he founded a Kansas City paper, the *Independent,* through which he fought the local political machine and worked for Progressive reforms, such as direct primaries, rights for women, and protection for factory workers. He then moved to the Progressive *Denver Post* and the *Rocky Mountain News,* where he suggested in one editorial that 11 state senators be lynched. In a 1914 article for *Harper's Weekly* titled "Poisoners of Public Opinion," he charged that Rockefeller's publicity staff had "neither truth nor any saving instinct of decency" (436). He decried Ivy Ledbetter Lee's depictions of strike leader Mother Jones as a whorehouse madam and argued that Lee had misrepresented the opinions of 317 newspaper editors in a pamphlet on the Ludlow, Colorado, coal mining strikes of 1913–14. In a 1915 muckraking article "How the Drug Dopers Fight," he vilified quack medicines by juxtaposing pictures of happy patients from advertisements with those patients' actual death certificates. His co-authored book against child labor, *Children in Bondage,* vividly described children stunted and maimed by factory machinery. After working for Wilson in the 1916 campaign, contributing a tract *Wilson and the Issues,* he was made chair of the CPI because of his demonstrated abilities in collecting data and presenting it persuasively and because of his knowledge of journalism, public relations, and advertising.

Like Roosevelt and La Follette, Creel realized that in the Progressive era citizens had to be brought to an understanding of and enthusiasm for the nation's actions:

> The *war-will,* the will-to-win, of a democracy depends upon the degree to which each one of all the people of that democracy can concentrate and consecrate body and soul and spirit in the supreme effort of service and sacrifice. What had to be driven home was that all business was the nation's business, and every task a common task for a single purpose. (Creel, *How We Advertised* 5)

In response to the ethics codes that had recently been adopted by most fields of public rhetoric, Creel claimed that his publicity machine did educational work, providing citizens with the right information so they could make the right decisions. His was thus a morally ethical form of persuasion:

We wanted to reach the people through their minds, rather than through their emotions, for hate has its undesirable reactions. We wanted to do it, not by over-emphasis of historical appeal, but by unanswerable arguments that would make every man and woman know that the war was a war of self-defense that had to be waged if free institutions were not to perish. (Creel, *How We Advertised* 100)

Thus the democratic theory of Progressive leaders, involving respect for citizens and the "right" education of them as in the Wisconsin Idea, was now being employed in a war effort that many of these leaders initially denounced, as certainly Bob La Follette did.

War information came to newspapers in official news releases, just as press bulletins had been sent by the University of Wisconsin and the Forest Service to create a persuasive picture of the "right" side. The division's section on women's war-work, which muckraker Ida Tarbell joined, created bulletins on women's service, the homefront, and American values of courage and self-sacrifice, for reprint on women's pages and in news columns. The committee's Division of News created a running record of the war effort, available each day to news bureaus and correspondents over the telegraph wires. This division involved creative writers, such as Arthur Bullard, Ernest Poole, and Wallace Irwin, as well as Edgar G. Sisson, who had been a muckraker at *Cosmopolitan*. These regular reports enabled newspapers to document the glory of each day's battles without having to send reporters to the front (Creel, *How We Advertised* 70–83, 212–21). Those correspondents who went to Europe were hampered by official restrictions, kept back from the fighting and informed of troop movements only through official communiques. Will Irwin, the first writer to report the Battle of Ypres, got the news several days after the event. In 1918 in France, reporters accredited through a bond and deposit were finally allowed at the front, but their stories were censored by the Military Intelligence Service.

To force any recalcitrant newspapers to consistently support the cause, Wilson and Creel used increasingly stringent laws. The Espionage Act of June 15, 1917, declared unconstitutional by the Supreme Court after the war, mandated heavy fines and imprisonment for anyone who "shall willfully cause or attempt to cause ... disloyalty ... or shall willfully obstruct recruiting." During the act's first year, more than 75 papers were investigated by the post office, which decided on the journals that should be judged unmailable and then sought convictions from the Department of Justice. The Trading-With-the-Enemy Act of October 6, 1917, primarily aimed at the German-language press, authorized censorship of all messages sent abroad and required any newspaper or magazine containing articles in a foreign language to file sworn translations with the local postmaster. Next came the Sedition Act of May 16, 1918, which imposed heavy fines and imprisonment for the writing or publication of "any disloyal, profane, scurrilous, or abusive language about the form of government of the United States or the Constitution, military or naval forces, flag, or the uniform of the army or navy of the United States" (Counter-Espionage Laws). Enforcement of these acts caused socialist journals, like the *The New York Call* and Victor L. Berger's Milwaukee *Leader*, to lose their mailing privileges and the number of German-language papers to decline by half during the war. Three editors of the Philadelphia *Tageblatt* went to prison for disloyal articles.

Even though laws could force compliance, journalists generally chose to adhere to the vision of reality provided by bulletins from the front, putting persuasion before verified facts, as many muckrakers had done for the Progressive cause. Most newspapers had been neutral or pro-Ally at the beginning of the war: in the third month of American involvement 240 newspapers were neutral, 105 pro-Ally, and 20 pro-German. Six months later, after the sinking of the *Lusitania* and the first impositions of censorship, few remained neutral or published any governmental criticisms although Hearst's *Journal* and *American*, the *Chicago Tribune*, the *Washington Post*, the Cincinnati *Inquirer*, the Cleveland *Plain Dealer*, the Milwaukee *Sentinel*, the *Los Angeles Times*, and *La Follette's Weekly Magazine* continued to oppose Americn participation in the war. In this climate, as *The New Republic* argued in a piece reprinted in *La Follette's Weekly Magazine*, no thesis but the American thesis would be tolerated:

> Any attitude of criticism on the question of the war, one even of intellectual speculation on its fundamental issues, anything which could be interpreted as pacifism, internationalist Socialism, religious nonresistance, has, to a large part of the newspaper mind of America, become merely treason. ("Public Opinion in War Time" 3)

Lincoln Colcord of the *Philadelphia Public Ledger* described the lack of investigative research and social criticism as "the press, the whole voice of the press shouting away on the war idea, making public opinion something which is not public opinion at all, but merely lack of vision in the newspapers" ("Public Opinion in War Time" 3).

Like the University of Wisconsin, the Forest Service, and railroad lines, the CPI also used "informative" pamphlets: to give citizens "a fundamental understanding of the causes of the war and of the absolute justice of

America's position" (Creel, *How We Advertised* 99). Most of the pamphlets were written by university professors (Blakely). *How the War Came to America* began the series of Red, White, and Blue books, which included many pamphlets about the barbaric Prussian state written by history, sociology, and English professors from Minnesota, Princeton, Wisconsin, and Syracuse. Another publication, the *War Cyclopedia*, provided citizens with practical information they needed at home. Seventy-five million copies went to American homes; excerpts were reprinted in newspapers and translated for publication abroad (Creel, *How We Advertised* 114). The President's Flag Day speech from June of 1917, a statement of the reasons the United States went to war, came out as an appendix to *How the War Came to America*, of which 6,227,912 copies were circulated. This booklet was then reprinted with footnotes documenting German atrocities (Cornwell 50). Boy Scouts were asked to be "dispatch bearers" to circulate the right values from door to door along with pamphlets on American government. Special pamphlets were also written for foreign countries: to reveal Germany's savage goals, provide practical information, and champion the American cause. In Vladivostok, Russia, for example, the CPI distributed a million publications in six months, sounding alarms against typhus as well as against Lenin and Trotsky. Airplane crews shot mortar guns holding paper messages and pamphlets, and they bombarded the German front with armistice balloons.

Like La Follette and Roosevelt, Creel realized that pamphlets and news items could not replace public speaking aimed at reaching listeners immediately with emotion and fact. Wilson had the bad tendency to lecture as he had done as a university professor; he often went into the intricacies of proposed legislation or war decisions without emotional appeal or human example. As a busy President in these years before radio, he could not reach the entire nation regularly, and Creel knew that other speakers and speech types would be needed. He thus instituted the Four-Minute Men, involving 75,000 speakers, among them many college professors (Creel, *How We Advertised* 85). E. T. Gundlach, head of a Chicago advertising agency, ran this project. Muckraking novelist Samuel Hopkins Adams and Bertram G. Nelson, professor of public speaking at the University of Chicago, served on the board of directors, helping to choose, train, and evaluate speakers. Every week or two, the board sent out a bulletin to local representatives for distribution to their roster of speakers, outlining the topic, providing appropriate quotations and catch phrases, and offering sample speeches. Speakers wrote their own talks, following the guidelines provided, to be persuasive in their own style to their own local audiences (Cornwell 51). Topics included reasons for fighting, German propaganda, savings bonds, the Red Cross, and the meaning of America. Four-minute men—and women—spoke in thea-tres, schools, churches, lodges, union meetings, and other forums. Their verbatim reading of Wilson's July Fourth message of 1918 came as close to approximating a presidential radio speech as was possible before network radio. In New York City alone, 1,600 speakers addressed 500,000 people each week—in English, Yiddish, and Italian (Mock and C. Larson 125). Creel estimated that nationally during the war trained speakers gave one million addresses to audiences totalling 400 million (Cornwell 52). At 153 colleges, students studied the bulletins and practiced speaking to qualify for the College Four-Minute Men, a program through which college students addressed their peers.

The advertising division of the CPI involved representatives from major firms, the Associated Advertising Clubs of the World, and the National Advertising Advisory Board. Following the "Chicago Plan" designed by agency owner William H. Rankin, individuals or groups purchased space in newspapers and magazines, for billboards or for window displays, and then donated it to the government. American advertisers themselves purchased and donated $340,981 worth of space, with their contribution generally noted in the ads (Creel, *How We Advertised* 159). Artist Charles Dana Gibson led a group, through the division of Pictorial Publicity, that contrib-uted artwork for magazine advertisements, posters, and window displays. Their first large campaign recruited 250,000 shipyard volunteers for the army by using appeals to patriotism and monetary gain. To curb turnover of labor and increase production, this group also initiated a factory campaign, stressing that "The Right Men in the Right Jobs Will Win the War." Dramatic posters emphasized the crucial need for liberty loans: Walter Whitehead's "Come On!" showed a huge, determined soldier standing over a dead German; F. Strothman's "Beat Back the Hun with Liberty Bonds" revealed a Hun holding a bloody bayonet and looking over the edge of Europe towards the United States. Red Cross ads employed emotional appeals to get wives and mothers involved with the war effort: "One Member of a Family Is Not Enough" and "Make This a Red Cross Christ-mas." Anti-German ads, like the "Spies and Lies" ads that began "German agents are everywhere," increased suspicion against German Americans and lead to their persecution. James Montgomery Flagg created the posters of Uncle Sam with the pointing finger and the caption reading "I Want You for the U.S. Army" (*World War I*). With the cause being America and proper ethics thus assured, no exaggeration went untried: Patent medicine ads never went this far.

Herbert Hoover, head of the United States Food Administration during the war, declared, "There is no publicity organ in the world like the motion picture. We look upon it as a Godsend" (C. W. Campbell 68). Films had begun dealing with the war even before it was declared. In 1915, for example, J. Stuart Blackton's *Defenceless America* was released with help from Roosevelt to put pressure on Wilson to declare war. It portrayed a peacenik father speaking at a rally along with foreign agents while the enemy bombed New York and killed his family. Roosevelt, Admiral Dewey, and others appeared on film at the end stating the need for preparedness at the least. The theme of war readiness pervaded other features, like 1916's *The Hero of Submarine D-2*, *Defense or Tribute?*, and *The Flying Torpedo*, which ended with a peace society endorsing military readiness and singing the national anthem. The *New York Tribune* sponsored publicity for this film in newspapers throughout the country. Non war films also praised readiness and strength: In *The Pacifist (1916)*, for example, a weakling gained respect when he beat up a bully and defended his own rights. In this period of mounting patriotism, the woes of labor no longer appealed to audiences. In fact, many films, like *The Son of His Father* (1918), began featuring rich sons of capitalists becoming heroes not by altering working conditions but by instigating the new levels of production needed for preparedness.

After Wilson broke diplomatic relations with Germany in February of 1917, the public relations professionals of the Associated Motion Pictures Advertisers joined with the War Department to urge theatres to include patriotic films in their weekly programs. One popular film was Cecil B. DeMille's *The Little American* (1917), in which Mary Pickford defiantly opposed German soldiers who torpedoed her ship and occupied her French chateau that was serving as a hospital for allied soldiers: She remained calm and determined even when they forced her to clean their boots. The CPI also encouraged the independent making of war documentaries: *Protecting the Ships at Sea* and *Are We Prepared?*, for example, acquainted Americans with military training and national defense; *Making Steel Rails for the Allies* and *Making Rifles* dealt with military manufacturing. Several series featuring famous movie stars urged Americans to buy Liberty Bonds. Weekly newsreels also carried the war message to theatergoers (C. W. Campbell 36–42, 58–61).

In 1917, the CPI took charge of patriotic filmmaking, asking directors to continue their documentary and feature work under the committee's auspices and to donate most of the profits to the war effort. Films went to

American theatres, meetings, Four-Minute Men training sessions, military camps, and groups abroad. Yale's playwriting teacher George Pierce Baker headed the scenario department and wrote *The Remaking of a Nation,* filmed at Camp Sherman in Ohio. By 1918, 10 feature films were being made each month for showing at home and throughout the world, even on the firing lines. Among the early features were *The 1917 Recruit, American Ambulances, Ship Building,* and *Women's Part in the War. America's Answer* contained scenes of American ship building, government and military leaders, and the glorious progress of troops in France (C. W. Campbell 70–79). The *New York Times* reviewer realized its impact: "Not a man and not a woman in the crowd that filled the seats failed to feel the pull of the war, the urging of its influence, the sense of participation in it" (qtd. in C.W. Campbell 79).

Along with ads, articles, and films for adults, Creel invested in war education for children, recognizing, like La Follette, Van Hise, and Pinchot, that young people had to be persuasively introduced to a cause. The National School Service, a twice monthly brochure, was mailed out to 600,000 teachers with the goal of reaching 20 million homes (Cornwell 54). Each issue contained articles on America and the war, applicable quotations, and directions for classroom lessons designed to convey important war messages to children of various ages. The service sent out eight issues before the CPI was terminated at the end of the war.

By working for the school service and for all the other committees, college writing professors and extension administrators helped craft wartime rhetoric. J. J. Pettijohn, who had been director of the extension division of Indiana University and in charge of the Indiana State Speakers' Bureau, headed the Speaking Division, which enlisted nationally known speakers, like Ida Tarbell and Jane Addams, to give longer and more individual presentations than the four-minute speeches. When the Speaking Division merged with the Four-Minute Men in September of 1918, he became associate director of that combined division. He also headed a state speakers' bureau for Indiana and the National School Service in 1919 (Vaughn 31, 101).

Frank Aydelotte, who taught technical writing in the English department at MIT and had, like Wisconsin's Karl Young, experimented with courses on the engineer's role in society, organized and became in 1918 national director of the "War-Aims Course," a brief course for soldiers on the historical background of the war and the dangerous social philosophies of the belligerent nations. When his syllabus was tried out in May 1918 in Boston, it succeeded so well at enhancing morale that it was made mandatory for servicemen in basic training. Under the Students' Army Training

Corps plan announced in May 1918, with Aydelotte as a chief planner and MIT's president Richard C. Maclaurin as director, army enlistees were encouraged to go to college for a short period before reporting to their bases; universities agreed to provide 10 hours a week of military training—six of practical work and four of academic studies of military value. More than 500 universities participated, with 3,120 student-soldiers registered at Minnesota, 2,250 at Wisconsin, and 2,000 at Columbia. Under Aydelotte's direction, English departments devoted their courses to the writing of military reports (Gruber 214–34).

James W. Searson, professor of English and journalism at Kansas State University, managed the editorial work for the CPI, turning out war pamphlets and encyclopedias with the assistance of over 100 freelance writers and investigators (Mock and Larson 159). He hired Stuart B. Sherman, an English professor from Illinois, and Elmer E. Stoll, an English professor from Minnesota, to work on war pamphlets. Sherman wrote a pamphlet for the War Information Series, *American and Allied Ideals: An Appeal to Those Who Are Neither Hot Nor Cold,* in which he quoted Cicero and Milton to prove the purity of the allies. Searson also served as managing editor for national school service publications, working along with William C. Bagley, an education professor from Columbia. He set up state editorial boards, consisting of the state education superintendents and four other members, to offer advice to the central advisory board in Washington. He also wrote to over 300 teachers requesting help with making the bulletins more successful (Vaughn 100).

Other writing specialists received training during the war that they employed later to teach college students. Edward Bernays was born in Vienna, served as press agent for the Russian Ballet, Enrico Caruso, and other top artists, and worked as a medical journalist. For the CPI, he headed the news bureau for Latin America. He helped enlist American businesses into the war effort and then took charge of the Latin American news service. He persuaded Ford, Studebaker, Remington, National City Bank, International Harvester and other corporations to turn their Latin American branches virtually into outposts of the CPI. Their customers received anti-German pamphlets; posters and other displays filled their windows; newspapers with the right attitude on the war got their advertising business (Mock and C. Larson 321–22).

Bernays taught public relations at New York University in 1923, a course that he incorrectly spoke of as the first one in the country. He taught that a business should find out what the public thinks of it, examine what it really is, and bridge that gap by changing what it is or changing the conception (I. Ross 56–57). Bernays believed that in a modern democracy, as in Latin America during the war, individuals were not making reasoned judgments but instead acting from human needs and desires manipulated by an "invisible government," by propaganda that determined the career and friends citizens chose, the products they bought, the candidates they voted for. Modern businesses and politicians produced this government through a "consistent, enduring effort to create or shape events to influence the relations of the public to an enterprise, idea, or group" (*Propaganda* 25). Well-trained students would be the next generation of event shapers.

The CPI's massive propaganda effort also involved many professional writers, allowing them to witness the ultimate power of their craft and the monolithic results of the genres functioning together. After seeing the impact of each genre, many writers changed fields after the war. Creel's associate chair was Harvey O'Higgins who had attended the University of Toronto. For *McClure's, Collier's, Scribners,* and other reform magazines, he had written detective stories and essays on political and social issues, unmasking the vested interests or "invisible government" of the United States. His full-length studies included *The Beast* (1910) on the plight of city youth and *Under the Prophet in Utah* (1911) on corruption in the Mormon church. His wartime pamphlet for the CPI, *The German Whisper,* sounded a strong warning against German propaganda. After the war, he turned his attention away from politics, and instead, aided by study of psychoanalysis, he undertook in-depth character analyses in novels such as *Julie Cane* (1924) and *Clara Barron* (1926).

Carl Byoir worked as a reporter for the *Iowa State Register* and as a city editor for the *Waterloo Times-Tribune* in high school. Entering the University of Iowa in 1906, he negotiated contracts for college yearbooks for a living. In 1913, he became publisher of a read-aloud magazine for preschool children, *John Martin's Book.* In 1914 he began working for Hearst, and in 1916 he became circulation manager for *Cosmopolitan.* As associate chair of the CPI, he was involved in nearly all aspects of the committee's work. As a Washington liaison officer for the advertising division, he helped to direct advertising campaigns and secure free space. He then became associate director of the foreign section under Sisson and associate chair of the CPI. After the war, he became one of the country's leading public relations consultants, founding the firm of Carl Byoir and Associates to serve the Cuban government as a promoter of tourism. He crafted a "United Action

Campaign" for the American Legion and an advertising campaign for the Great Atlantic and Pacific Tea Company (Vaughn 26).

L. Ames Brown, who had been a reporter for the Nashville *Tennessean* and a White House correspondent for the New York *Sun* and the Philadelphia *Record*, headed the Division of Syndicated Features, which used leading writers to provide stories for Sunday editions, and after the war became president of the public relations firm of Lord, Thomas, and Logan. Reporter Will Irwin of the *Saturday Evening Post*, who had been managing editor of *McClure's* during 1906–07 and in 1908 a columnist for *Collier's Weekly*, was viewed by Creel as the best war reporter, covering the American, British, and Italian armies in realistic terms; he also served as director of the foreign section of the CPI in 1918 (Vaughn 36). After the war he abandoned newspaper work and instead wrote books that exposed various institutions, such as *The House That Shadows Built* (1928) on the film industry. His *The Next War* (1921) pleaded for the elimination of horrific wars from civilized societies; in *Propaganda and the News*, Irwin treated the "inner workings of journalism" and the "methods and ruses employed by successful publicity men" (5). Walter Lippmann served as a military intelligence officer during the war bringing propaganda behind enemy lines, experience he drew on after the war in writing *Public Opinion* and other works about the power of propaganda. All of these writers moved beyond the war into new persuasion fields, for which they had the theoretical and practical tools of experts.

While a mammoth rhetorical effort aimed at enveloping Americans into the war spirit, it also curbed the activities of those who remained unconvinced. Special targets were the man and institution, Bob La Follette and the University of Wisconsin, that had taught modern persuasion techniques to the nation. Vigorously opposed to American entry into the war, La Follette was the victim of an unsuccessful attempt to expel him from the Senate. With constant pressure applied by the Senate and the press, the university eventually turned on its mentor, using La Follette's own propaganda techniques against him.

La Follette judged the war as advancing causes of an aggressive Great Britain and providing profits for the rich, especially those involved in the munitions trade, while poor boys died in battle. His filibuster prevented the passage of armed merchant-ship legislation at the close of a short Senate session in 1917, and he spoke and voted against declaration of war with Germany although he did favor equipping the army well once it was engaged in battle so that American men and women would be protected. In September 1917, an incorrect report of his speech at a Non-Partisan League meeting increased antagonism toward him and led to an expulsion attempt in the Senate. His words, "I would not be understood as saying that we didn't have grievances [against Germany]. We did," were reported by the Associated Press and thus by many newspapers as "we had no grievances [against Germany]." Dozens of newspapers vilified him; the *Cincinnati Post* dubbed him "von La Follette." Under attack on the Senate floor, La Follette spoke for freedom of speech and made "the war-mad press and war extremists" another of his Iagos. The Senate protracted the proceedings, making La Follette a national symbol of anti-Americanism but never voting to remove him (La Follette and La Follette 762–72; Burgchardt 92).

When Assistant Secretary of Agriculture Carl Vrooman spoke at the University of Wisconsin in November 1917, the poor student response led him to report that La Follette's university was also insufficiently militant, "guided by a milk and water patriotism, a kind of platonic patriotism" (qtd. in Gruber 104). The Wisconsin press quickly publicized this criticism. Van Hise, aided by John Commons, who had been involved in crafting La Follette's Progressive legislation, wrote Wilson eight typewritten pages of defense, describing in detail the university's mobilization for war. Then in the spring of 1918, Princeton professor Robert McNutt McElroy, chair of the National Security League Committee on Patriotism through Education, accused the university of being unpatriotic and harboring traitors.

With Bleyer's help, Van Hise then started an elaborate propaganda campaign against La Follette, involving a pamphlet and letters sent to Congressmen, faculty, regents, alumni, newspapers, and magazines (Gruber 104–05; Curti and Carstensen, *University of Wisconsin* II, 115–18). These documents reported on a "round robin" faculty resolution, brought to each teacher's office by members of a committee, that renounced La Follette's opposition to the war. Over 90% of the faculty on campus at that time, more than 400 people, including Birge, Bleyer, Hyde, Cairns, and Young, were among its signees. The resolution denounced La Follette personally and echoed the Constitution's definition of treason:

> We, the undersigned resident members of the faculty of the University of Wisconsin of the rank of instructor and above, protest against those utterances and actions of Senator Robert M. La Follette which have given aid and comfort to Germany and her allies in the present war; we deplore his failure loyally to support the government in the prosecution of the war. In these respects, he has misrepresented us, his constituents. (University of Wisconsin)

By going from office to office followed by reporters and then further publicizing the signed document, university officials created and exploited a powerful symbolic event.

To further demonstrate the entire university's contempt for La Follette, Van Hise secured help from Richard Ely, a frequent early contributor to *La Follette's Weekly Magazine* who had been attacked by the Board of Regents for advocating academic freedom and the rights of labor. With John Commons, he established the Madison chapter of the Wisconsin Loyalty League "to purge the state politically ... [to] put La Follette and all his supporters out of business" (Gruber 208). Ely first initiated an unsuccessful campaign to find evidence in German periodicals of La Follette's assistance to the enemy. Then Ely and Commons designated faculty who would visit with their colleagues and sign them into the league; they both also supported the "round robin." Following the end of the war, the faculty asked for this document to be withdrawn from the files of the State Historical Society of Wisconsin, but La Follette preferred for it to remain there and so it did.

By making La Follette an enemy, university officials disassociated themselves from the prime traitor and thus maintained their patriotism. He became their Philetus Sawyer, whom La Follette had publicly and repeatedly denounced years earlier for attempting to lead him down a wicked path, an enemy to vilify and stand apart from. First the CPI and then the Wisconsin faculty employed the propaganda organs of La Follette's own Progressive campaigns, such as speeches, bulletins, articles, reported quotations, advertisements, and staged events. As these techniques were turned on La Follette, the master persuader became persuasion's victim.

The CPI was dismantled as soon as possible after the war ended because Congress would not continue to approve its totalitarian powers during peacetime and because Republicans objected to its role as publicity agent for a Democratic president. Congress criticized its powers as though they were dealing with just a one-time war machine, not with a new form of rhetoric that would not go away. H. L. Mencken later labeled academicians who served the CPI as "star spangled" men and women who prostituted their professional ethics (Herold 17). But the manipulation they participated in was backed by belief in the cause and methods, just as La Follette's and Roosevelt's had been. These professors had used persuasion to motivate action, creating a potent combination of service and strong-arm that could make citizens feel needed and important if they joined, or alone and ashamed if they did not. The committee's vast persuasive powers led to the negative connotation now given to the word *propaganda;* this label for manipulation of beliefs and attitudes had been coined by the Catholic church in 1622 to describe its missionary efforts, but modern politics and advertising made the concept seem far less benign than before. National rhetoric that combined facts and persuasion had shown itself to be perhaps the fiercest of all powers; the strategies of influence that La Follette and Roosevelt had created were now forcefully serving many other causes.

6

After World War I: A Cacophony of Persuasion

Bob La Follette was elected to the Senate in 1916 and would be again in 1922, by which time Americans were reexamining the war's costs and thus its opponents. In 1922, he initiated Senate investigation of oil leases at Teapot Dome, Wyoming, and other sites for which Warren Harding's Secretary of the Interior had been accepting bribery payments, and he ran for president on an independent ticket in 1924. During World War I, as during the 1924 election, he was an independent rhetor steadfastly battling for his vision of a democratic, peaceful nation, continually provoking opposition, such as Wilson's declaration that La Follette led "a little group of willful men, representing no opinion of their own" after their filibuster in the Senate blocked the passage of a bill that would have authorized the arming of merchant ships, a key step toward war (Thelen 133–34). Dos Passos repeated Wilson's line in his eulogy for La Follette in *The 42nd Parallel*:

> In nineteen-twentyfour La Follette ran for President and without money or political machine rolled up four and a half million votes
> but he was a sick man, incessant work and the breathed out air of committee rooms and legislative chambers choked him
> and the dirty smell of politicians,
> and he died,
> an orator haranguing from the capitol of a lost republic;
> but we will remember
> how he sat firm in March nineteen-seventeen while
> Woodrow Wilson was being inaugurated for the second time, and for three days held the vast machine at deadlock. They wouldn't let him speak; the galleries glared hatred at him; the Senate was a lynching party,
> a stumpy man with a lined face, one leg stuck out in the aisle and his arms folded and a chewed cigar in the corner of his mouth
> and an undelivered speech on his desk,
> a willful man expressing no opinion but his own. (425–26)

Willful men and women expressing opinions—or hiring others to do so for them—were creating the cacophony of modern persuasion by the time of La Follette's death in 1925. The strategies of writing and speaking learned in World War I and before had created the modern American media—that could change a company's reputation, publicize new developments, and sell any product including war. Between the world wars, in the professions and the universities, the genres were separating, with their own codes and purposes, but they still shared the often contradictory missions of explanation and persuasion. With separation, they became more critical of each other: Each genre claimed that it alone tried to tell a story responsibly and thus offer service, whereas the others tried only to manipulate. At odds but mutually dependent, they all had a strong impact on the United States, shaping the reality that its citizens perceived. Although these professionals often turned on each other, as can be seen for example in their reaction to public relations counsel Ivy Ledbetter Lee, together they were creating America.

The war had certainly demonstrated the power of public relations and advertising campaigns to teach Americans about the "right way" and to manipulate them into endorsing it. The victories of the women's suffrage and the prohibition movements offered further evidence of this power. H. L. Mencken called the Anti-Saloon League "an enormously effective fighting organization, with a large staff of highly accomplished experts in its service" (244). The boom of the 1920s also led to rapid growth in corporate advertising and public relations campaigns, involving the print media, radio, and staged public events. By 1929, advertising was a billion dollar industry involving psychological analyses of targeted groups; appeals to pity, belonging, and other values; well-crafted images and copy; and campaigns combining ads with promotional gimmicks.

In the 1920s, politicians also continued to call on persuasion specialists to help deliver their message. In 1928, after losing the presidential election, the Democratic party established its first permanent publicity bureau. The Republicans soon followed. Lobbying by special interests began in Washington and state capitals, with press agents creating propaganda campaigns that relied on psychological models of voter preference. Walter Lippmann in *Public Opinion* argued that political manipulation had become so dominant that people no longer formed their own opinions about public policy, but instead held opinions supplied to them by the media.

Events from the Depression demonstrated the importance of public support for survival in a bad economy. Churches, Community Chest, the

YMCA, and the American Red Cross hired agencies or set up their own publicity departments, mostly by engaging former newspaper reporters and editors. Roosevelt's New Deal agencies created work for advertising firms in popularizing the TVA, Civilian Conservation Corps, and Farm Security Administration, with support from new data sources like the Gallup Poll, introduced in 1935. In the Depression, also, corporations found the need for more and better publicity as did colleges and universities suffering from financial woes. During that decade, many small and large companies also had to defend themselves against public mistrust, a discontented labor force, and Roosevelt's regulations. In Washington and New York, more trained journalists were hired for these public relations activities than by newspapers (Herold 18).

By 1940, university teaching of advertising and public relations reflected the increasing sophistication of these professions. A 1946 survey of 34 prominent schools found 11 had advertising courses within the journalism sequence, five had turned them over to the business school, 17 divided them between the two, and one involved four departments in teaching advertising: business, journalism, psychology, and art (Burton). Like the universities surveyed, almost all schools with programs in journalism or business offered advertising courses. They emphasized developing prospects, analyzing their values and needs, and testing their reactions to ads; working with samples, coupons, contests, and events; combining emotive copy and art work; and deciding on the best media and proper frequency of advertising (*Printer's Ink Refresher Course*). By 1930, over half of all business schools also required a business writing class, which concerned letters and reports as well as stylistics, to further improve informative and persuasive communication with clients (Russell 127). Public relations courses developed more slowly although by the 1940s at least 30 colleges and universities were listing 47 courses with that label, and many advertising and journalism courses covered campaign techniques (A. M. Lee 83). This instruction focused on campaign management, planning and evaluation, psychological tactics, communication channels, and business law as well as writing. Both fields developed their tactics secure in the belief that in a democracy they had a right, or even an obligation, to state each claim and represent each client as well as possible. During the 1930s in his many presentations to students and young professionals, Arthur Wilson Page, vice president of AT&T and in-house public relations expert, stated that a business' opinion research and publicity efforts simply allowed it to accomplish the task "of fitting itself to the patterns of public desires" (qtd. in Newsom, Scott, and Turk 47).

With the power of advertising and public relations becoming abundantly clear, creative writing and journalism often viewed themselves as the loyal opposition, using persuasion also of course, but for more noble causes. Although all of these genres were interlocked in the business world and in university departments, and they all shared many of the same techniques, reporters and fiction writers generally viewed themselves as standing on higher ground.

For these writers, their own discipline was not just one means but the only moral way to influence the masses. In decrying the moneyed interests, they responded harshly to propagandists in other fields like advertising and public relations, to professionals like Ivy Lee who in the 1920s and 1930s was portrayed as the epitome of public manipulation for profit. A central character of John Dos Passos' *The 42nd Parallel* (1930), the first novel of his USA trilogy, is J. Ward Morehouse, an immoral purveyor of lies, an artificial man in an artificial job whose success rests on his ability to do and say whatever will work. This character seems to have been modeled on Lee, whom Dos Passos met in the Moscow Hotel in 1928: The resemblance is made clear in Morehouse's involvement with strikes in Colorado mines similar to Lee's famous Ludlow case (Ludington 259, 269).

After the failure of his first marriage, which offered him financial security, Morehouse decides that newspaper work is not lucrative enough and he sets out to be a "clean-cut young executive" in public relations, advertising, and labor negotiation (243). He prepares for this new career through the proper furnishings:

> Ward rented an office at 100 Fifth Avenue, fitted it up with Chinese porcelain vases and cloisonné ashtrays from Vantine's and had a tigerskin rug in his private office. He served tea in the English style every afternoon and put himself in the telephone book as J. Ward Morehouse, Public Relations Counsel. (311)

Morehouse's publicly insists that American capitalists are "firm believers in fair play and democracy and are only too anxious to give the worker his share of the proceeds of industry if they can only see their way to do so in fairness to the public and investor," but in private he relentlessly pursues the priorities of whatever client pays his wages (317). Dos Passos evinces a begrudging kind of respect for these amoral skills in his portrayal of the ever struggling and ambitious Morehouse and in his ironic declaration to Edmund Wilson that he had "finally come to the conclusion that, since the Communist party with its pedantic Marxism is impossible, the thing to do is to persuade some radical millionaire to hire an Ed Bernays or Ivy Lee to use American publicity methods to convert the Americans to Communism" (qtd. in Ludington 290).

In his biography of John D. Rockefeller, *God's Gold* (1932), John T. Flynn portrayed Lee as an all-powerful diabolical manipulator, able to put an entirely changed vision of Rockefeller and thus of Standard Oil before the American people by recreating Rockefeller as a mythic persona:

> The figure of the striding, ruthless monopolist in high hat and long coat gripping his walking stick and entering a court house has been replaced by pictures of a frail old man, playing golf with his neighbors, handing out dimes to children, distributing inspirational poems, and walking in peace amid his flowers. (484)

In this attack on Lee, as in their critiques of American society, biographers and novelists sought their own power as the representative of "right" values, relying on tools, however, that they shared with advertisers and public relations consultants: persuasive examples and scenes, affecting stories, interpretations of history, portrayals of heroes and villains, appeals to audiences, emotive language. But, in their vision, they were the only ones who used these techniques sincerely, for the "good" of the people, and the only ones removed from the din of business and politics.

Journalists also viewed themselves as the true voice of the nation, presenting reality and the right interpretations of it. During the 1920s and 1930s, they would cover, through various mixtures of reason and sensationalism, the attempted enforcement of the prohibition amendment, oil scandals resulting from the Teapot Dome lease, the exploits of organized crime, and the progress of facism in Europe along with the Scopes monkey trial, the kidnapping of the Lindbergh baby, and the birth of the Dionne quintuplets.

The newspaper's influence on society was reflected in the huge growth in college journalism instruction before World War II. In 1941, the American Association of Teachers of Journalism listed 542 colleges and universities that offered journalism instruction, with more than 100 junior colleges also providing basic instruction; over 200 teachers were members of the association. By that year, 383 colleges and universities also offered courses on radio work, primarily as a supplement to their news instruction, a huge jump for an instruction type that began in the early 1930s (Charnley 376). College instruction concerned the writing and editing of serious news stories along with the more sensationalized pieces that would attract busy readers: Journalism professors thus offered classes in investigative reporting as well as feature articles, human interest pieces, reviews, the women's page, sports articles, and photography. In a growing number of courses on newspaper management, students further learned about the news media as large corporations.

As newspaper reporting and editing gained a secure professional status, their identity was also undergoing change, with many allegiances complicating their stated mission of service to the community. For Ivy Lee, "news is that which the people are willing to pay to have brought to their attention" (*Publicity* 9–13). As he noted, editors and reporters were certainly influenced by the local citizens themselves, what they might want to read about and care about. Edward Wyllis Scripps, owner of the Scripps-McRae chain, for example, viewed his midwestern audience as "that large majority of people who are not so rich in worldly goods and native intelligence as to make them equal, man for man, in the struggle with the wealthier and more intellectual citizens" (Cochran 235–36). With this group in mind, at the beginning of the century Scripps' reporters crusaded against local political bosses and for the rights of labor, news which his readers were willing to have brought to their attention. Individual journalists certainly also had their own biases. As E. B. White commented in disclaiming the possibility of objectivity, "all writing slants the way a writer leans, and no man is born perpendicular, although many men are born upright" (72). Another very real influence was that of advertisers, who contributed 64.9% of the newspaper's income in 1914 and 74.1% by 1927 (Willey and Rice 175). Bob La Follette, in fact, had discussed the practical, business controls on the press in a controversial 1912 speech at a publishers' meeting:

> There is here and there a "kept sheet" owned by a man of great wealth to further his own interests. But the papers of this class are few. The control comes through that community of interests, that interdependence of investments and credits which ties the publisher up to the banks, the advertisers and the special interests. ("The Undermining of My Candidacy" 13)

Other critics, like John Flynn, recognized the power of advertisers to control coverage of any news that affected their interests:

> The modern press belongs to business. It is on the side of business. It is very naturally on the side of the advertiser, particularly the big advertisers. Standard Oil is a very big advertiser. Stories criticizing Rockefeller are not now desired. Stories critical of business are not now desired. What is called "constructive" material is what is wanted. We have seen not merely the sale

of Mr. Rockefeller to the public but all business and along with it the
once-hated master of Standard Oil. (484)

In such a complicated landscape, journalists frequently retreated to a
view of their role as similar to that of the creative writer. Even though their
field was intertwined financially with advertising and public relations and
shared the same techniques of exposition and persuasion, they often cast
themselves as the only heroes working doggedly against corruption. Journalists' attack on Ivy Lee brought into focus their discomfort at depending
on the same information and rhetorical strategies as did those mercenary
and corrupt public relations counsels and advertisers.

One uncomfortable interrelation certainly pertained to hiring. As we have
seen, people frequently changed jobs from journalism to public relations and
advertising, and all of these specialists certainly knew each other's techniques.
In his book *The Goose-Step* (1923), Sinclair devoted part of his chapter on
"Jabbergrab in Journalism" to Lee, the "super-professor of prevarication," and
to his profession's terrible stranglehold on journalists and journalism schools:

> Being curious to know what kind of ethics Mr. Pulitzer's school is teaching, I
> pick up a publication of the Alumni Association, "Clean Copy." The title
> page contains a list of officers, and I note the chairman's name, and his
> address—prepare yourself for laugh!—care Ivy Lee, 61 Broadway, New York
> City! So we learn that the Columbia School of Journalism is preparing
> students to work in the offices of "Poison Ivy"! Its standards are such that it
> is willing for a employee of "Poison Ivy" to be chairman of its Alumni, and to
> advertise that fact in its paper! (323)

As Sinclair mockingly noted, even the top journalism schools prepared public
relations counsels and courted their influence even as they publicly distanced
themselves from these counsels' methodologies and goals.

Journalists frequently expounded on the duplicity involved in public
relations. In a 1915 article about the Ludlow strike in *The New York Call*, a
reformist newspaper "devoted to the interests in the working people," Carl
Sandburg branded Lee a "paid liar" and asked, "How shall the labor
movement handle this form of human snake, and how meet the poison
scattered by this subtle tongue?" (2). Lee's manipulation of the dispute,
according to Sandburg, was

> dirty work. It was coarse. It was cheap. It was desperately bold and overplayed.
> It was done by the cunning, slimy brain of a cunning, slimy charlatan

. . . . Ivy L. Lee is below the level of the hired gunman and slugger. His sense of right and wrong is a worse force in organized society than that of the murderers who shot women and burned babies at Ludlow. (2+)

Chester M. Wright, in The *New York Call*, spoke out against Lee's use of symbols and stunts to purify John D. Rockefeller, Jr., and other capitalists. To conclude his attack on "the money master" Rockefeller, Wright urged his readers to

> Let not his Ivy Lee tell you Ludlow is white. Let not the press that thinks as he thinks tell you bullets do not kill. . . . Be one of the "crowd," but help the crowd to stand erect in full possession of its own sense. At last the crowd will think right—and then the day of the class struggle will reach its eventide. (14)

In this portrait of Lee, the implication is that only hard-working journalists would tell the "objective" truth about strikes and unions and thus only they deserve the public's trust.

One of journalists' chief objections to public relations campaigns concerned the press release, the "handout" or "canned statement," as it was called. Henry Pringle, a reporter for the New York *World*, thoroughly described Lee's manipulation of this form of information. When, for example, John D. Rockefeller, Jr., offered "the unappreciative Egyptians a museum," first one of Lee's secretaries contacted the newspapers and wire services. Then, at the appointed hour, reporters came to Lee's office, received typewritten statements, and were asked if they had any questions, which Lee would answer briefly. The reporters then pocketed their handouts, "one or two of them protesting *sotto voce* against the role of messenger boy," and were escorted out the door (145). Lee and his press releases thus served as a controversial "buffer," protecting Rockefeller and other clients from real investigation while producing an aura of cooperation.

Reporters like Pringle also objected to the press conference as a "journalistic atrocity." In a time of crisis, when access to Rockefeller could not be denied, Lee announced a time for a meeting with him. When the reporters arrived for the short conference, they first received a formal statement. Then Rockefeller entered, everyone was introduced, and the questioning began. When a question was asked that Rockefeller preferred to evade, Lee coughed, Rockefeller smiled, and Lee indicated that the matter was confidential and thus could not be discussed. He also made sure to allot time to those reporters who were not looking for "hard-news":

> Some jackass from the tabloids invariably asks Joseph Conrad for his wife's favorite recipe ... and the Crown Prince of Sweden whether he believes in Swedish massage. The efforts of the more intelligent newspaper men present are buried under the avalanche of imbecility.

When the ceremony ended, journalists often found they had "little to print but the statement handed them at the beginning of the session," Lee's plan all along (Pringle 146–47). Neil MacNeil, an editor of the *New York Times*, felt that in this venue Lee, "the idol of every worker in his strange profession," gave "the press only the facts he wanted it to have and only when he was good and ready" (312).

Whereas critics like Pringle and MacNeil stressed journalism's complete separation from these tactics and its independent portrayal of news, other writers recognized that journalists were in fact involved daily with telling the stories that press agents proffered. In his critique of the press system in the United States entitled *Ballyhoo*, Silas Bent decried the control that public relations had on the press, claiming that in average issues of the New York *Herald Tribune* and *New York Times*, as examples, over 60% of the stories came from press agents. Concerning Lee, he argued that this "king of the press agents" was "a disingenuous propagandist," using as a typifying example Lee's $200,000 contract with New York's Interborough State Transit Commission, paid for with tax money, to promote fare increases that a public referendum had overwhelmingly opposed (144–45). But Bent recognized that even with such trickery clearly documented, newspapers still accepted most of his press releases as factual, not having the staff, time, or inclination to check them out.

In his own answer to criticisms, Lee often spoke of public relations' key service role in providing for communication between citizens and businesses: "[There must be] someone to assist corporations and large interests in so framing their policies that they would be in accord with an enlightened public sentiment." In this high-minded summary of his own occupation, Lee sounded very much like the creative writer or journalist. He answered specific criticisms of his handling of the Rockefellers in a letter to Stanley Walker, city editor of the *New York Herald Tribune*: "I am not aware of ever having been non-committal when anyone asked me about the Rockefellers," Lee said. "If a question is one that can be answered, I answer it. If it is a question that cannot be answered, I say that we have no comment to make" (qtd. in Hiebert 301–02). Lee told Walker that the only subject on which he usually refrained from making a comment was Rockefeller's investments, which for the stability of the market could not be discussed publicly.

When it was suggested to him that news releases be outlawed, Lee judged the proposal as an indication of the reporters' need to assert their own viewpoints and priorities. He told the American Association of Teachers of Journalism in 1924:

> If I were an editor and had offered to me any kind of information, I would welcome it with open arms. . . . I would do anything I pleased with the material offered to me; but as to objecting to having information offered me, it seems to me that by so doing I should convict myself of stupidity. (*Publicity* 31)

In an address to the Columbia School of Journalism in 1932, Lee again acknowledged the press's responsibility to analyze handouts, conduct their own investigations, and respond sensibly to news presented to them as "breaking" or "exclusive":

> You know, the press is sometimes a little naive, with all of its sophistication. . . . if I or anyone sends them a document which represents an advanced proof of something which is going to be distributed anyway, and here is a chance for the papers to print it first, the newspaper instinct is immediately aroused, and it is amazing how often the newspaper will print material submitted to them in that form that they would not when sent in any other. (qtd. in Hiebert 305)

Even his staunch critic Henry Pringle admitted that Lee simply capitalized on "the laziness which newspaper men share with the rest of the human race" (147).

Although attacks on Lee were commonplace, many journalism professors, and especially those in administrative positions, recognized the ongoing connections between the two careers and relied on Lee's guidance. Ralph Casey, a Wisconsin graduate and head of the journalism school at the University of Minnesota, and James Melvin Lee, director of journalism at New York University, were close associates of Lee. Even the Pulitzer School of Journalism at Columbia, as Upton Sinclair recognized, came under the influence of this "super-professor of prevarication" (*The Goose-Step 323*). Columbia's Dean Carl Ackerman was a close friend of Lee who depended upon him for guidance in planning the curriculum and finding jobs for graduates. J. W. Cunliffe, a Columbia professor of journalism and former chair of English at Wisconsin, defended Lee and publicists in general and suggested that criticism might be directed at the newspaper instead. "The fact is," he said, "the reporting organization has fallen down on its job. I do not say that it has been the fault of the reporters, but it has become incapable of dealing with the vast, complex, modern life of a great city" (qtd. in Lee, *Publicity* 30). These teachers saw the power of the public relations as a challenge to their own teaching; Students had to learn to respond with the same sophistication with which these counsels dealt with them.

Many established members of the press also came to Lee's defense and recognized the mutual dependency that others wanted to ignore. Walter M. Harrison, president of the American Society of Newspaper Editors, declared in 1928 that Lee's propaganda was an appropriate tool for a business or government and argued that journalists must independently determine its worth:

> People used to sneer at or condemn the work done by Ivy Lee. . . . I believe that today, newspapers recognize Mr. Lee's work as perfectly legitimate and usually helpful. That form of propaganda which takes the shape of reasonable arguments or of securing publicity for demonstrated facts is only helpful. When it attempts to distort facts or to substitute threats or cajolery for arguments, it becomes contemptible and should be ignored by the journalist to whom it is directed. (qtd. in Lee, *Occasional Papers* 20)

Here Harrison posits the need for journalists' active initiatives in a complex communication network: Their job should be to uncover the facts and expose distortions.

Journalists' full distrust of Lee and his occupation surfaced after news of his appearance before Congress came out in July of 1934. Beginning in 1929, Lee had begun doing public relations work for the German Dye Trust, helping the company to market its products and improve its image in the United States. In 1933, this company enlarged Lee's role, asking him for advice on German–American relations in a new fascist regime. Along with the firm's top administrators, Lee met with Joseph Goebbels, minister of propaganda; Baron Konstantin Von Neurath, foreign minister; and with Hitler himself. As with the Rockefellers, he advised these leaders to "make authoritative utterances which would receive publicity in the normal way," thus to use radio addresses, articles in magazines, and press conferences. When he fully realized the German agenda, in 1934, he ended this relationship with the Dye Trust.

In 1934, the Special Committee on Un-American Activities questioned Lee concerning this involvement and cleared him of wrongdoing. But the release of the story brought on a maelstorm of criticism in the press under headlines such as "Lee Gives Advice to the Nazis," "Lee's Firm Revealed as Reich's Press Advisor," and "Lee Exposed as Hitler's Press Agent" (Hiebert

310). Reporters barraged him and politicians vilified him until his death that November. Journalists perhaps reacted so strongly because they knew that effective public relations and advertising could control what the country bought and believed even if they had not done so in this case. Although the Congress judged that Lee had no effect on Hitler's rise to power, his colleagues knew that he could have. Even more than before, he became the utmost symbol of persuasion's possible misuse in the hands of skilled and ambitious experts.

Although Lee did withdraw from the German Dye Trust once he recognized Hitler's goals, if he had remained with the company perhaps he would have argued that he was only portraying a viewpoint as well as he could, like other members of the communication world. He had similarly defended the Rockefellers and their business agenda; journalists followed the political goals of Edward Wyllis Scripps; advertisers certainly tried to make the bicycle, cigarette, and lightbulb look good. As Franklin Roosevelt worked at selling the New Deal with help from public relations expert Louis McHenry Howe, he recognized, as Hitler did also, that there could be no strong leadership without effective persuasion. During World War II, for a propaganda operation much larger than Creel's, Roosevelt engaged former newscaster Elmer Davis as director of the Office of War Information; the prestigious public relations firm Hill and Knowlton represented war industry groups such as the Aviation Corporation of America; a well-organized War Advertising Council drew on professionals to create campaigns for war bonds and enlistment; filmmakers and novelists glorified the cause; and newspapers stood ready to report any victory and demonize the enemy.

By the 1930s and World War II, powerful persuaders like Franklin Roosevelt and Arthur Wilson Page of AT&T had absorbed the lessons of La Follette, Pinchot, Theodore Roosevelt, Steffens, Creel, and Lee. Universities provided them with graduates well trained at telling citizens what to think and do and at disparaging persuaders who did so for other, presumably less noble, purposes. Each genre as well as each company might view itself as having only the best interest of the public in mind; its methodology and message were the only ones to be trusted. Attacking other persuaders was easier and more satisfying than recognizing the fuller picture of interdependence.

The experts that La Follette, Van Hise, and Bleyer envisioned as improving the lot of all citizens competed for those citizens' allegiance, but with widely disparate messages and goals. In a highly complex manner, Wilson and Roosevelt sold world wars, muckrakers sold political reform, filmmakers sold the American dream, and advertisers sold luxury products. Despite their different messages, all of them relied on sophisticated persuasion techniques. The task of coping with this rhetoric fell to the mass of the citizenry whose only rhetoric training, whether they were college graduates or not, consisted of reading model essays, writing five-paragraph themes, and completing grammar exercises. Unfortunately, Progressive reformers had assumed that advanced knowledge of rhetoric and skill at persuasion were not necessary for average citizens who would be called upon, not to write professionally, but to act in concert to improve their own communities on the basis of information given to them by experts. Although the public could thus be a willing audience for the "right" perspective as envisioned by the Progressives, they could also be an audience vulnerable to the cacophony of perspectives and techniques that increasingly bombarded them with each subsequent decade.

7

"The Unknown Citizen"*: A Conclusion

(To JS/07/M/378 This Marble Monument is Erected by the State)

He was found by the Bureau of Statistics to be
One against whom there was no official complaint,
And all the reports on his conduct agree
That, in the modern sense of an old-fashioned word, he was a saint,
For in everything he did he served the Greater Community.
Except for the War till the day he retired
He worked in a factory and never got fired,
But satisfied his employers, Fudge Motors Inc.
Yet he wasn't a scab or odd in his views,
For his Union reports that he paid his dues,
(Our report on his Union shows it was sound)
And our Social Psychology workers found
That he was popular with his mates and liked a drink.
The Press are convinced that he bought a paper every day
And that his reactions to advertisements were normal in every way.
Policies taken out in his name prove that he was fully insured,
And his Health-card shows he was once in a hospital but left it cured.
Both Producers Research and High-Grade Living declare
He was fully sensible to the advantages of the Installment Plan
And had everything necessary to the Modern Man,
A phonograph, radio, a car and a frigidaire.
Our researchers into Public Opinion are content
That he held the proper opinions for the time of year;
When there was peace, he was for peace; when there was war, he went.
He was married and added five children to the population,
Which our Eugenist says was the right number for a parent of his generation,
And our teachers report that he never interfered with their education.
Was he free? Was he happy? The question is absurd:
Had anything been wrong, we should certainly have heard.
                                        —W. H. Auden (1939)

*From The Collected Poetry of W. H. Auden by W. H. Auden. Copyright © 1940 and renewed 1968 by W. H. Auden. Reprinted by permission of Random House, Inc.

By World War II, the United States was a nation of rhetoric, its citizenry barraged by well-trained persuaders combining exposition and persuasion freely to make their case and oppose other possible influences. With the overriding goal being to convince a given group of a cause or value, any technique might be employed that could achieve the desired effect.

In 1939, two months after he moved to the United States from England, W. H. Auden created a portrait of that powerful public rhetoric and its dominion over individuals. "The Unknown Citizen," written as a tombstone epitaph, portrayed a man at the mercy of those trained to record data concerning him, to inform him of any important events, and to persuade him about products and wars.

Auden's poem concerns an urban, blue-color worker who led the more prosperous life envisioned by Progressive social reformers. His steady factory job offered benefits, such as good medical care and insurance, negotiated by his well-established union. With credit and installment plans, he had luxuries unknown to earlier generations of workers: "everything necessary to the Modern Man, / A phonograph, radio, a car and a frigidaire." He could also afford a daily newspaper, which he had the education to read, and a regular evening out.

But if Auden here notes some benefits of modern urban living, he also totaled up the costs of Progressive improvements. The movement, as Jane Addams or Bob La Follette represented it, posited "the citizenry" in a new theoretical manner, in an attempt to subdue the power of an ever more consolidated American business and government complex. This vision entailed an odd kind of modern power. Reformers did not seek a return to separate farms and towns; they also did not believe that government should too aggressively hamper business growth. Instead of advocating agrarianism or socialism, they steadfastly argued for education and social action as power. In the new democracy, "citizens" would work together to better their own communities and maintain independence from corrupt government officials and corporations, thus limiting encroachments of the establishment by concerted action. Their active education involving regular group problem solving would fit them for this role. Although citizens would not be writers themselves, they would glean from professional writing the information and values that would aid their progress. In the view of John Dewey and Bob La Follette, persuasion would thus go out to well-educated and active Americans who would be able to judge which candidate or scientific innovation would help them to achieve a better future. Citizens would want independence and fairness, and so they would choose only those options that would make them strong.

By the time Auden came to the United States, Progressive democracy had brought about Big Persuasion, with techniques that all the power sectors knew how to employ. In 1910, Progressive speeches, ads, and pamphlets, in the hands of a La Follette or Pinchot, were viewed as a method of wrestling control from corrupt government and business and empowering the average citizen. But as politicians and journalists assailed the establishment, its own college-trained rhetors rose to meet the challenge. Auden's poem makes clear all the applications stemming from this sophisticated training. Newspapers, advertisements, credit agreements, union contracts, job evaluations, marketing surveys, public opinion polls, phonographs, and radio—all forms of high-tech persuasion—were as much a part of the citizen's life as his job, family, car, and Frigidaire: He thus had become fully immersed in the persuasion taught in journalism, advertising, creative writing, and public relations programs. His reactions to products could be forecasted and evaluated; his work history monitored; his needs as a consumer researched and met—by Producers Research and High-Grade Living. And in the line "when there was war, he went," Auden recognizes that professional writing caused this citizen not just to buy a certain beer or take out a loan but to fight in World War I. As Auden indicates, every form of communication in this environment had a persuasive purpose—journalists told stories that would sell a daily paper, advertisers marketed products, technical writers pushed installment plans, politicians sold wars. The great powers of government and business, in fact, could only sell Frigidaires and patriotism to consumers and voters through communication systems: They had to seek the public's cooperation through words and pictures.

As Auden assesses the results, the Progressive vision of trained persuaders had been embraced by every interest that grappled for power and financial success and had thus achieved a more far-reaching and malignant power than reformers ever imagined. And what became of the Progressive vision of an educated and independent citizenry who could counter such a powerful influence? How well trained were Americans at assessing this information and persuasion and making their own judgments? By the 1920s, the active educational goals of listening, speaking, and acting together had begun to recede as the pressure of increased numbers of students and concern for the growing content of various fields created classrooms much more geared to listening to teachers and reading about a set content area than to acting communally to blend knowledge with experience. Beyond experimental schools such as Lincoln High School at Teachers' College, Columbia University and new kindergarten classrooms, Progressive theories of active instruction had little long-range institutional impact (Russell 199–235). Instead by 1930, most of the experimentation with new techniques had ceased, and high schools and junior high schools were relying on grammar, vocabulary, spelling, forms of discourse, and literary study to structure courses in English that were completely separated from the work in other disciplines and that primarily involved lecture and drill. Although an integrated approach to active instruction remained in some elementary schools, Progressive goals had failed to overturn the more controlled and segmented approach to education that remained the tradition everywhere.

Within the accepted school curriculum, twentieth-century students have received very little experience with real persuasion. Where the five-paragraph theme and grammar instruction thrive, the goals have been clarity and correctness much more frequently than an idea's effect on a particular group of readers. Discussion of appeals to the values and beliefs of an audience, the ethos of the speaker, and the logical arguments that could change attitudes and actions—paramount ingredients of classical rhetoric and of the modern persuasion genres—have rarely penetrated the schools. The teacher as expert, grade deliverer, or friendly coach has generally been the only audience for the exercises in writing that accompany regular work in grammar, vocabulary, and spelling.

By the end of the nineteenth century and the beginning of the twentieth, the growing content of college majors meant that even the best educated Americans felt deficient in presenting their own ideas and persuading others to change their attitudes and actions. In 1879, A. S. Hill complained of the new inattention to writing quality at the upper division: "The professor, absorbed in a specialty, contented himself with requiring at recitations and examinations knowledge of the subject-matter, however ill-digested and ill-expressed" ("An Answer to the Cry" 234). Hill recognized that juniors and seniors in the arts and sciences fields were doing less written work as larger class sizes, new textbook materials, and lab sessions changed the college class structure. Faculty concerned with research, graduate teaching, and professional training had "a license to complain about poor student writing but an institutionally sanctioned excuse for not devoting time to their undergraduates' writing" (Russell 63). With specialization, only those students in the professional writing fields such as journalism, advertising, public relations, and creative writing received regular assignments and instruction on persuasive writing: In the new English departments the earlier four-year commitment to theory and practice of rhetoric dwindled into a one-course rehash of the essay forms taught in high school. As the new professional majors developed further in each decade of the twentieth century, even though writing-across-the-curriculum proponents tried to turn the tide, upper-division classes often involved very little writing, with objective tests serving as the more common determiner of grades and with those writing assignments that remained tending to be expositions of course content and not persuasive renderings of ideas.

As a product of this education system, the Unknown Citizen supported his country's war and peace and cooperated with his union, but he never planned any political action with his colleagues and never used writing or speaking to express any views of his own. He becomes, in fact, a modern saint by cooperating and by not voicing any opinion at all: an anathema to what Progressives wanted for the working man and woman. Ironically, this citizen's only means of responding appears to be by providing data to persuaders, to the governmental Bureau of Statistics, union and factory officials, social psychologists, hospital and bank statisticians. When Auden asks, "Was he free? Was he happy?" and answers that "The question is absurd:/ Had anything been wrong, we should certainly have heard," he implies that "we" would have heard through official conduits of information and certainly not by the direct action of the citizen himself. The representative Unknown Citizen clearly has no tools with which to respond to the official discourse—or even to understand how it controls him.

When persuasion became a professional specialty at the beginning of the century, separate from any language arts, English, rhetoric, or composition instruction offered to all students, citizens were losing access to even the knowledge of classical rhetoric that earlier generations had possessed. The training in writing and speaking that students received by the beginning of the twentieth century was much more likely to focus on thesis statements, topic sentences, and grammar—on clear school writing—than on persuasive techniques. Thus, as the public persuasion aimed at graduates became ever more sophisticated, they became less adept at replying to it or coping with it. Aristotle realized that for his students to succeed in Greek society, they would need to be able to take apart the speeches of others as well as to argue persuasively. The naiveté of Phaedrus in Plato's dialogue is demonstrated as he is taken in by the tricks of older rhetors: they can seduce him without his understanding how it was done or even that it was done. Good sense or a general education alone will not protect a young Phaedrus; study of rhetoric will.

In 1939, as is also true today, citizens had persuasion foisted on them but had little awareness of its techniques, the interconnectedness of its genres, and its impact on their own lives. The Unknown Citizen, like his fellow students, was not well served by "their education," a structure in which he remained passive: "He never interfered." English departments and teachers today, the descendents of earlier rhetoric teachers, are cooperating with mass persuasion, this Wizard of Oz, by rarely acquainting students with what lies behind the curtain, by failing to offer even basic instruction on persuasion in our culture. Thus the educational system has allied itself with advertisers and politicians, allowing the citizenry to remain vulnerable to their techniques. E. B. White claimed that the "slants and the twists and the distortions" of modern rhetoric were ultimately scrutinized by the reader who could "sift and sort and check and countercheck in order to find out what the score is" (72). Given the morass of rhetoric portrayed in Auden's poem, however, it seems more likely for such distortions to be simply overwhelming. The Unknown Citizen's employers are pleased that he is not "odd in his views": perhaps he does not hold or expouse odd views because he is not forming them and acting for himself. He is not following the reader's process that E. B. White maintained is central to democracy.

Certainly, powerful interests sponsor mass persuasion, and individuals do not have an equivalent form of access to communication means. But a powerful countering influence to this swirl of words could come from citizens trained not just in how to write correctly but in how mass persuasion works. For citizens to be able to express their views or analyze the complex messages with which they are assaulted, they need to understand persuasion in its real forms: how Hitler led Germans into World War II, how MacDonald's sells hamburgers to single mothers or older citizens, how Tupac Shakur's lyrics attracted such a large audience, why yellow ribbons appeared on trees during Desert Storm, why Reagan and Clinton seemed so charismatic to voters. The Progressive era presented an optimistic picture of active citizens benevolently aided by persuaders, but citizens should not be at the mercy of those who control words. When education about persuasion became solely an advanced specialty, from which training in composition in the earlier grades was almost completely divorced, the schools enabled a few graduates to wield a mighty power without providing the others with the means to "sift and sort and check and countercheck." To fulfill those crucial evaluative goals for citizens in a democracy and to give them the means to express themselves, they must receive an education on how those slants, twists, and distortions work.

Works Cited

Abbott, Edwin A. *How to Write Clearly: Rules and Exercises on English Composition*. Boston: Roberts, 1875.

Abbott, Edwin A., and J. R. Seeley. *English Lessons for English People*. Boston: Roberts, 1872.

Adams, Katherine H. *A History of Professional Writing Instruction in American Colleges: Years of Acceptance, Growth, and Doubt*. Dallas: Southern Methodist UP, 1993.

America's Answer. CPI, 1918.

Applegate, Edd. *The Ad Men and Women: A Biographical Dictionary of Advertising*. Westport, CT: Greenwood, 1994.

Are We Prepared? From series *Uncle Sam at Work*, 1915–16. Universal Film, 1915. Based on Frederic J. Haskin's *The American Government*.

Arnold, Matthew. *Culture and Anarchy*. london: Smith, Elder, 1869.

Aroauld, Antoine. *The Art of Speaking*. London: Taylor and Clements, 1708.

Asker, William. "Does Knowledge of Formal Grammar Function?" *School and Society* 17 (1923): 109–11.

Aydelotte, Frank. *English and Engineering*. New York: McGraw, 1917.

Bain, Alexander. *English Composition and Rhetoric: A Manual*. London: Longmans, 1866.

Baker, Ray Stannard. "Railroads on Trial." *The Muckrackers*. Ed. Arthur Weinberg and Lila Weinberg. New York: Putnam's, 1961. 300–05.

Bent, Silas. *Ballyhoo: The Voice of the Press*. New York: Boni and Liveright, 1927.

Berlin, James A. *Rhetoric and Reality: Writing Instruction in American Colleges, 1900–1985*. Carbondale: Southern Illinois UP, 1987.

——. *Writing Instruction in Nineteenth-Century American Colleges*. Carbondale: Southern Illinois UP, 1984.

Bernays, Edward L. *Propaganda*. New York: Liveright, 1928.

Birge, E. A. Letter to Willard Bleyer. 27 June 1910. ms. Archives, U of Wisconsin, Madison.

Black, Ruby A. "Teaching Women's Features." 1922. ms. Archives, U of Wisconsin, Madison.

Blair, Hugh. *Lectures on Rhetoric and Belles Lettres*. Edinburgh: Strahan, 1783.

Blair, Karen. *The Torchbearers: Women and Their Amateur Arts Associations in America, 1890–1930*. Bloomington: Indiana UP, 1994.

Blakey, George T. *Historians on the Homefront: American Propagandists for the Great War*. Lexington: UP of Kentucky, 1970.

Bledstein, Burton J. *The Culture of Professionalism*. New York: Norton, 1976.

Bleyer, Willard Grosvenor. "Answers to Correspondents in Early English Journalism." *Journalism Quarterly* 7 (1930): 14–22.

——. "The Beginning of the Franklins' *New-England Courant*." *Journalism Bulletin* 4.2 (1927): 1–5.

——. "A Constructive Program for the Association of Teachers of Journalism." Annual Convention, 1921. ms. Archives, U of Wisconsin, Madison.

——. Digest of Talk on "Methods of Teaching News Gathering and News Writing." American Association of Teachers of Journalism, Madison, December 1921. ms. Archives, U of Wisconsin, Madison.

——. *The High School Course in English*. Madison: U of Wisconsin, 1906.

——. *How to Write Special Feature Articles*. Boston: Houghton, 1919.

——. *Journalism.* Reading with a Purpose, 49. Chicago: ALA, 1929.

——. Letter to Charles Van Hise. 9 January 1909. ms. Archives, U of Wisconsin, Madison.

——. Letter to Charles Van Hise. 3 May 1911. ms. Archives, U of Wisconsin, Madison.

——. Letter to E. A. Birge. 21 January 1909. ms. Archives, U of Wisconsin, Madison.

——. Letter to E. A. Birge. 28 June 1910. ms. Archives, U of Wisconsin, Madison.

——. Letter to Franklin W. Scott. 2 April 1909. ms. Archives, U of Wisconsin, Madison.

——. Letter to George E. Vincent. 14 April 1909. ms. Archives, U of Wisconsin, Madison.

——. Letter to Reading Publishers, 1910. ms. Archives, U of Wisconsin, Madison.

——. *Newspaper Writing and Editing.* Boston: Houghton, 1913.

——. "Outline for Analysis of News Report and of the Use of It by Papers." 1913. ms. Archives, U of Wisconsin, Madison.

——. *The Profession of Journalism.* Boston: Atlantic, 1918.

——. "The Relations of the University to the Press." Wisconsin Press Association, February 1905. ms. Archives, U of Wisconsin, Madison.

——. "Report of the Chairman of the Course in Journalism." 1918. ms. Archives, U of Wisconsin, Madison.

——. "Research Problems and Newspaper Analysis." *Journalism Bulletin* 1.1 (1924): 17-22.

——. *Types of News Writing.* Boston: Houghton, 1916.

——. "The University That Is the Mecca of Good Government Pilgrims." *St. Louis Star,* 1913. ms. Archives, U of Wisconsin, Madison.

——. "University of Wisconsin Extension." 1913. ms. Archives, U of Wisconsin, Madison.

——. "What Schools of Journalism Are Trying to Do." *Journalism Quarterly* 8 (1931): 35-44.

Brereton, John. "Sterling Andrus Leonard." *Traditions of Inquiry.* Ed. John Brereton. Oxford: Oxford UP, 1985. 81-104.

Brewster, Arthur Judson, and Herbert Hall Palmer. *Introduction to Advertising.* New York: McGraw-Hill, 1924.

Buck, Gertrude. "'Make-Believe Grammar.'" *School Review* 17 (1909): 21–33.

Burgchardt, Carl R. *Robert M. La Follette, Sr.: The Voice of Conscience.* New York: Greenwood, 1992.

Burton, Philip Ward. "Advertising Instruction in Schools and Colleges of Journalism." *Journalism Quarterly* 23 (1946):381–83+.

Butterfield, Roger. *American Past.* New York: Simon and Schuster, 1947.

Cairns, William B. *The Forms of Discourse.* Boston: Ginn, 1896.

Campbell, Craig W. *Reel America and World War I.* Jefferson, NC: McFarland, 1985.

Campbell, George. *The Philosophy of Rhetoric.* London: Strahan, 1776.

Campbell, JoAnn, ed. *Toward a Feminist Rhetoric: The Writing of Gertrude Buck.* Pittsburgh: U of Pittsburgh P, 1996.

Canfield, James H. *Taxation: A Plain Talk for Plain People.* New York: Society for Political Education, 1883.

Carey, James C. *Kansas State University: The Quest for Identity.* Lawrence: Regents Press of Kansas, 1977.

Carpenter, Stephen H. *An Introduction to the Study of the Anglo-Saxon Language.* Boston: Ginn and Heath, 1878.

Carruth, William Herbert. *Verse Writing: A Practical Handbook for College Classes and Private Guidance.* New York: Macmillan, 1917.

Cashman, Sean Dennis. *America in the Age of the Titans: The Progressive Era and World War I.* New York: New York UP, 1988.

Charnley, Mitchell V. "Education for Radio in Professional Schools and Departments of Journalism." *Journalism Quarterly* 19 (1942): 376–82.

"Claiming Our Privilege to Serve." *La Follette's Weekly Magazine* 9 Jan. 1909: 3–4.

Clark, Gregory, and S. Michael Halloran. Introduction. *Oratorical Culture in Nineteenth Century America*. Ed. Gregory Clark and S. Michael Halloran. Carbondale: Southern Illinois UP, 1993. 1–26.

Cochran, Negley D. *E. W. Scripps*. New York: Harcourt, 1933.

Connors, Robert J. Composition-Rhetoric: Backgrounds, Theory, and Pedagogy, Pittsburgh: U of Pittsburgh P, 1997.

———. "Historical Inquiry in Composition." Conference on College Composition and Communication. New York, March 1984.

Cornwell, Elmer E., Jr. *Presidential Leadership of Public Opinion*. Bloomington: Indiana UP, 1965.

Counter-Espionage Laws of the United States. Washington: The League, 1918.

Craik, George. *The English of Shakespeare*. London Chapman and Hall, 1857.

Creek, Herbert L. "How I became an Expert on Business Letter Writing." *ABWA Bulletin* 17 (1952): 5–7.

Creel, George. "How the Drug Dopers Fight." *Harpers Weekly* 60:30 Jan. 1915. 110-12.

———. *How We Advertised America*. New York: Harper, 1920.

———. "Poisoners of Public Opinion." *Harper's Weekly* 7 Nov. 1914: 436–38+.

Creel, George, Benjamin Barr Lindsey, and Leonore MacKay. *Children in Bondage*. New York: Hearst, 1914.

Crowley, Sharon. *The Methodical Memory: Invention in Current-Traditional Rhetoric*. Carbondale: Southern Illinois UP, 1990.

Curti, Merle, and Vernon Carstensen. *The University of Wisconsin: A History, 1845–1925*. 2 vols. Madison: U of Wisconsin P, 1949.

Darwin, Charles. *On the Origin of Species by Means of Natural Selection, or Preservation of Favoured Races in the Struggle for Life*. London: Murray, 1859.

Davis, Kenneth C. *Don't Know Much About History: Everything You Need to Know About American History But Never Learned*. New York: Avon, 1990.

Davis, W. N., Jr. "United States 27. The Age of Industrial Growth." *Encyclopedia Americana*. Deluxe Library Edition. 1990.

Day, Henry N. *Elements of the Art of Rhetoric*. New York: Barnes, 1850.

Defenceless America. Dir. J. Stuart Blackton. Vitagraph, 1915.

Defense or Tribute? Dir. and Writ. Oscar I. Lamberger. Radio Film, 1916.

Dewey, John. *The Child and the Curriculum*. Chicago: U of Chicago P, 1902.

———. "Fred Newton Scott." *John Dewey: The Early Works, 1882–1894*. Ed. Jo Ann Boydston. Vol. 4. Carbondale: Southern Illinois UP, 1971. 119–22.

———. "The New Psychology." *Andover Review* 2 (1884): 278–89.

———. "Psychology and Social Practice." *Psychological Review* 7 (1900): 105–24.

———. "The University Elementary School: History and Character." *John Dewey: The Middle Works, 1899–1924*. Ed. Jo Ann Boydston. Vol 1. Carbondale: Southern Illinois UP, 1976. 325–34.

Dickinson, Thomas. *The Case of American Drama*. Boston: Houghton, 1915.

———. , ed. *Wisconsin Plays*. New York: Huebsch, 1914.

Dos Passos, John. *The 42nd Parallel*. Boston: Houghton, 1930.

Dreiser, Theodore. *The Financier*. New York: Burt, 1912.

———. *The Stoic*. Cleveland: World Publishing, 1947.

———. *The Ttan*. New York: John Lane, 1914.

Drewry, John E. "Journalistic Instruction in the South." *Journalism Bulletin* 4.4 (1927): 31–39.

Dugard, William. *Rhetorices Elementa Quaestionibus et Responsionibus Explicata*. London: William Dugard, 1648.

Dygert, Warren B. *Advertising: Principles and Practice*. New York: Longmans, 1936.

Dykhuizen, George. *The Life and Mind of John Dewey*. Carbondale: Southern Illinois UP, 1973.

Edney, Clarence W. "English Sources of Rhetorical Theory in Nineteenth-Century America." *A History of Speech Education in America.* Ed. Karl R. Wallace. New York: Appleton, 1954. 80–104.

Eisenach, Eldon J. *The Lost Promise of Progressivism.* Lawrence: UP of Kansas, 1994.

Emery, Edwin, and Michael Emery. *The Press and America: An Interpretive History of the Mass Media.* 4th ed. Englewood Cliffs: Prentice, 1978.

Emery, Michael, R. Smith Schuneman, and Edwin Emery. *America's Front Page News: 1690–1970.* New York: Doubleday, 1970.

Fehlman, Frank E. *How to Write Advertising Copy That Sells: Principles and Practices.* New York: Funk and Wagnalls, 1950.

Final Programme for the American Conference of Teachers of Journalism, Madison, 1913. ms. Archives, U of Wisconsin, Madison.

The Flying Torpedo. Dir. and Writ. Robert M. Baker and John Emerson. Triangle Film, 1916.

Flynn, John T. *God's Gold: The Story of Rockefeller and His Times.* Chautauqua, NY: Chautauqua, 1932.

Fox, Stephen. *The Mirror Makers: A History of American Advertising and Its Creators.* New York: Morrow, 1984.

Frederick, John T. "A Maker of Songs." *American Prefaces* 2 (1937): 83–84.

Froebel, Friedrich. *The Education of Man.* Trans. W. N. Hailmann. New York: Appleton, 1887. Trans. of *Die Menschenerziehung die Erziehungs.* 1826.

Gale, Zona. "Civic Problems in the Small City and Village." *La Follette's Weekly Magazine* 7 Aug. 1909: 12–13.

——. *Miss Lulu Bett.* New York: Appleton, 1920.

Gardner, Edward Hall. *Effective Business Letters.* New York: Ronald, 1915.

——. "What Makes a Good Letter Good?" *System* 36 (July 1919): 56–58.

Garland, Hamlin. *A Member of the Third House: A Dramatic Story.* Chicago: Schulte, 1892.

——. *A Spoil of Office: A Story of the Modern West.* Boston: Arena, 1892.

Goldman, Eric F. *Two-Way Street: The Emergence of the Public Relations Counsel.* Boston: Bellman, 1948.

Grabo, Carl H. *The Art of the Short Story.* New York: Scribner's, 1913.

Griffin, Clifford S. *The University of Kansas: A History.* Lawrence: UP of Kansas, 1974.

Gruber, Carol S. *Mars and Minerva: World War I and the Uses of Higher Learning in America.* Baton Rouge: Louisiana State UP, 1975.

Guthrie, Warren. "The Development of Rhetorical Theory in America, 1635–1850." *Speech Monographs* 13 (1946): 14–22; 14 (1947): 38–54; 15 (1948): 61–71; 16 (August 1949): 98–113; 18 (March 1951): 17–30.

Hall, Samuel R. *Writing an Advertisement.* Boston: Houghton, 1915.

Halloran, S. Michael. "From Rhetoric to Composition: The Teaching of Writing in America to 1900." *A Short History of Writing Instruction: From Ancient Greece to Twentieth-Century America.* Ed. James J. Murphy. Davis, CA: Hermagoras, 1990. 151–82.

Herbart, Johann F. *The Application of Psychology to the Science of Education.* Trans. Beatrice C. Mulliner. New York: Scribner's, 1898.

The Hero of Submarine D-Z. Dir. Jasper Ewing Brady. Vitagraph, 1916.

Herold, David. "Historical Perspectives on Government Communication." *Informing the People: A Public Affairs Handbook.* Ed. Lewis M. Helm et al. New York: Longman, 1981. 14–21.

Herrick, Robert. *The Common Lot.* New York: Grosset, 1904.

——. *A Life for a Life.* London: Macmillan, 1910.

——. *The Memoirs of an American Citizen.* New York: Macmillan, 1905.

Hiebert, Ray Eldon. *Courtier to the Crowd: The Story of Ivy Lee and the Development of Public Relations.* Ames, IO: Iowa State UP, 1966.

Hill, Adams Sherman. "An Answer to the Cry for More English." *Good Company* 4 (1879): 233–40.

——. "English in Our Colleges." *Scribner's Magazine* 1 (1887): 507–12.

——. *The Principles of Rhetoric and Their Application.* New York: Harper, 1878.

Historical Statistics of the United States: Colonial Times to 1970. Part 1. Washington, D.C.: U.S. Department of Commerce, Bureau of the Census, 1975.

Hochmuth, Marie, and Richard Murphy. "Rhetorical and Elocutionary Training in Nineteenth-Century Colleges." *A History of Speech Education in America.* Ed. Karl R. Wallace. New York: Appleton, 1954. 153–77.

Hope, M. B., *The Princeton Text Book in Rhetoric.* Princeton, NJ: Robinson, 1859.

Hotchkiss, George Burton. *An Outline of Advertising.* New York: Macmillan, 1933.

Howar, Ralph M. *The History of an Advertising Agency: N. W. Ayer and Son at Work, 1869-1949.* Cambridge: Harvard UP, 1949.

Howells, William Dean. *My Literary Passions.* New York: Harper, 1895.

——. *A Traveler from Altruria.* New York: Harper, 1894.

Hyde, Grant Milnor. *A Course in Journalistic Writing.* New York: Appleton, 1922.

——. *Handbook for Newspaper Workers.* New York: Appleton, 1921.

——. "Journalism in the High School." *Journalism Bulletin* 2.1 (1925): 1-9.

——. "Raising the Quality of Students." *Journalism Bulletin* 4.1 (1927): 15–22.

——. "Taking Stock after Twenty-Four Years." *Journalism Quarterly* 6 (1929): 8–12.

——. "What of the High School Class?" *Journalism Bulletin* 2.3 (1925): 22–23.

Irwin, Will. *The House That Shadows Built.* Garden City, NY: Doubleday, 1928.

——. *The Next War: An Appeal to Comon Sense.* New York: Dutton, 1921.

——. *Propaganda and the News or What Makes You Think So?* New York: Whittlesey, 1936.

"John Dewey, Ph.D." *Chronicle* 21 (1890): 327-28.

Johnson, Nan. *Nineteenth-Century Rhetoric in North America.* Carbondale: Southern Illinois UP, 1991.

Johnson, Walter. *Gifford Pinchot: Forester-Politician.* Princeton: Princeton UP, 1960.

Keller, Morton. *Regulating a New Society: Public Policy and Social Change in America, 1900–1933.* Cambridge: Harvard UP, 1994.

Kitzhaber, Albert R. *Rhetoric in American Colleges, 1850-1900.* Diss. U of Washington, 1953. Dallas: Southern Methodist UP, 1990.

LaCapra, Dominick. *History and Criticism.* Ithaca: Cornell UP, 1985.

La Follette, Robert M. *La Follette's Autobiography: A Personal Narrative of Political Experiences.* 1911. Madison: U of Wisconsin P, 1968.

——. "Pinchot or Ballinger—Which." *La Follette's Weekly Magazine* 9 October 1909: 3–4.

——. "The Undermining of My Candidacy." *La Follette's Weekly Magazine* 19 October 1912: 9–17.

La Follette, Belle Case, and Fola La Follette. *Robert M. La Follette: June 14, 1855–June 18, 1925.* Vol. 1. New York: Macmillan, 1953.

Larson, Robert W. *Populism in the Mountain West Town.* Albuquerque: U of New Mexico P, 1986.

Lathrop, John. Inaugural Address. U of Wisconsin, 1850. ms. Archives, U of Wisconsin, Madison.

Lazell, Fred J. "Weeding Out the Unfit." *Journalism Bulletin* 4.1 (1927): 25–30.

Lee, Alfred McClung. "Trends in Public Relations Training." *Public Opinion Quarterly* 11 (1947): 83–91.

Lee, Ivy Ledbetter. *Occasional Papers.* New York: Ivy Lee, 1934.

——. *Publicity: Some of the Things It Is and Is Not.* New York: Industries, 1925.

Lee, James Melvin. *Instruction in Journalism in Institutions of Higher Education.* Department of the Interior Bureau of Education Bulletin 18. Washington: GPO, 1918.

Leonard, Sterling. "As to the Forms of Discourse." *English Journal* 3 (1914): 201–11.

———. *The Atlantic Book of Modern Plays.* Boston: Atlantic Monthly, 1921.

———. *Current English Usage.* Chicago: NCTE, 1932.

———. *The Doctrine of Correctness in English Usage, 1700-1800.* Madison: U of Wisconsin Studies in Language and Literature. No. 25, 1929.

———. *English Composition as a Social Problem.* Boston: Houghton, 1917.

———. *Essential Principles of Teaching Reading and Literature in the Intermediate Grades and the High School.* Philadelphia: Lippincott, 1922.

———. *Poems of the War and the Peace.* New York: Harcourt, 1921.

Lippmann, Walter. *Public Opinion.* New York: Harcourt, 1922.

The Little American. Dir. Cecil B. DeMille. Writ. Jeanie MacPherson. With Mary Pickford. Artcraft Pictures, 1917.

Locke, John. *An Essay Concerning Humane Understanding: In Four Books.* London: Bassett, 1689.

Lovett, Robert Morss. *All Our Years: The Autobiography of Robert Morss Lovett.* New York: Viking, 1948.

Ludington, Townsend. *John Dos Passos: A Twentieth Century Odyssey.* New York: Dutton, 1980.

MacKaye, Percy. "Theatre and University: How They May Help Each Other." *La Follette's Weekly Magazine* 17 February 1912: 7–8.

MacNeil, Neil. *Without Fear or Favor.* New York: Harcourt, 1940.

Making Rifles. International Film Service, 1917.

Making Steel Rails for the Allies. International Film Service, 1917.

Manley, Robert N. *Centennial History of the University of Nebraska. I. Frontier University.* Lincoln: U of Nebraska P, 1969.

McMurry, Charles A. *The Elements of General Method Based on the Principles of Herbart.* Bloomington, IL: Public-School Publishing, 1893.

McMurry, Charles, A., and Frank M. McMurry. *The Method of the Recitation.* Bloomington, IL: Public School Publishing, 1897.

Mencken, H.L. *A Book of Prefaces.* Garden City, NY: Garden City, 1927.

Mich, Daniel D. Editorial, Wisconsin *State Journal.* November 1935. ms. Archives, U of Wisconsin, Madison.

Mock, James R., and Cedric Larson. *Words That Won the War: The Story of the Committee on Public Information, 1917–1919.* Princeton: Princeton UP, 1939.

The Money Master. George Kleine, 1915. Based on the play by Cleveland Moffett.

Morison, Samuel Eliot. *The Development of Harvard University since the Inauguration of President Eliot, 1869–1929.* Cambridge: Harvard UP, 1930.

Mott, Frank Luther. *American Journalism: A History of Newspapers in the United States through 260 Years: 1690–1950.* Rev.ed. New York: Macmillan, 1950.

———. *A History of American Magazines: 1885–1905.* Cambridge: Harvard UP, 1957.

Mulligan, John. *Structure of the English Language.* New York: Appleton, 1852.

Nelson, Harold L. "Founding Father: Willard Grosvenor Bleyer, 1873–1935." *AEJMC: Seventy-Five Years in the Making—A History of Organizing for Journalism and Mass Communication Education in the United States.* Ed. Edwin Emery and Joseph P. McKerns. Journalism Monographs No. 104. Columbia, S. C.: AEJMC, 1987. 5–6. ED 292 091.

Nevius, Blake. *Robert Herrick: The Development of a Novelist.* Berkeley: U of California P, 1962.

Newsom, Doug, Alan Scott, and Judy Vanslyke Turk. *This Is PR: The Realities of Public Relations.* Belmont, CA: Wadsworth, 1993.

Nichols, Charles Washburn. "Teaching Shakespeare to Engineers." *English Journal* 2 (1913): 366–69.

Norris, Frank. *The Octopus.* New York: Nelson, 1900.

——. *The Pit.* New York: Doubleday, 1903.

O'Dell, De Forest. *The History of Journalism Education in the United States.* New York: Columbia University Teachers College Bureau of Publications, 1935.

O'Higgins, Harvey. *Clara Barron.* New York: Harper, 1926.

——. *The German Whisper.* Washington: GPO, 1918.

——. *Julie Cane.* New York: Grosset and Dunlap, 1924.

O'Higgins, Harvey, and Benjamin B. Lindsey. *The Beast.* New York: Doubleday, 1910.

O'Higgins, Harvey, and Frank J. Cannon. *Under the Prophet in Utah: The National Menace of a Political Priestcraft.* Boston: Clark, 1911.

Ohmann, Richard. *English in America: A Radical View of the Profession.* New York: Oxford UP, 1976.

The Pacifist. Dir. Henry Beaumont. Essanay Film, 1916.

Pegram, Thomas R. *Partisans and Progressives: Private Interest and Public Policy in Illinois, 1870–1922.* Urbana: U of Illinois P, 1992.

Pestalozzi, Johann H. *Leonard and Gertrude.* Trans. Eva Channing. Boston: Heath, 1885.

Pimlott, J. A. R. *Public Relations and American Democracy.* Princeton: Princeton UP, 1951.

Phillips, David Graham. *The Great God Success; A Novel.* New York: Stokes, 1901.

——. *The Plum Tree.* Indianapolis: Bobbs-Merrill, 1905.

——. *The Second Generation.* New York: Appleton, 1907.

——. *Susan Lenox.* New York: Appleton, 1919.

Pinchot, Gifford. *Breaking New Ground.* New York: Harcourt, 1947.

Piper, Edwin Ford. *Barbed Wire, and Other Poems.* Chicago: Midland, 1917.

——. *Barbed Wire and Wayfarers.* New York: Macmillan, 1924.

——. *Paintrock Road.* New York: Macmilan, 1927.

Ponder, Stephen. "Progressive Drive to Shape Public Opinion, 1898–1913." *Public Relations Review* 16.3 (1990): 94–104.

Pope, Daniel. *The Making of Modern Advertising.* New York: Basic, 1983.

Potter, W. J. Themes and Forensics, 1854. ms. Pusey Library, Harvard U.

Pringle, Henry F. "His Master's Voice." *American Mercury* 9 (1926): 145–53.

Printer's Ink Refresher Course in Advertising, Selling, and Merchandising. New York: Funk and Wagnalls, 1947.

Programs for the 1923 and 1924 Annual Conference, Association of Schools and Conferences of Journalism. ms. State Historical Society of Wisconsin Library, Madison.

Protecting the Ships at Sea. From series *Uncle Sam at Work,* 1915-16. Universal Film, 1916. Based on Frederic J. Haskin's *The American Government.*

"Public Opinion in War Time." *La Follette's Weekly Magazine* Oct. 1917: 3+.

Raucher, Alan R. "Public Relations in Business: A Business of Public Relations." *Public Relations Review* 16.3 (1990): 19–26.

Requirements for Admission to the Freshman English Course. 1910. ms. Archives, U of Wisconsin, Madison.

Roosevelt, Theodore. *An Autobiography.* New York: Macmillan, 1919.

——. "The Man with the Muckrake." *The Muckrackers.* Ed. Arthur Weinberg and Lila Weinberg. New York: Putnam's, 1961. 58–65.

——. "Wisconsin: An Object Lesson for the Rest of the Union." *La Follette's Weekly Magazine* 3 June 1911: 6+.

Ross, Donald Keith. "W. G. Bleyer and the Development of Journalism Education." MA Thesis. U of Wisconsin, 1952.

Ross, Edward Alsworth. *Social Control: A Survey of the Foundations of Order.* New York: Macmillan, 1901.

Ross, Irwin. *The Image Merchants: The Fabulous World of Public Relations.* New York: Doubleday, 1958.

Rudolph, Frederick. *Curriculum: A History of the American Undergraduate Course of Study since 1636*. San Francisco: Jossey, 1977.

Russell, David R. *Writing in the Academic Disciplines, 1870–1990: A Curricular History*. Carbondale: Southern Illinois UP, 1991.

Sandburg, Carl. "Ivy Lee—Paid Liar." *New York Call* 7 Mar. 1915, sec. 2: 2+.

Sarasohn, David. *The Party of Reform: Democrats in the Progressive Era*. Jackson: UP of Mississippi, 1989.

Scott, Fred Newton. "English Composition as a Mode of Behavior." *English Journal* 11 (1922): 463–73.

——. "The Standard of American Speech." *English Journal* 6 (1917): 1–11.

Scott, Fred N., and Gertrude Buck. *A Brief English Grammar*. Chicago: Scott, Foresman, 1905.

Scott, Fred N., George R. Carpenter, and Franklin T. Baker. *The Teaching of English in the Elementary and the Secondary School*. New York: Longmans, 1903.

Scott, Fred N., and Joseph V. Denney. *Paragraph-Writing*. Ann Arbor: Register, 1891.

Scott, Fred N., and Gordon A. Southworth. *Lessons in English, Book Two*. Boston: Sanborn, 1906.

Sherman, Stuart P. *American and Allied Ideals; An Appeal to Those Who Are Neither Hot Nor Cold*. War Information Series No. 12. Washington: US Committee on Public Information, 1918.

Sinclair, Upton. *The Goose-Step: A Study of American Education*. Pasadena: Upton Sinclair, 1922.

——. *The Jungle*. New York: Doubleday, 1906.

Smart, Walter Kay. *How to Write Business Letters That Win*. Chicago: Shaw, 1916.

Smith, Duane A. *Colorado, Wyoming, and Montana, 1859–1915*. Albuquerque: U of New Mexico P, 1992.

The Son of His Father. Dir. Victor Schertzinger. Writ. Ridgwell Cullum. Thomas H. Ince, 1918.

Spencer, Herbert. *Philosophy of Style: An Essay*. New York: Appleton, 1900.

Spencer, M. Lyle. *Editorial Writing: Ethics, Policy, Practice*. Boston: Houghton, 1924.

——. *News Writing: The Gathering and Handling of News Stories*. New York: Heath, 1917.

Steffens, Lincoln. *The Autobiography of Lincoln Steffens*. New York: Harcourt, 1931.

——. "Chicago: Half Free and Fighting On." *McClure's Magazine* Oct. 1903: 563-77.

——. *The Shame of the Cities*. New York: Heinemann, 1904.

——. *The Struggle for Self-Government*. New York: McClure, 1906.

——. "Wisconsin: Representative Government Restored." *McClure's Magazine* Oct. 1904: 563-79.

Storr, Richard J. *Harper's University: The Beginnings*. Chicago: U of Chicago P, 1966.

Sutton, Albert. *Education for Journalism in the United States From Its Beginning to 1940*. Northwestern University Studies in the Humanities 10. Evanston: Northwestern U, 1945.

Talon, Omer. *Audomari Talaei Rhetorica as Carolum Lotharingum Cardinalem Guisianum*. Paris: Matthaei Davidis, 1549.

Thelen, David P. *Robert M. La Follette and the Insurgent Spirit*. Boston: Little, Brown, 1976.

Thompson, Lawrance, and R.H. Winnick. *Robert Frost: A Biography*. New York: Holt, 1981.

Thurber, Edward A. "Composition in Our Colleges." *English Journal* 4 (1915): 9–14.

Tipper, Harry, Harry L. Hollingworth, George Burton Hotchkiss, and Frank Alvah Parsons. *The Principles of Advertising*. New York: Ronald, 1915.

University of Wisconsin Faculty Round Robin, 1918. ms Archives, State Historical Society of Wisconsin Library, Madison.

Van Hise, Charles R. *The Conservation of Natural Resources in the United States*. New York: Macmillan, 1910.

Varnum, Robin. *Fencing with Words: A History of Writing Instruction at Amherst College during the Era of Theodore Baird, 1938–1966.* Urbana: NCTE, 1996.

Vaughn, Stephen. *Holding Fast the Inner Lines: Democracy, Nationalism, and the Committee on Public Information.* Chapel Hill: U of North Carolina P, 1980.

Veblen, Thorstein. *The Theory of Business Enterprise.* New York: Scribner's, 1904.

Veysey, Laurence. "Stability and Experiment in the American Undergraduate Curriculum." *Content and Context: Essays on College Education.* Ed. Carl Kaysen. New York: McGraw, 1973. 1–63.

Wallace, Karl R. *A History of Speech Education in America: Background Studies.* New York: Appleton, 1954.

Wallace, Una. "A Singing Professor." *Daily Iowan* 6 December 1931, Sunday Magazine Section: 1+.

Ward, Lester F. *Dynamic Sociology.* New York: Appleton, 1883.

Watt, Homer. *The Composition of Technical Papers.* New York: McGraw, 1917.

Wayland, Francis. *Report to the Corporation of Brown University.* Providence: Whitney, 1850.

Weinberg, Arthur, and Lila Weinberg. Introduction. *The Muckrakers.* Ed. Arthur Weinberg and Lila Weinberg. New York: Putnam's, 1961.

Welch, Kathleen E. "Writing Instruction in Ancient Athens after 450 B.C." *A Short History of Writing Instruction: From Ancient Greece to Twentieth-Century America.* Ed. James J. Murphy. Davis, CA: Hermagoras, 1990. 1–17.

Wendell, Barrett. Notes of Lectures in English 12, 1885-87. ms. Pusey Library, Harvard U.

——. "Of Education." *The Privileged Classes.* New York: Scribner's, 1908. 181–274.

White, E. B. "Letter from the East." *New Yorker* 18 Feb. 1956: 66–79.

White, William Allen. *A Certain Rich Man.* New York: Grosset and Dunlap, 1909.

Wilbers, Stephen. *The Iowa Writers' Workshop: Origins, Emergence, and Growth.* Iowa City: U of Iowa P, 1980.

Willey, Malcolm W., and Stuart A. Rice. *Communication Agencies and Social Life.* New York: McGraw, 1933.

Williams, Sara L. *Twenty Years of Education for Journalism.* Columbia, MO: Stephens, 1929.

"Wisconsin Alumni Want School." *Journalism Bulletin* 2.4 (1925): 12.

Woolley, Edwin C. "Admission to Freshman English in the University." *English Journal* 3 (1914): 238–44.

——. *Exercises in English.* Boston: Heath, 1911.

——. *Handbook of Composition.* Boston: Heath, 1907.

——. *The Mechanics of Writing.* Boston: Heath, 1909.

——. *Written English.* Boston: Heath, 1915.

World War I: The Home Front. Washington: National Archives Trust Fund Board, 1970.

Wozniak, John Michael. *English Composition in Eastern Colleges, 1850–1940.* Washington, DC: UP of America, 1978.

Wright, Chester M. "Rockefeller's Barricade of Ink." *New York Call* 13 June 1915, sec. 2: 1+.

Young, Frances Berkeley. *A College Course in Writing from Models.* New York: Holt, 1910.

Young, Frances Berkeley, and Karl Young. *Freshman English: A Manual.* New York: Holt, 1914.

Young, Karl, Norman Foerster, and Frederick A. Manchester. *Essays for College Men: Education, Science, and Art.* New York: Holt, 1913.

Author Index

A

Abbott, Edwin A., 9, 10
Adams, Katherine H., 13
Applegate, Edd, 117, 118
Arnold, Matthew, 3, 7, 8
Aroauld, Antoine, xiii
Asker, William, 17
Auden, W. H., 145–150
Ayedelotte, Frank, 77, 125, 126

B

Bain, Alexander, 6, 8, 9, 33
Baker, Franklin, 31, 32
Baker, Ray Stannard, 106, 111
Bent, Silas, 140
Berlin, James A., xiv–xvi, 17, 83
Bernays, Edward L., 38, 59, 84, 110,
    126, 127, 136
Birge, E.A., 54, 56–59, 129
Black, Ruby A., 52, 56
Blair, Hugh, xi, xv, 3, 4
Blair, Karen, 78
Blakey, George T., 122
Bledstein, Burton J., 19
Bleyer, Willard Grosvenor, 44–64, 66,
    68, 69, 89, 99, 100, 109, 112,
    118, 129, 143
Brereton, John, 35
Brewster, Arthur Judson, 92, 114–116
Buck, Gertrude, 5, 16, 33
Burgchardt, Carl R, 41, 42, 129
Burton, Philip Ward, 134

Butterfield, Roger, 110

C

Cairns, William B., 7, 129
Campbell, Craig W., 108, 112, 124, 125
Campbell, George, xi, xv, xviii, 4, 6
Campbell, JoAnn, 5
Canfield, James, 78, 79
Cannon, Frank J., 127
Carey, James C., 75, 76
Carpenter, George, 8, 31, 32
Carpenter, Stephen, 9
Carruth, William Herbert, 89, 90
Carstensen, Vernon, 56, 129
Cashman, Sean Dennis, 18, 23
Charnley, Mitchell V, 136
Clark, Gregory, xv
Connors, Robert J., xiv, 1
Cornwell, Elmer E., Jr., 96, 123, 125
Craik, George L., 9
Creek, Herbert L., 92, 93
Creel, George, 118–25, 143
Crowley, Sharon, xv
Curti, Merle, 56, 129

D

Darwin, Charles, 17, 22
Davis, Kenneth C., 17, 18
Davis, W. N., Jr., 25
Day, Henry N., xiii, 6
Denney, Joseph V., 33
Dewey, John, xvi, xvii, 28–32, 35, 37,
    146

161

Dickinson, Thomas, 64, 68, 69, 78, 108
Dos Passos, John, 24, 132, 135, 136
Dreiser, Theodore, 107
Drewry, John E., 85
Dugard, William, xiii
Dygert, Warren B., 92
Dykhuizen, George, 31

E

Edney, Clarence W., xiii
Eisenach, Eldon J., xvi, xvii, 26
Emery, Edwin, 101–03
Emery, Michael, 101–03

F

Flynn, John T., 136–38
Foerster, Norman, 8
Fox, Stephen, 115
Frederick, John T., 91
Froebel, Friedrich, 27, 28, 30, 37

G

Gale, Zona, 107, 108
Gardner, Edward Hall, 65–67, 77, 89
Garland, Hamlin, 107
Goldman, Eric F., 109, 112
Grabo, Carl H., 89
Griffin, Clifford S., 71, 72, 78
Gruber, Carol S., 126, 129, 130
Guthrie, Warren, xii

H

Hall, Samuel R., 77
Halloran, S. Michael, xv, 20
Herbart, Johann F., 28, 30
Herold, David, 100, 130, 134
Herrick, Robert, 81, 82, 108
Hiebert, Ray Eldon, 112, 140, 142, 143
Hill, Adams Sherman, xi, xiv, 6, 7, 13, 15, 16, 33, 148
Hochmuth, Marie, xiii
Hollingworth, Henry L., 116
Hope, M. B., xiii
Hotchkiss, George Burton, 114–16
Howar, Ralph M., 105, 114
Howells, William Dean, 107, 108

Hyde, Grant Milnor, 50, 54, 55–57, 59–62, 66, 129

I

Irwin, Will, 106, 120, 128

J

Johnson, Nan, xiv, xv
Johnson, Walter, 97

K

Keller, Morton, xvi, xvii, 25, 26
Kitzhaber, Albert R., xiv, 17

L

LaCapra, Dominick, xviii
La Follette, Belle Case, 24, 40, 42, 43, 129
La Follette, Fola, 24, 40, 42, 129
La Follette, Robert M., xii, xvi, 24, 25, 39–44, 48, 49, 67–70, 72, 95–98, 108, 118, 128–33, 137, 143, 146, 147
Larson, Cedric, 123, 126
Larson, Robert W., 86
Lathrop, John H., 2
Lazell, Fred J., 90
Lee, Alfred McClung, 134
Lee, Ivy Ledbetter, 59, 112, 119, 135, 136, 138–43
Lee, James Melvin, xviii
Leonard, Sterling, 16, 35–37
Lindsey, Benjamin B., 127
Lippmann, Walter, 128, 133
Locke, John, 4
Lovett, Robert Morss, 81–83, 91
Ludington, Townsend, 135, 136

M

MacDougall, Curtis, 55, 56, 60
MacKaye, Percy, 68, 69, 78, 93
MacNeil, Neil, 140
Manchester, Frederick A., 8
Manley, Robert N., 78, 79
Mencken, H. L., 130, 133

Mich, Daniel D., 56
Mock, James R., 123, 126
Morison, Samuel Eliot, 13
Mott, Frank Luther, 102, 104, 114, 115
Mulligan, John, 9
Murphy, Richard, xiii

N

Nelson, Harold L., 56
Nevius, Blake, 82
Newsom, Doug, 134
Nichols, Charles Washburn, 79, 80
Norris, Frank, 107

O

O'Dell, De Forest, xviii, 72, 73
O'Higgins, Harvey, 127
Ohmann, Richard, 19, 20

P

Palmer, Herbert Hall, 92, 114–16
Parsons, Frank Alvah, 116
Pegram, Thomas R., xvi
Pestalozzi, Johann H., 27, 28, 37
Phillips, David Graham, 107
Pimlott, J. A. R., 110
Pinchot, Gifford, 96–100, 109, 111, 118,
    125, 143, 147
Piper, Edwin Ford, 80, 81, 91
Ponder, Stephen, 97–99
Pope, Daniel, 117
Potter, W. J., 3
Pringle, Henry F., 97, 139–41

R

Raucher, Alan R., 109, 111
Rice, Stuart A., 137
Roosevelt, Theodore, xvi, 25, 95–101,
    107, 111, 119, 122, 124, 130
Ross, Donald Keith, 45
Ross, Edward Alsworth, 23
Ross, Irwin, 126, 127
Rudolph, Frederick, 3, 19
Russell, David R., 34, 147, 148

S

Sandburg, Carl, 138, 139
Sarasohn, David, xvi, xvii, 26
Schuneman, Smith, 102, 103
Scott, Alan, 134
Scott, Fred Newton, xiv, xv, 14, 15,
    31–35, 37, 79, 83
Seeley, J. R., 9, 10
Sherman, Stuart, 126
Sinclair, Upton, 8, 12, 15, 105, 107, 138,
    141
Smart, Walter Kay, 89
Smith, Duane A, 86
Southworth, Gordon A., 33
Spencer, Herbert, 64
Spencer, M. Lyle, 89, 92
Steffens, Joseph Lincoln, 24, 25, 41–43,
    81, 96, 143
Storr, Richard J., 81
Sutton, Albert, xviii

T

Talon, Omer, xiii
Thelen, David P., 119
Thompson, Lawrance, 87
Thurber, Edward A., 23
Tipper, Harry, 106
Turk, Judy Vanslyke, 121

V

Van Hise, Charles R., 44–50, 57, 58,
    62–64, 68, 69, 72, 75, 79, 81,
    95, 97–100, 109, 118, 125,
    129, 130, 143
Varnum, Robin, 5
Vaughn, Stephen, 125, 126, 128
Veblen, Thorstein, 23
Veysey, Laurence, 37, 38

W

Wallace, Karl, xiii
Wallace, Una, 80, 81
Ward, Lester F, 23
Watt, Homer, 77
Wayland, Francis, 18, 19
Weinberg, Arthur, 23, 109
Weinberg, Lila, 23, 109

Welch, Kathleen E., 2, 3
Wendell, Barrett, xi, 13, 14, 16, 33, 81
White, E.B., 137
White, William Allen, 74, 107
Wilbers, Stephen, 80
Willey, Malcolm W., 137
Williams, Sara L., 90
Winnick, R. H., 93
Woolley, Edwin C., 10–12, 60, 61

Wozniak, John Michael, 14
Wright, Chester M., 139

Y

Young, Frances Berkeley, 8
Young, Karl, 8, 64, 65, 125, 129

Subject Index

A

Addams, Jane, xvi, 43, 81, 125, 146
Advanced composition, generic form,
    12–15
Advertising, 105, 113–118, 123, 124
    employment of journalism students,
        117, 118
    ethics codes, 116–117
    history of, 105, 113–118
    for World War I, 123, 124
Advertising instruction, 34, 51, 58, 73,
    77, 84–87, 92
Agricultural journalism instruction, 63,
    76, 77, 84–86
American Association of Teachers of
    Journalism, 59, 60
Auden, W. H., 145–150

B

Baker, Ray Stannard, 106, 111
Barnum, P. T., 109
Barton, Bruce F., 117
Bascom, John, 4, 40, 41, 56
Belles Lettres, 3, 4
Bernays, Edward, 38, 59, 84, 110, 126,
    127, 136
    on Progressive communication, 38
    as a public relations professional, 59,
        110, 126, 127, 136
    as a teacher of public relations, 84,
        126, 127
Birge, E.A., 54, 56–59, 129
Black, Ruby, 52, 56

Bleyer, Willard, 45–62, 89, 97–100, 129
    advocate of the Wisconsin Idea, 45
    attack on Bob La Follette during
        World War I, 129
    early education and job training, 45
    as journalism teacher and administra-
        tor, 48–62
    influence on Roosevelt's publicity ef-
        forts, 97–100
    textbooks, 56, 60, 89
    as university publicist, 45–48
Business writing. See Technical writing.
Byoir, Carl, 127, 128

C

Canfield, James H., 78, 79
Classical rhetoric, in the American col-
    lege curriculum, xi, xii, 1–3
College curriculum, nineteenth century,
    1–2, 18–19
    course requirements, 1,1
    industrialists' critique of, 18, 19
College newspapers, 58, 59, 73, 90
    University of Kansas *Kansan*, 73
    University of Missouri *Missourian*, 90
    University of Wisconsin's *Cardinal*,
        58, 59
Committee on Public Information
    (CPI), 118–131
Commons, John, xvi, 43, 44, 130
Cook, George Cram ("Jig"), 80
Creative writing instruction, 34, 68, 69,
    74, 77–83, 85, 87–91, 93

college courses, 34, 68, 69, 74,
        77–83, 85, 87, 88
teacher training, 80, 81, 93
textbooks, 89–91
Creel, George, 118–125, 143
    with the Committee on Public Infor-
        mation (CPI), 118–125, 143
    on ethical persuasion, 119, 120
    as a muckraker, 119
Cunliffe, John W., 57, 59

D

Dewey, John, xvi, xvii, 28–32
    college teaching, 31
    education, 28
    influence on Fred Newton Scott, 31
    school curriculum at the University
        of Chicago, 29, 30
    theory of education, xvi, xvii, 28–30,
        32
Dickinson, Thomas, 64, 68, 69, 78, 108
Dos Passos, John, 24, 132, 135, 136

E

Ely, Richard, xvi, 43, 44, 130
Emerson, Ralph Waldo, 19
Espionage Act of 1917, 120

F

Film–making, 98, 107, 108, 111, 112,
        124, 125
    for commercial products, 111, 112
    for the Department of Agriculture, 98
    for Progressive causes, 107, 108
    as World War I propaganda, 124, 125
Forms of discourse, xi, 5–7, 33
Freshman composition instruction,
        1–20, 33, 37
    criticisms of, 8, 12–20
    cultural significance of, 15–20
    grammar study in, 9–12, 33
    history of, xi–xvii, 1–12, 15–20, 33
    readings in, 7, 8
    rhetorical study in, 5–7, 15, 16, 33, 37
Froebel, Friedrich, 27, 28, 30, 37

G

Gale, Zona, 107, 108
Gardner, Edward Hall, 65–67, 77, 89

H

Harper, William Rainey, 81
Harvard University, advanced composi-
        tion courses, 12–14
Hearst, William Randolph, 99, 102, 103
Herbart, Johann, 28, 30
Herrick, Robert, 81, 82, 108
Hitler, Adolph, 142, 143
Hopkins, Edwin M., 72–74
Hyde, Grant Milnor, 50, 54, 55–57,
        59–62, 66, 129

I

Irwin, Will, 106, 120, 128

J

Jones, Will Owen, 79
Journalism instruction, 34, 50–62,
        72–74, 76, 77, 79, 85–93
    college courses, 34, 50–62, 72–74,
        76, 77, 79, 85–93
    graduate study, 53, 54
    high school courses, 61, 62
    press clubs, 52, 53
    standards, 54, 55
    teacher training for, 93
    textbooks, 60, 61, 89, 92
    "women's page" courses, 51, 52, 56

K

Kansas, Progressive era history, 71, 72
Kansas State University, advance writng
        curriculum, 75–78

L

La Follette, Belle Case, 24, 40, 42, 43,
        129
La Follette, Robert, xii, xvi, 24, 25,
        39–44, 48, 49, 67–70, 72,
        95–98, 108, 118, 128–133,
        137, 143, 146, 147

and advanced writing instruction, xii,
39, 48, 49
campaigns and elections, 24, 25
college career, 24, 40, 41
as eulogized by John Dos Passos, 132
and journalists, 42, 137
later years, 132, 133
and Lincoln Steffens, 24, 42, 43
opposition to World War I, 118,
128–130
Progressive platform, xvi, 146, 147
rhetorical skills, 40–42, 67
and Roosevelt's publicity campaigns,
95–98
and round–robin faculty resolution,
129–130
and the Wisconsin Idea, 43, 44, 48
La Follette's Weekly Magazine, 43, 68,
108, 121, 130
Lee, Ivy Ledbetter, 59, 112, 119,
135–143
criticisms of, 119, 135–139, 142, 143
and a "Declaration of Principles," 112
and the German Dye Trust, 142, 143
depiction by John Dos Passos, 135,
136
his response to criticisms, 140, 141
and the Rockefeller family, 112, 139,
140
support for, 141, 142
Leonard, Sterling, 16, 35–37
teaching career, 35
theory of teaching writing, 16, 35–37
Lippmann, Walter, 128, 133
Louisiana State University, advanced
writing curriculum, 84
Lovett, Robert Morss, 81–83, 91

M

MacKaye, Percy, 68, 69, 78, 93
McClure, S. S., 105, 106
McClure's Magazine, 24, 42, 96, 105,
106, 108, 128
Mencken, H. L., 130–33
Minnesota, Progressive era history, 79
Morrill Act, 71
Muckraking journalism, 104–107

N

Newcomb College, advanced writing
curriculum, 91
Newspapers, 45, 46, 74, 96–98,
101–105, 115, 116, 120–122
and advertising revenue, 115, 116
muckraking articles in, 104–106
nineteenth–century, 101–104
and Roosevelt's reform efforts, 96–98
and the Spanish–American War, 103,
104
technical developments, 102
and university publicity, 45, 46, 74
and World War I, 120–122
Nichols, Charles Washburn, 79, 80
Norris, Frank, 107

O

O'Higgins, Harvey, 127
Osborn, Alex F., 117

P

Pageants and pageantry courses, 77, 78,
87
Perrin, Porter, xiv
Pestalozzi, Johann, 27, 28, 37
Pinchot, Gifford, 96–100, 109, 111, 118,
125, 143, 147
Piper, Edwin Ford, 80, 81, 91
Populism, 22–24, 63, 71, 74–76, 84, 86
Press bulletins, 45, 46, 74, 97, 98
Progressive education, xvii, 31, 26–38,
48–94
advanced college writing instruction,
xvii, 31, 34, 35, 37, 38,
48–94
lower school language arts, xvii,
26–33, 35–37
vocational college curricula, xvii, 37,
38
Progressive era, history, xvi–xviii,
17–19, 22–26
Progressivism, xvi–xviii, 21–38, 68, 69,
77, 78, 106–108
dramatic theory, 68, 69, 77, 78
educational theory, xvii, xviii, 26–38
and film–making, 107, 108
and novel writing, 106, 107

political theory, xvi, xvii, 21–26
Public relations, 43–48, 95–101,
          109–113, 118–131, 133, 134
   during the Depression, 133, 134
   ethics codes, 112
   film–making for, 111, 112
   hiring of journalists, 112, 113, 127,
          128
   nineteenth–century history of,
          109–111
   for Theodore Roosevelt, 95–101
   for the University of Wisconsin,
          43–48
   for World War I, 118–131
Public relations instruction, 84–87, 126,
          127, 134
Publicity films, see Film–making
Pulitzer, Joseph, 103, 115

R

Rockefeller family, xvii, xviii, 17, 112,
          119, 136–140, 142
Roosevelt, Franklin, 134, 143
Roosevelt, Theodore, xvi, 25, 95–101,
          107, 111, 119, 122, 124, 130
   impact on the Committee for Public
          Information (CPI), 119, 122
   and the term "muckraker," 107
   as a Progressive reformer, xvi, 25,
          95–101, 111
   and pro–World War I film, 124

S

Scott, Fred Newton, xiv, xv, 14, 15,
          31–35, 37, 83
   composition curriculum at University
          of Michigan, 14, 15, 33, 35,
          83
   textbooks, xiv, 31–33
   theory of education, xiv, xv, 32, 33
Scripps, Edward Wyllis, 137, 143
Sedition Act of 1918, 121
Sinclair, Upton, 8, 12, 15, 105, 107, 138,
          141
   evaluation of freshman composition
          courses, 8, 12, 15
   evaluation of Ivy Lee and public rela-
          tions, 138, 141

as a muckraker, 105, 107
Speech, history of instruction in, xii, xiii,
          66, 67, 74, 77, 84, 85
Strong, Frank, 72–75

T

Technical and business writing, 34, 35,
          64–66, 77, 79, 80, 85–89, 92,
          93
   courses, 34, 35, 64–66, 77, 79, 80,
          85–88
   teacher training, 92, 93
   textbooks, 66, 77, 89
Thomas, Joseph, 79
Trading–with–the–Enemy Act of 1917,
          120, 121

U

University of California, advanced writ-
          ing curriculum, 87, 88
University of Chicago, 81–83, 91
   advanced writing curriculum, 81–83,
          91
   history of, 81
University of Florida, advanced writing
          curriculum, 85
University of Iowa, advanced writing
          curriculum, 80, 81, 91
University of Kansas, advanced writing
          curriculum, 72–75
University of Michigan, advanced writ-
          ing curriculum, 31, 33–35
University of Minnesota, advanced writ-
          ing curriculum, 79, 80
University of Montana, advanced writ-
          ing curriculum, 86, 87
University of Nebraska, advanced writ-
          ing curriculum, 78, 79
University of Texas, advanced writing
          curriculum, 85, 86
University of Washington, advanced
          writing curriculum, 88
University of Wisconsin,
   advanced writing curriculum, 48–69
   extension division, 47, 48
   freshman composition program, 6–12
   influence on other universities,
          70–73, 75, 78, 91, 94
   press bulletins, 45, 46

and the Wisconsin Idea, 43, 46–47,
    49–50

V

Van Hise, Charles, 44–50, 57, 58,
    62–64, 68, 69, 72, 75, 79, 81,
    95, 97–100, 129, 130
    and advanced writing instruction, 49,
        50, 57, 58, 62–64, 68, 69
    attack on Bob La Follette during
        World War I, 129, 130
    influence on other college presidents,
        72, 75, 79, 81
    influence on Roosevelt's publicity ef-
        forts, 95, 97–100
    and publicizing the University of Wis-
        consin, 44–48

W

War–Aims Course, 125, 126
Waters, Henry Jackson, 76, 77
Wendell, Barrett, xi, 13, 14, 16, 33, 81
Wheeler, Benjamin Ide, 87
White, William Allen, 74, 107
Wilson, Woodrow, 118, 119, 123, 124,
    130, 132
Wisconsin Idea, 43–49, 72, 85, 120
Woolley, Edwin, 10–12, 60, 61
World War I, publicity effort for, 118–131

Y

Young, Karl, 8, 64, 65, 125, 129